SONGS OF DEGREES

SONGS OF DEGREES

Essays on

Contemporary

Poetry and Poetics

John Taggart
With a Foreword by Marjorie Perloff

THE UNIVERSITY OF ALABAMA PRESS

Tuscaloosa and London

Copyright © 1994
The University of Alabama Press
Tuscaloosa, Alabama 35487–0380
All rights reserved
Manufactured in the United States of America
Designed by Paula C. Dennis

∞

The paper on which this book is printed meets the minimum requirements of American
National Standard for Information Science-Permanence of Paper for Printed Library
Materials, ANSI Z39.48-1984.

Library of Congress Cataloging-in-Publication Data

Taggart, John, 1942–
Songs of degrees : essays on contemporary poetry and poetics /
John Taggart; with a foreword by Marjorie Perloff.
p.   cm.
Includes bibliographical references and index.
ISBN 0-8173-0713-3 (alk. paper)
1. American poetry—20th century—History and criticism—Theory,
etc. 2. Experimental poetry, American—History and criticism.
3. Poetics.   I. Title.
PS323.5.T34   1994
811'.509—dc20   93-41326

British Library Cataloguing-in-Publication Data available

Contents

Foreword

Marjorie Perloff

John Taggart belongs to that remarkable generation of poet-theorists who came of age in the seventies and eighties. I say poet-theorists (rather than poet-critics) advisedly, for unlike the poets of the previous generation—Robert Lowell, Robert Duncan, Robert Creeley, to name just three—who regarded the production of critical essays as a kind of left-handed activity, a holiday from their "real" poetic vocation, today such poets as David Antin, Charles Bernstein, Susan Howe, Steve McCaffery, Leslie Scalapino, and Rosmarie Waldrop don't always distinguish between the writing of a theoretically informed poetry and a poetically inspired theory. Susan Howe's *Melville's Marginalia* (1993), for example, is a meditation on the aporias of American colonial history and its legacy that combines "poetry" and "prose" in ways not unlike those that animate her 1993 book of poems *The Nonconformist's Memorial*.

In "A Picture of Mystery and Power," his own meditation on Susan Howe's earlier *My Emily Dickinson,* John Taggart hails Howe's experiment as a corrective to the contemporary "obscuring of poetry by an ever-increasing overlay of prose commentary." "Criticism," he observes drily, "turns poetry into prose that misremembers its source," a source which is, in Taggart's view, equivalent to *vision.* This is what Taggart's own critical essays, collected here for the first time, are all about: an imaginative and visionary re-creation of a particular body of poetry, with an eye, not just toward explication or documentation or the now-fashionable use of the literary work as social and cultural text, but toward the discrimination of poetic, which is to say spiritual, value. Again and again, Taggart examines a group of poems or a particular oeuvre and raises the question: Why is this work so *valuable,* and what can it do for us as readers and writers?

The essays in *Songs of Degrees* were written over a fifteen-year period—roughly the same period that begins with the publication of Taggart's first major collection of poems, *Dodeka* (1979). In 1974 the poet completed a doctoral dissertation on objectivist poetics under the direction of the noted modernist scholar Walter Sutton at Syracuse University. The objectivists—notably Louis Zukofsky and George Oppen—have been the wellspring of his writing, whether poetic or critical, since that time. Six of Taggart's eighteen essays included here are devoted specifically to the poetry of Zukofsky and Oppen, but the others also bear their imprint, poets like William Bronk, Bruce Andrews, Susan Howe, and Theodore Enslin, coming out of the objectivist tradition, even as the essays on Robert Duncan and Charles Olson deal with closely related poetic phenomena and the short pieces on his own work chart the process whereby Taggart has adapted the lessons of the objectivists (and via Zukofsky, of Wallace Stevens) so as to Make It New.

Much recent work on "Writers on the Left" like Oppen and Zukofsky is concerned with the "political unconscious" of their poetry, but ideological analysis is not Taggart's game. Indeed, although Taggart has always kept his distance from the mainstream of confessionalism and "scenic" poetry (Charles Altieri's term) that dominates the magazines, his lyric is equally detached from the political engagement that has characterized so-called language poetry. Thus the essay "Deep Jewels," which opens the collection, has as its epigraph, not a citation from Marx or Gramsci, Benjamin or Bataille, as is the case with many radical poetries today, but Blake's famous lines from *The Book of Thel,* "Can Wisdom be put in a silver rod, / Or Love in a golden bowl?" The opening paragraph announces that the great thing about George Oppen's poetry is its "organic and iridescent density"—hardly fashionable terms in the language poetry lexicon.

Since the first essay announces certain strains that are typical of the whole collection, I want to look at it a little more closely. Taggart begins by distinguishing Oppen's "density" from what he considers the pseudo-density of a poet like William Empson, "a critic as poetaster whose work seems to have its single motive power in an admiration for metaphysical wit and complexity, so that his own poems read as literally senseless, voiceless puzzles, but not as poems." Oppen, in contrast, "does not

propose to entertain or to amaze by playing upon ideas already at
hand, but to think, 'naked,' in the poem to some purpose." This bold
distinction—a value judgment academic critics of the nineties would be
reluctant to make, lest they be accused of "aesthetic fetishism" or a
chauvinistic nationalism (Empson being British)—is buttressed, not, as
the reader might expect, by recourse to Ezra Pound and William Carlos
Williams, Oppen's ostensible masters, but to Andrew Marvell's "On a
Drop of Dew," which "gains its density from complex variation and
restatement of the equation: drop of dew = human soul, from tightly
interlocked end rhymes with iambic lines kept supple by the ripple play
of mono/poly syllable combinations within the line, and from frequent
line-length alterations." However commonplace the linking of dewdrop
and soul, Taggart observes, its articulation in the poem is as perfect as that
of a Bach fugue.

But Oppen's "density," Taggart posits, is not Marvell's, however mar-
velous the latter's metaphysical wit, nor, in a series of brilliant aperçus, is
it judged to be akin to Pound's "juxtaposition by displacement." Rather,
Taggart links Oppen to Blake, whose "ability to startle by an unannounced directness [and] by an 'unreasonable' pursuit of exact statement" is precisely the driving force behind Oppen's work. At the same
time, the mythic synthesis of Blake's Prophetic Books was no longer
available to a poet of the mid-twentieth century. "Oppen's refusal to
construct a mythic universe . . . places him at the disadvantage of continually refinding his subject in each new poem." Hence the elaborate
construction of a poem like *The Four Zoas* gives way to the serial
organization of *Of Being Numerous,* the individual segments refusing to
build toward "bravura rhetorical climaxes," much less to comprehensive
Answers.

The resulting poetry, the essay posits, is nothing if not "brave." "Oppen
is always beginning again out of a relative poverty of poetic resources
with each new poem; 'relative' because, while deliberately avoiding the
multilayered richness of Blake's myth universe, the clean slate per se is
not really possible. All our acts have histories." Indeed, *density* is
achieved by the use of devices that allow the reader to "witness . . . a
mind in actual serious process." The chief such devices are ellipsis and,
in the later poems in *Seascape: Needle's Eye,* the "literal space gap" or
"silence." Here is Taggart's take on the opening poem of *Seascape:* "From
a Phrase of Simone Weil's and Some Words of Hegel's":

Where there once were ellipses, gaps of white space, "silence," now appear. Does this mean anything? I think it does: a further move toward the substantive, the atomization of facts' totality now laid down like the giant stones of Macchu Picchu, no mortar between them, only a few verbs of being remaining here and there. Poets as opposed as Frost and Pound are agreed that the sentence is a form of power. When you alter syntax out of recognizable subject-verb-object order, you run the risk of losing that torque/torsion energy transfer that Fenollosa long ago perceived as gram-mar's replication of the whole physics of nature.

This is as good an account as I have seen of Oppen's particular form of minimalism. Taggart recognizes that the Pound-Fenollosa love affair with the simple declarative sentence (e.g., "farmer pounds rice") as the em-bodiment of "direct treatment of the thing," suggesting as it does that "the sentence is a form of power," has no attraction for the more stringent and austere Oppen, whose use of "bare" substantives connected by "only a few verbs of being" and embedded in white space has its own "torque/torsion energy transfer." It is an energy transfer Taggart makes his own. Instead of invoking authority, as do most critics ("As Foucault says . . . ," "As Derrida has shown . . . "), Taggart turns to the authority of metaphor and simile: the nouns are "laid down like the giant stones of Macchu Picchu, no mortar between them." The reading of Oppen he gives us is admittedly subjective, and yet he obviously hopes that it will be per-suasive to us: "The advantage of a near-verbless poetry is solidity. And the snare of the poem become solid object is that it may actually become just that, an object—voiceless box—stuck in the three-dimensional statue space of unvisited public parks. What saves Oppen from this objectivist trap is, again, his mind, his voice as his mind's agent, insistent to state the truth."

Such insistence does not make for a poetry of immediate gratification or accessibility. In a later essay called "George Oppen and the An-thologies," Taggart takes up the vexed issue of Oppen's reception. For Oppen has never made it into the Norton (or comparable) anthology canon; to this day, he remains largely unknown, even to the Poetry Establishment. His work, like Zukofsky's, and like that of Taggart himself, is too uncompromising: it gives us neither the "clear, visual images" Eliot regarded as a sine qua non of poetry nor the fiction-making we find in Stevens and Williams: "Rather than set up structures only to collapse them by internal contradiction or ironic subversion, Oppen builds what might be called tentative structures that remain tentative. His poems betray no confidence in a final outcome, but the voice that emerges from them has a tone which suggests that, however intransigent the difficulties, one might still attempt to use language 'constructively' and to come to knowledge (measure) of the world."

But—and this is the other side of Taggart's critique—objectivism, or any other ism, can also be a trap. Hence the need for critique as well as for sympathetic reading. In "How to Do Things with Words," Taggart praises Bruce Andrews's creation of a "heightened experience of language," his use of the individually "designed" page as measure, but he is uneasy about the tendency, in language poetry, to use words as ends not means: "[Abstraction] can force or encourage a more conscious experience of language; it can produce varieties of irony in the process. It is not clear that it can do anything else." Similar questions are raised about the work of Clark Coolidge and, in a long brilliant essay, about William Bronk, whose reworking of a Stevensian poetics, Taggart argues, increasingly gives short shrift to what Stevens called the real, turning inward at its own peril.

Even if one doesn't agree with Taggart (I don't, in the case of Andrews and Coolidge), one cannot help but find his arguments extremely provocative and interesting. For Taggart, poetry suffers if it ignores what he repeatedly refers to as the visionary, the spiritual. No doubt, this predilection stems from his religious upbringing. The son of a Methodist minister, Taggart recalls that he was literally raised in church, and although he has remarked drily that the church was not "a place where I wished to maintain residence," he continues to find the secularism of his fellow poets unsatisfactory, turning to Stevens, but even more to Eliot, for exemplars of what a "spiritual" poetry might be. In an essay on Frank Samperi called "The Spiritual Definition of Poetry," he remarks, "The answer is seeing—not belief, but the experience of seeing for ourselves what has already been seen by another. . . . What engenders seeing is the imagination's power to connect one thing with some other thing, fusing them fast, to produce a new third thing. The process is metaphor."

If this comment sounds merely traditional, a return to the New Critical privileging of metaphor, Taggart's particular spin on metaphoricity is all his own. His is a vision based on invocation and incantation—an intricate incantation produced by permutating sounds and silences in ways that recall John Cage or Jackson MacLow rather than the Eliot and Stevens who are Taggart's acknowledged mentors. I conclude with the opening lines of "The Game with Red," a poem from Taggart's volume *Loop* (1991).

> Deepened by black red made deep by black
> deepened and dark darker at the top
> doorway without a door's always darker
> deep red dark red always darker at the top.

Why should it always be darker at the top? The poem yields its meanings only slowly (and never surely) as we trace the permutations from "deep" to "dark" to "darker." Taggart's critical writing moves in similar ways, refusing to explicate, to summarize, to paraphrase. If poetry is, in Stevens's words, the scholar's art, the reverse is also true; the scholarly investigation, passionately undertaken, becomes a central component of the poet's art. Metaphor—Oppen's unmodified abstract nouns, "laid down like the giant stones of Macchu Picchu"—this is the connecting link between Taggart's "verse" and "prose," and it is the poetic dimension of these "Songs of Degrees" that makes reading them such a special pleasure.

SONGS OF DEGREES

Deep
Jewels

Can Wisdom be put in a silver rod,
Or Love in a golden bowl?
—William Blake, *The Book of Thel*

It is well that George Oppen's *Seascape: Needle's Eye* is of very few pages. For these poems, even more than those in *Of Being Numerous*, possess a surpassing density, a coordinate density of syntactic surface and of undistracted reflection. It is my sense that both densities devolve without constraint into each other, betraying no spot-welding; that the initial difficulties a reader may encounter are worth enduring for the reward of words put in unusual, often exhilarating combinations and of a thought process which is terrifying in its honesty. If the book were longer, we might be tempted to read for striking single lines or images—how most poetry is read most of the time—thereby missing the truly organic and iridescent density of Oppen's poetry.

Density was not originated in poetry by Oppen. Our century has prided itself upon the refurbishment and near-idolatry of the seventeenth-century metaphysical poets. An indication of this is the denatured poetry of William Empson, a critic as poetaster whose work seems to have its single motive power in an admiration for metaphysical wit and complexity, so that his own poems read as literally senseless, voiceless puzzles, but not as poems. The object for the reader of an Empson poem, like the college student in a poetry class, is to "figure it out." Its satisfactions are those of the crossword puzzle. If it, and the only slightly less arid work of Tate and Ransom, were restricted to the crossword pages of newspapers, they would occupy their proper zone and provide their proper pleasure of riddle solving. The density of George Oppen's poetry, however, is of a wholly different order because his thought is of a different order. It is truly his own; he does not propose to entertain or to amaze by playing upon ideas already at hand, but to think, "naked," in the poem to some purpose. To make the distinction clear, consider a metaphysical set piece, Marvell's "On a Drop of Dew," which may well have served as a model for the above worthies.

Marvell's poem gains its density from complex variation and re-statement of the equation: drop of dew = human soul, from tightly interlocked end rhymes with iambic lines kept supple by the ripple play of mono/poly syllable combinations within the line, and from frequent line-length alterations. The idea underlying the equation is a near-commonplace. Marvell links the dewdrop with the soul because it comes from heaven—"the bosom of the morn"—is whole and complete in itself, but is nevertheless restless and "unsecure" because "so long divided from the sphere." And as the dewdrop lies within the blowing roses, so the soul—"that drop, that ray / Of the clear fountain of Eternal Day"—is "within the human flower." In typical metaphysical conceit fashion, the dewdrop and Christian soul unite in

> . . . how coy a figure wound,
> Every way it turns away:
> So the world excluding round,
> Yet receiving in the Day.
> Dark beneath, but bright above,
> Here disdaining, there in love.

Marvell's poem ends, having coyly assumed something of a literal sphere shape itself, by interpreting the dewdrop's fragility as a soullike longing to leave this world—"It all about does upward bend"—and by identifying the dew with sacred manna, which congeals on earth only to dissolve and "run / into the glories of th'Almighty Sun." Marvell's density comes from the further and further outreaching series of variations made (and ending) on the first identification/equation, which in itself is "simple." In fact, it is a principle of such composition that the theme, for its variations to affect, must be uncomplex. Bach's "Musical Offering" doesn't suffer because its fugue subject was dictated without forethought by a merely competent amateur, Frederick the Great.

Oppen is most commonly associated with Pound, Zukofsky, and Williams. Though the work of each man is whole and distinct, Oppen, as well as Zukofsky and Williams, writes within the technical "understanding" of Pound. It's useful to look at the *Cantos* to see just how distinct Oppen's density is from Marvell's and from that of his most forceful contemporary master. Pound's density develops from his ideogramic method. An example of this is the following excerpt from Canto LXXX:

> as he walked under the rain altars
> > or under the trees of their grove
> > or would it be under their parapets
> in his moving was stillness
> as grey stone in the Aliseans
> > or had been at Mt Segur
> And it was old Spencer (, H.) who first declaimed me the Odyssey
> with a head built like Bill Shepard's
> on the quais of what Siracusa?
> > Or what tennis court
> near what pine trees?

The procedure is juxtaposition by displacement: or, or, or. The reader must locate "he" in a quick succession or montage of settings without indication whether first or last is any more "the" setting than any of the others. Pound's lines are written so as to transform the reader into a camera operator constantly adjusting the focus as to follow an event, a movement, and as a consequence is moved in the process. The act of adjustment is maintained if the scenes are extremely opposite one another, an oppositeness made emphatic by word-sound syncopation: *under* rain al*tars, under trees, under* pa*rapets;* Ali*seans,* Mt *Segur, Sp*encer, *Shepard's, Sir*acusa; *tennis* court, *pine trees.* Pound's density is generated by the cumulative scene/sound pattern or mesh (vortex/ideogram), a "patterned energy" in Hugh Kenner's phrase, which is made up of rhetorical reversal displacements, abrupt juxtapositions of people and places not usually connected in their own space-time made to seem even more so by close repetition of single words and near-sprung-rhythm syncopation of subword sounds.

Despite the brevity of this example (from a canto that contains Washington, Debussy, Symons remembering Verlaine at the Rabarin, Santayana, Waterloo, Andy Jackson, the author's curiosity that Mr. Eliot has not given more time to Mr. Beddoes, the obligatory Chinese ideograms and Greek tags, *plus* all the standard axes of Pound's mind), the means of achieving density are no more complex than those found in Marvell. In fact, they are probably simpler. Pound's variations are made upon Pound. As one reads through the *Cantos,* there are fewer and fewer surprises. Both themes and variations tend to assume, amid constellations of ever-multiplying exotic reference, fixed identities. Quantity and strangeness of reference with masterly control of cadence are the elements of Pound's density.

My suggestion has been that Oppen's density is somehow distinct, and therefore particularly valuable, from the metaphysical play upon received ideas and from Pound's self-ideogramic method. To be sure, he is much closer to Pound than to Marvell. I think this is because Oppen has chosen to stand fast to the conception of image as center, foundation, and base for composition. Which, if not Pound's original notion, is surely his emphasis. Oppen's task as a poet sympathetic with this emphasis has been to avoid flat-out duplication, to turn it to his own use. What he, along with Zukofsky and Williams in their different ways, has successfully attempted is "to construct a method of thought from the imagist technique of poetry—from the imagist intensity of vision." (The statement comes from Oppen's interview with L. S. Dembo in the Spring 1969 issue of *Contemporary Literature.*)

This is the necessary achievement, what every poet conscious of tradition and "self-conscious," must manage: to adapt an existent body of technique and thus gain access "into" language and one's own mind. The language is the poet's to begin with, but only as a public trust; without a current, viable technique, it remains only as so much potential for the living writer, containing only what is already known. There is also the chance, then, not simply for "expression," but rather for search and discovery in one's own voice and through one's own vision. Such an adaptation (of image from Pound, of overall form consciousness from Zukofsky) allows Oppen to *think actively in his poetry.* Is this not the true goal, beyond the superficial release from closed metrical writing, of Olson's composition by field, of Duncan's desire that the poem contain all the "incidentals" of its composition process? For if we cannot do this, no matter how fine the style, nothing will be done. Poetry will lapse, as it has lapsed with a Swinburne, with a Robert Bridges, with each gentleman's present-day equivalents, from its high heuristic function to pinching the cheeks of a perennially debased "beauty." Historically, Pound's "desuetizing" and the whole modernist cleansing of tools have been useful. Now, however, the time has come to stop echoing "no ideas but in things" and to engage the poem directly that the searching mind may find there its rightful place for discovery. Let the poetics take care of themselves.

The peculiar density I would claim for the *Seascape* poems is a by-product of Oppen's willingness to so engage the poem. Not endlessly to prepare for its never-to-be hyperpurified state, but to use it now. What finally distinguishes Oppen's work from that of his immediate sources is the character of his own mind. I will evade psychoanalysis and argue that the mind most resembling Oppen's is that of William Blake. What's most striking about Blake is his incredible "freedom of statement." The man is capable of saying anything in pursuit of exact statement. Who else in English poetry would write serious conversations between a clod of clay, a worm, and a daughter of beauty *(Book of Thel)?* Who else can put down such terrifying questions as in "The Tyger" or be as religiously vindictive ("The death of Jesus set me free: / Then what have I to do with thee?" in "To Tirzah")? Who else can insistently point out social injustice ("London," "The Chimney-Sweeper") and at the same time write the flat-out platitudes that make up most of the *Songs of Innocence?* The answer is not George Oppen; it can only be William Blake.

Oppen, however, is equally capable of saying absolutely anything. For here is a veteran of all the "make it new" wars who can still write the near-sentimental "Sparrow in the cobbled street, / Little sparrow round and sweet" ("Stranger's Child"—*The Materials*), who can register social protest: "Now we do most of the killing / Having found a logic / Which is Control" ("Power, The Enchanted World"—*Of Being Numerous*), and not least a poet who can write a poem of quiet affection for a woman "Clear minded and blind / in the machines / And the abstractions and the power" who

> . . . sought for a friend
>
> Offering gently
>
> A brilliant kindness
> Of the brilliant garden

("A Kind of Garden: A Poem for My Sister"—*Of Being Numerous*). Oppen is also the poet of moral warning:

> Wolves may hunt
>
> With wolves, but we will lose
> Humanity in the cities
> And the suburbs, stores
> And offices
> In simple
> Enterprise.
>
> ("A Narrative"— *This In Which*)

If Blake and Oppen mirror one another in a shared ability to startle by an unannounced directness, by an "unreasonable" pursuit of exact statement, which is not so much irrational as unmannered in traditional modes of procedure, there are also differences. The most important of these is Oppen's refusal to construct a mythic universe, a reduction of the universe in which we all live, for a richer poetry. The splendor of, say, *The Four Zoas* comes from Blake's mythic synthesis, which is a little familiar in its separate parts and yet remains strange as a whole. It is Blake's preoccupation with his synthetic myth universe which makes Eliot's remark that he did not see enough of the universe decently accurate.

Oppen is placed by his refusal to make such a synthetic construction at the disadvantage of continually refinding his subject in each new poem. (This may explain why he is drawn to serial organization, e.g., "Image of the Engine," "A Language of New York," the title poem from *Of Being Numerous;* the series permits any number of variations without forcing new beginnings and without losing sight of the object.) There's positive gain, though, in that each poem demands great effort, each potentially as crucial as others of the past, so that a sense of the "problem" seen whole—there are no bravura rhetorical climaxes in Oppen's poems—emerges.

Earlier I cited a section from "Power, The Enchanted World" as an instance of social protest. When quoted more fully, it becomes more complex.

> Now we do most of the killing
> Having found a logic
>
> Which is control
> Of the world, "we"
> And Russia

> What does it mean to object
> Since it will happen?
> It is possible, therefore it will happen
> And the dead, this time dead

"Complex" is hardly the word. For the difficult question and its sad, hard answer offer us no relief—as they should not—there is no "answer." This is what cannot be found in Blake, who has all the answers, and what, though the word sounds nearly freakish, makes Oppen's poetry "tragic." It is not Aristotle's tragedy, nor a tragedy of any time other than our own, when neither heroic victory nor defeat can be had but only never-ending struggle, the terms of which are never quite clear.

> One had not thought
> To be afraid
>
> Not of shadow but of light
>
> Summon one's powers

The tone remains brave, though none of Blake's angels will appear to light our way. There's no requirement for such a tone. It is a gift, humane and generous, from Oppen's persisting mind. What good can it do? Only what all great art does: to lay out the human facts a little more clearly. Not salvation. We *may* see more if we listen closely to this man who has dedicated himself to "the rare poetic of veracity."

That last phrase comes from "West," one of the poems in *Seascape*. It belongs with another phrase, this one from a later poem in the same book, "Song, The Winds of Downhill": "out of poverty / to begin / again." Together, the two phrases define Oppen's practice from *Discrete Series to Seascape*. Thus Oppen is always beginning again out of a relative poverty of poetic resources with each new poem. "Relative" because, while deliberately avoiding the multilayered richness of Blake's myth universe, the clean slate per se is not really possible. All our acts have histories. The result of such a consciously assumed attitude is a density even more intense than that of the previous books.

An indication of this is Oppen's use of the ellipsis. Prior to *Seascape* it serves to indicate shifts in cadence which are also shifts in the downward thought progression of the poem. As a result, the reader can follow the composing mind more directly, the removes of cookie-cutter syllogistic form reduced, can feel that one is witness to a mind in actual serious process, a process unrehearsed for the cultural occasion of "poetry," deliberately impoverished and resolutely active. The ellipsis connects the moves of this process and reminds us that something has been left out— that for all his sincerity, both poet and reader are still involved with artifice—. Reading Oppen's poems, we must try to fill in these indicated gaps if we are truly to read them. This is not a strategem à la Robbe-Grillet or Nathalie Sarraute to engage readers more intimately but to inform them simply (and forcibly) of the process, of the development, of the choices that are being made.

The ellipsis becomes a literal space gap in the *Seascape* poems. Consider number 4 of "Route" from *Of Being Numerous:*

> Words cannot be wholly transparent. And that is the
>   "heartlessness" of words.
>
> Neither friends nor lovers are coeval . . .
>
> as for a long time we have abandoned those in
>   extremity and we find it unbearable that we should
>   do so . . .
>
> The sea anemone dreamed of something, filtering the sea
>   water thru its body,
>
> Nothing more real than boredom—dreamlessness, the
>   experience of time, never felt by the new arrival,
>   never at the doors, the thresholds, it is the native
>
> Native in native time . . .
>
> The purity of the materials, not theology, but to present
>   the circumstances

And then "From a Phrase of Simone Weil's and Some Words of Hegel's," the first poem in *Seascape:*

> In   back   deep the jewel
> The treasure
> No   Liquid
> Pride of the living life's liquid
> Pride in the sandspit wind this ether this other this element all

It is I or I believe
We are the beaks of the ragged birds
Tune of the ragged bird's beaks
In the tune of the winds
Ob via   the obvious
Like a fire of straws
Aflame in the world or else poor people hide
Yourselves together   Place
Place where   desire
Lust of the eyes the pride of life and foremost of the storm's
Multitude moves the wave belly-lovely
Glass of the glass sea shadow of water
On the open water no other way
To come here the outer
Limit of the ego

Where there once were ellipses, gaps of white space, "silence," now appear. Does this mean anything? I think it does: a further move toward the substantive, the atomization of facts' totality now laid down like the giant stones of Macchu Picchu, no mortar between them, only a few verbs of being remaining here and there. Poets as opposed as Frost and Pound are agreed that the sentence is a form of power. When you alter syntax out of recognizable subject-verb-object order, you run the risk of losing that torque/torsion energy transfer that Fenollosa long ago perceived as grammar's replication of the whole physics of nature.

So the question becomes what does Oppen lose by this intensified noun-upon-noun, phrase-upon-phrase stone mason poetry and what possible advantage, beyond the occasional brilliancy, can be so obtained? The loss is not shimmer, flex of a metal-jointed fish in sunlight. That and many other effects can be got by nouns and phrases held in fine rhythmic control. What can only be compensated for is the propulsion of quickened emotion:

> Thou mak'st the vestal violate her oath;
> Thou blow'st the fire when temperance is thaw'd;
> Thou smother'st honesty, thou murd'rest troth;
> Thou foul abettor! thou notorious bawd!
> Thou plantest scandal and displacest laud.
>   Thou ravisher, thou traitor, thou false thief,
>   Thy honey turns to gall, thy joy to grief!
>
> (Shakespeare, "The Rape of Lucrece")

There is significant emotion in the *Seascape* poems, but even more than Oppen's previous work they tend toward the meditative and, ultimately, toward the tragic. These poems typically close very quietly as if their author had seen "everything" and, knowing the odds against anyone's vision being whole, would hazard a statement however qualified and tentative. It's no accident that none of the final lines for these poems has end punctuation. Things *could* end differently.

The advantage of a near-verbless poetry is solidity. And the snare of the poem become solid object is that it may actually become just that, an object—voiceless box—stuck in the three-dimensional statue space of unvisited public parks. What saves Oppen from this objectivist trap is, again, his mind, his voice as his mind's agent, insistent to state the truth. The language of my claim is a little ridiculous. Who doesn't wish to state the truth? But if the desire is common, few have given us such a sustained effort, which at the same time makes no apologetics for itself nor rhetorical flourishes of solution. Reading the *Seascape* poems, one cannot escape the feeling that they were written very slowly, perhaps with a difficulty beyond "craft," bringing as much pressure/compression to bear as possible so that the image may be revelation—a problem or situation literally revealed in its parts and their connections, but not necessarily "resolved"—. It is almost as if the verbs would too much hurry this centering down, causing the image's weight to fall too soon or off the mark.

There is another factor which prevents Oppen's poetry from turning into so much verbal masonry: the reader. If you are to read him at all, it must be done actively, yourself involved in the statement's gradual composition. This involvement means that the reader necessarily contributes to the poem's final density. To a degree, this is true of all writing. Dickens' *Our Mutual Friend* and Dostoyevsky's *The Possessed* are whole worlds made to seem even more inclusive by their length and by the proportionate amount of time we must spend with them. We must likewise spend considerable time with Oppen's much briefer poems.

Returning to "From a Phrase of Simone Weil's and Some Words of Hegel's," for example, we are immediately caught up in

            In   back   deep the jewel
            The treasure
            No   Liquid

> Pride of the living life's liquid
> Pride in the sandspit wind this ether this other this element all

The first line's gaps are for depth, the cadence counterpointing the two set-off words with the longer phrase so that the jewel is truly withdrawn, the last thing to be found. It is as buried treasure, but "No   Liquid": it has the place and value of treasure without being solid coin or necklace. "Pride of the living life's liquid" suggests something totally opposite, like plasma, yet this too is off as the next line makes clear. The treasure is somehow human and almost, more than that, "metaphysical," the object of this pride nearly equivalent to an élan vital, a sweeping inclusive consciousness.

We are not allowed, however, to rest on this understanding.

> It is I or I believe
> We are the beaks of the ragged birds
> Tune of the ragged bird's beaks
> In the tune of the winds

"It is I" = all, all of that grand long line's items so that pride is not simply an energetic hubris, but an awareness *in* consciousness of the all/whole, which must still be contained in, originate from the singular I. "Or": Oppen believes we are merely birds' beaks, a tune of the winds; insignificant things, not the apex of all creation, yet nevertheless parts of the whole. The "or" does not belong to an either/or.

This is the tendency ("Ob via"), the way toward which all things obviously go

> Like a fire of straws
> Aflame in the world or else poor people hide
> Yourselves together

For if the world is not like this, if we and the world are not all parts of an Heraclitian flux, some process, then surely we shall be destroyed. What we must have, to be certain that we do indeed "belong," is place.

> Place where   desire
> Lust of the eyes the pride of life and foremost of the storm's
> Multitude moves the wave belly-lovely

> Glass of the glass sea shadow of water
> On the open water no other way
> To come here the outer
> Limit of the ego

It is therefore place that we desire with a visual lust—it is not within us, despite Christianity's attempt at transference—almost as if it were a warrant for our existence, proof that we do belong here. We accordingly take pride in the place we have assumed in/on the world, coming in time to believe that it is actually ours. (This perception is one of several Oppen shares with William Bronk; see Bronk's essay "The Occupation of Space—Palenque" in his *The New World.*) It is place by which the pride of life manifests itself. We can combat this pride—which is not the crucial thing, which is the static, deathlike posture we take on with pride of place—but not finally evade it by living as a sailor lives on the sea in a necessary harmony of close attention and adjustment.

No matter how strong our desire, we can never transform the sea, the very source and most fundamental metaphor of life, into "our place." (Oppen's "glass sea" may be even a little too positive.) We may act as though we have control, but it is merely a negative achievement disguising the ever-present chance of the I's obliteration by the sea, massive and featureless force of the anti-I. We do not actually lose the ego here, its deadly presumption and finally stupid territorial defense of self, but at least we are living in a way that makes such presumption difficult and momentary at best, ourselves now nearly fluid at the ego's outer limit.

This is not what the people came to hear the evangelist say. Oppen's abiding perception of the tragic—which can now be defined as the ceaseless conflict that cannot be won but only continued between the ego I, presuming to seize and hold life as a property, and life itself as the sea pounding on and on—will not tolerate any easy resolution. What is to be hoped for is very modest:

> To find now depth, not time, since we cannot, but depth
> To come out safe,   to end well
>
> ("Anniversary Poem")

We have begun very simply and have ended at a point so far removed from, and yet so inextricably connected with, the poem's beginning brief words that it is difficult to describe the journey by which we got there. Certainly, none of it could have been predicted beforehand. That it could not is an indication of the surpassing density, beyond "surprise" in its cadences and in the thought they carry, of George Oppen's poetry. This density is unlike Marvell's or Pound's or any other because its originating mind is unique in its passion for exact statement and in its "illogical" compassion for the ego's sad predicament. I have said these poems tend toward the tragic. It is no contradiction to say they are also radiant, "deep jewels," where wisdom and love are securely conjoined.

The Spiritual Definition of Poetry

Fable or allegory are a totally distinct and inferior kind of poetry. Vision or imagination is a representation of what eternally exists, really and unchangeably.
—William Blake, *Notebook*

The aim of the poet is to state a vision, and no vision of life can be complete which does not include the articulate formulation of life which human minds make.
—T. S. Eliot, "Dante"

The imagination of Frank Samperi's trilogy *(The Prefiguration, Quadrifariam, Lumen Gloriae)* is essentially visionary. By visionary I mean a quality associated with the perception of a whole that is complex, organized, and dynamic. Kathleen Raine, in the second volume of her memoirs *The Land Unknown,* describes such perception in detail.

> I was looking at the hyacinth, and as I gazed at the form of its petals and the strength of their curve as they open and curl back to reveal the mysterious flower-centres with their anthers and eyelike hearts, abruptly I found that I was no longer looking *at* it, but *was* it; a distinct, indescribable, but in no way vague, still less emotional, shift of consciousness into the plant itself. Or rather I and the plant were one and indistinguishable; as if the plant were a part of my consciousness. I dared scarcely breathe, held in a kind of fine attention in which I could sense the very flow of life in the cells. I was not perceiving the flower but living it. I was aware of the life of the plant as a slow flow of circulation of a vital current of liquid light of the utmost purity. I could apprehend as a simple essence formal structure and dynamic process. This dynamic form was, as it seemed, of a spiritual not a material order; or of a finer matter, or of matter itself perceived as spirit. There was nothing emotional about this experience which was, on the contrary, an almost mathematical apprehension of a complex and organized whole, apprehended *as* a whole. This whole was living; and as such inspired a sense of immaculate holiness.

What analysis would sort into separate dead categories, the visionary imagination apprehends as a single organic whole, the parts of which all fit and which are in motion, not static, but dynamic and living. Buckminster Fuller's word "synergy" is an attempt to deal with such experience. Phenomenology is a like attempt by formal philosophy. The past has dealt less awkwardly with it as the holy, the numinous, the mythic. Even Lévi-Strauss, whose *Mythologiques* typifies what may be regarded as a fundamentally futile predilection in basing a "science of mythology" on algebraic analysis, organizes his analysis according to musical analogy (e.g., one of his studies is entitled "A Short Symphony" and consists of first movement: Ge, second movement: Bororo, third movement: Tupi; others are modeled after such forms as the toccata and fugue, the double inverted canon, and the sonata). Such analysis recognizes the nature of myth, which is the product of visionary imagination, as a harmonious and active whole. The visionary imagination may not be consciously spiritual, but its product—myth, vision—will always be so by its very nature.

These poems are informed by a similar recognition. As Samperi writes in *Lumen Gloriae,* what he desires to attain through his poetry is "glorified body spiritual man undivided." His desire is to live within the vision of his imagination, which is Christian generally and Dantesque specifically. Thus (from the "Paradiso *Canto Primo*" prose section of *Quadrifariam*): "The Commedia is Eternal Form—not medieval art; therefore, any critical evaluation is out of the question." And from a poem in the same volume:

> the theological poet
> indirectly reveals
> the user and maker
> in harmonious relation to
> the Holy Spirit
> because the true object
> of the theological poet
> is Eternal Form
> Species in the Image

Eternal form is not terza rima, but that through which species (the imagery of individual poems or in Samperi's concise sentence: "Imagery in toto is species in the Image") secures apprehension of the larger Christian Image, the vision of eternity, which is the spiritual condition of the whole experienced by Kathleen Raine. Critical evaluation of the

Commedia is irrelevant because it *has* presented such vision. This is not a matter of belief, but of experience, seeing. Boccaccio reports that old women touched Dante's garments in wonder at this man who had walked through hell. Samperi would say he saw in or through the *Commedia* a vision of eternity. There can be no argument.

It may be that critical evaluation is also irrelevant for Samperi's own poems. Certainly it serves no purpose to question whether poets have actually undergone visionary experience. What can be asked is whether their images contain or somehow suggest a vision. Or, reading their images, what do we see?

The imagery of these poems is constructed by linear culmination—"dripping words," in Zukofsky's phrase. They read as severe catalogues of particulars, each line a single, separate word or brief phrase. Occasionally, a stripped-down subject-verb-object word order is retained as a sentence spine. This depositing of isolates in a series of isolates produces a formal structure that is sculptural in its vertical severity. Without the delay of horizontal rhythms and syntax, the reader is drawn down through the poem with ever-increasing speed as if subject to some absolute gravitational effect upon the mind and eye, a sensation reinforced by the trilogy's unusually long and narrow page size (10⅛" × 5¼"). Thus the image coheres only at (or after) the poem's close. It becomes an image by virtue of the participating reader who puts it together as a glance configures a rose window. All imagery is complex, but Samperi's multiplies the terms of relation into an even further collective complex. It is not incidental that most of the poems have no final periods. The isolates collect into an image outside the poem proper in the reader's head.

The most extended example of this image process, which is also a structure, is the series of poems that make up "Triune," the first book of *Quadrifariam.* In an explanatory note, Samperi writes that "Triune" seeks to delineate book, canzone, song (and their equivalents: eternity, image, gift), "only in the end to let go, release boundary." These terms define a range of poetry as their equivalents define a spiritual range made up of what could be understood as condition (eternity, wherein the soul belongs and wishes to dwell), the vision of that condition (image, of which there may be several enactments or perspectives—as many as there are perceptors—within the Image), and grace (gift from the spirit to the poet in terms of what will encourage his ability to render his vision visible). Finally, the boundary terms of both ranges must be exceeded, the poet's meditation ended, if he is to be taken up, absorbed into the divine. "Image / signifies / release."

Samperi characterizes the transcendent movement through these ranges as a descent. This reverses the usual representation of spiritual release as a radiating out or upward. But it is not personal idiosyncrasy; it is precisely the movement the reader must make to configure the poem's image to see what there is to see.

The following is one page, which I read as a single poem, from "Triune."

Leaf revealing water
reflected
angel
reflecting
water
revealing
hills
woods
lake beyond
dark
everywhere light
everywhere
closed
reflecting
fall
revealing
linear
bird
shadow
ocean
shore extension
intension
collapse
city
visually
crystalline
revealing
reflecting
angels
animals

revealing
a man
his reflection
person
trapped

The water reflected the angel, who is thus positioned as one thing among others in the material universe. (Though as real as these other things, the angel does not forfeit its spiritual nature by being included in the poem's catalogue.) The reflecting water now reveals hills, woods, lake beyond. The reflection, in contrast to the angel (elsewhere described in the poem as "angel completely / light"), is dark and itself reflects "fall," a season, a motion, a loss of grace, a state of unredeemed material existence. The fall-reflection reveals the "linear" which ends with intension, what is presumed to matter in a universe controlled by causal laws, the sign for which is the collapsing city.

Yet even this once-supreme, but now-ruined, object of the causal universe is visually crystalline and reflects angels and animals, who in turn reveal the final reflection of the poem: the trapped man. Reflect/ reveal: these are two modes of seeing. All the objects in the universe reflect one another, implying some connection between them. What they reveal is a deeper sense of what is there, *within* the reflection.

Further: individual object reflects individual object like so many apparently random mirrors until the whole light (or the light's source) is revealed. (The poem's last revelation is actually a reflection because the eventual deeper seeing must be done by the reader; the progression is from reflection to revelation, but the final revelation will always be "virtual.") The mirrors participate in and point toward that revelation until all isolate elements have been transformed into total transcendent light.

The poem should not be read as a dangling chain of mirror reflections with a single pendant revelation. Rather, it and "Triune" in its entirety proceed as linear clusters of reflections-revelations. The closing reflection of the poet as trapped man is not the sum revelation which, again, can only be immanent or virtual for the entire poem. Thus there is no contradiction between the closing reflection and the poem's overall revelation or image. And there is no trap (as there can be little comprehension for Samperi's constant attitude of "sorrowing" throughout the trilogy) unless we are aware where he is (in the collapsing city) and where he desires to be (with the angel).

The subject of this poem allows for and encourages a continuous reflexive play between the objects serving as mirror-reflectors and the image they collectively reveal. In fact, it is this never-exhausted series of reversible equations which is the constantly shifting, but always the same "subject" of "Triune." Each poem offers a slightly altered position for understanding the equations which consequently make the image ever more inclusive and complex. This fuguelike reiteration of similar elements from poem to poem contributes a growing resonance and depth to the book's emerging reflection-image.

Yet however refulgent the light, the poet paradoxically remains the trapped man. As one object in the universe, he can offer partial reflection that will point toward the whole, but he cannot *be* in that whole (despite his desire, despite his awareness). So that:

> vision full
> everything else empty
> vague
> necessary
> poverty the gift
> the city man
> dreamer
> poet
> an image
> center
> no guide
> invocation
> useless

This is standard religious paradox: while the vision may be full, not lacking, the poet is not living within it. Instead, he leads a life of poverty in the collapsing city, where as poet he dreams an image that could provide him a center, the whole of his vision. But there is no guide to help him (or us) get there. Invocation—to call out for either guide or center—is useless as a means of escaping the material. So: "every move man makes for confraternity with angels is a movement toward 'specific difference.'"

Nonetheless, reading through "Triune," we discover that both image and vision are announced at the book's end. They come one after the other on facing pages.

(image/revelation)	(vision/reflection)
Sea no horizon teleology	Light
background	intelligence
intensification	light
past	hill
the heroic	pool
the proletarian	concave
an identification	convex
if the intelligential	mind
the movement	crystal
the relation	return
therefore the theological	presupposition
use the gift	center
the clarification	angels
background	water
intensification	objects
species	transcendentals
image	forms
then rock	undefined
a boy below amidst grass	experience
the father on a bench	individual
the hills beyond intelligence	universal
spheres undivided	identity
the hierarchical	eternal form
apparential	supposition
the eternal	image
integral	shadow
river	trace
plain	information
hill	lover
valley	contemplative
processional	speculation
father	participative
son	reason
eternity	visional
image	beatific

The first fifteen lines of the image-revelation poem may be crossed out. They present nothing that can be seen. They function as instances of a quick, abstract shorthand method for reference back to other poems (an abstract fugal memory), and they can only suggest the visible in recollection. We do see the boy and father in a setting that, like a film dissolve, is rapidly abstracted into the spiritual. The hills never described in any local detail become spheres undivided, then simply "apparential" indicators (mirrors/reflectors) for the eternal.

Likewise, the processional of nominal river-plain-hill-valley reflects the integral father-son relation that is also the divine relation or supreme unity characteristic of eternity, the destination of the contemplative soul released from all boundaries imposed by the causal-material universe. (Those familiar with the alchemical tradition of Boehme and Paracelsus may read the poem as a Christian parallel to its teaching that, in Blake's words, "god is in the lowest effects as well as in the highest causes.")

Image signifies release. Revelation provides the last reflection, which then provides the reader-composed final revelation, the ultimate image. What we see within the reflection is light, hill and pool in concave-convex (complete) balance, which forms an angelic center where all isolated objects are subsumed in the transcendental eternal form. The image is an informing shadow trace for this state. To perceive it, as opposed to being assumed into it, one must be as an attentive lover, contemplating upon and participating within what reflection would give for the revelation that will be "visional / beatific."

When I look into the "Triune" image, however, I see Blake's "Soul embraced by divine lover" at the end of *Jerusalem*. It could easily have been "When the Morning Stars sang together" or any other of Blake's illustrations for the Book of Job. The fact that I saw these "old" visions and not Samperi's "new" one is indication that his cumulative linear shadow trace is not sufficient to render spiritual vision visible. It would be wrong and impossible to demand an original vision that shows no connection with those of the past. But this is not what we demand nor what the formal care of these poems would lead us to expect, which is seeing. Samperi: "if a work is primarily addressed to God, then it follows that the audience isn't essential." This neatly obliterates the reader, who I would argue is most definitely essential for these poems, and it comes close to committing hubris. Regardless of the declared eternity image and visional beatific, signs like petitions for belief of nonimage and nonvision, God has no need to complete or to see the Godhead.

I have cited the literally visual. There are even more vivid literary examples.

> Nel suo profondo vidi che s'interna,
>   legato con amore in un volume,
>   cio che per l'universo si squanderna;
> sustanzia ed accidenti, e lor costume,
>   quasi conflati insieme per tal modo,
>   che cio ch'io vidi, e un semplice lume.
> La forma universal di questo nodo
>   credo ch'io vidi, perche piu di largo,
>   dicendo questo, mi sento ch'io godo.
> Un punto solo m'e maggior letargo,
>   che venticinque secoli alla impresa,
>   che fe'Nettuno ammirar l'ombra d'Argo.

There are points of similarity, including the use of abstractions, between Samperi's visional beatific and Dante's experience of the scattered leaves of the universe ingathered by love into one simple flame. Both exist on a level of suggestion. And both must be judged on a scale of that level. That is: what divides bare-bones autosuggestion—whatever aura of association, necessarily personal and arbitrary, a word or phrase may be felt to possess—from formed incompletion so formed to hold us within its outline, inciting an active, expanding, and deepening response? When has the poet participated too much, leaving nothing to be filled in—or too little, the incomplete outline not even recognizable as incomplete—within the poem?

The answer is seeing. I repeat: not belief, but the experience of seeing for ourselves what has already been seen by another. If we are asked to believe that vision has occurred, then the very request seems to signify an inability to realize the "inapprehensible" in visual images. If, however, we see, there is no need for belief. What engenders seeing is the imagination's power to connect one thing with some other thing, fusing them fast, to produce a new third thing. The process is metaphor; the new third thing is the image. The image comes as the result of what we see, having looked at the first thing through the lens or screen of what we may know about the second. That looking, made compelling by the deliberate overstatement of identity that characterizes the imagination's power in metaphor, is what produces whatever seeing we may do. When what is seen suggests a whole, as opposed to any number of atomically separate objects of perception, there can be vision. Or, to reclaim a phrase from the recent past, there may be a "deep image."

This power is merely latent in Samperi's trilogy. The component "things" are not made luminous in their own distinctness, and the catalogue form does not generate a rhythmic coherence strong enough to fuse them together. Vague and nominal imagery can yield only a vague and nominal Image, a blurred vision.

The history of poetry in our century is only superficially the history of the struggle to make it new. More enduring is the struggle to regain the definition of poetry as spiritual ascesis, a definition obscured equally by the decadence of nearly all postromantic poetry, by its technical corrective as instigated by Pound, and by the diffuse mystical atmosphere manufactured by *écoles des Sages ou Mages* in the present. Lacking this definition's assurance of a method for work and a mode for discovery, Yeats' investigations into Irish mythology and the Kabbala are made to seem merely the eccentric hobbies of a crank. Lacking this definition, Pound cannot make it cohere; Williams rants about no ideas but in things and must labor in *Paterson* to find a means of transcending those same things for the possibility of larger and different perception; and Stevens is forced to invent a private aesthetic symbolism whereby poetry itself, as an interpenetration of costumed imagination and reality, is the ever-evasive symbolic goal. And the instances of solitary and often-failed struggle to realize the spiritual definition of poetry, as this trilogy demonstrates, do not cease in the supposedly more enlightened present.

There are two ways to secure this definition for poets who would write from the visionary imagination: (1) arduous study of and complete immersion in mythic and spiritual literature; (2) a like immersion in language. Poets will have to find their own path in the first area. They may choose to follow Plato through Plotinus on to Thomas Taylor and Blake (or follow Blake to Plato). Which text, whether a part of their own culture or not, does not matter. Eventually, they will have developed a sense of the entire literature and will have found what they specifically need, a discovery recognized by a sympathy of vision. That is, the visions encountered do not (and cannot) exactly duplicate the poets', but by their relative degree of congruence compel poets, like metaphor itself, to reexamine their experience, to look again. Thus poets will have found a context beyond the necessary present one for their single imagination, a context that may not be the traditional one of Curtius and Eliot and, if they stay awake, a basis for growth.

One danger to be avoided is secondary literature. We live in a time when there are more guides than mountains. The elaborations of the secondary guides are most useful as maps to (and not "of") the original sources. If there is something to see in a poet's vision, we cannot afford to settle in the middle distance of commentary.

Where the poet can and must settle is language, which not so much contains but *is* the great memory, *anima mundi,* the collective consciousness. For it is ourselves in a present that is always forgetful who are unconscious and who must dig and discover in language for what eternally exists, really and unchangeably. (Cf. Robert Duncan: "The creative experience of Man is a Word in its Mutations barely overheard in generation after generation, lost into Itself in Its being found.")

It is my own experience that, if followed with the persistent contemplation of Samperi's theological poet, language will reveal (or reflect) the contents of its memory, will inform the poet what the poem is actually about as opposed to a presumed subject, and will direct the poet as how to fulfill (not "fill") the form it gives as imperative. The notion of free will, the choosing that Duchamp would make the artist's essential function, is trivial in such experience. Those who would claim this freedom for the writer have elected to remain unconscious. Form (content) is not imposed upon language but received from it. It chooses you.

The failure of these poems is a failure to engage the imagination at sufficient depth and duration in the complex, organized, and dynamic whole that is language. The shadow trace is not enough. It may be that Samperi knows this and, fearing he would be directed outside the scope of his Christian/Dantesque belief, deliberately limits his involvement. Whether or not that is true, the result is nominal imagery and blurred vision. The failure is serious because the sincere desire of Samperi's theological poet is shared by all other poets who have either sought or have had given to (or imposed upon) them the spiritual definition of poetry: glorified body spiritual man undivided. We cannot be this man unless we are clear that to see means a conscious and continuous living in the myth of language.

Reading
William
Bronk

Reading William Bronk's poetry is a dark progress. Or, to make an obvious turn on the title of his first published collection, *Light And Dark* (Origin Press, 1956; reprinted 1975 by Elizabeth Press), it is a progress from light to dark, to a dark light. By light I mean a poetry possessing the qualities of light and of those qualities especially clarity of definition and distinction.

The agent of this clarity is always a single recognizable voice, related as it must be to certain voices around or before it, but recognizable nonetheless, its intelligence—active and alert beyond the passivity of "reflection"—visibly working with problems we come to feel identify a special and definite zone of operation. And we are justified in our expectation that, reading such poetry, we may experience those qualities: to perceive more, to perceive with a greater sense of depth, to perceive the possibility for conversation on what it all means to continue (with the past, with the present). By light I mean something more than simply "good" poetry, though its opposite is not poetry at all.

The first book in the chronology of the poems' actual writing is not *Light And Dark* but *My Father Photographed With Friends* (written in the 1940s, but not published until 1976 by Elizabeth Press). As its subtitle "and other pictures" indicates, it is a very typical first collection. Most of the effort has gone into getting down the description of what's seen and felt with some precision, without too many words or emotional histrionics. So "Growth of Alder":

> In its secret thickets consorting with rabbits
> and the hushed mice,

> meeting its dark reflection in any water,
> alder compounds its branches,
> its intricate cones.

And there are the typical formal recital pieces, the sonnets and syllabics (see "The Delineation," "Benedicite Omnia Opera"). Yet amid all this student modesty there is also an attempt to think actively and personally in the poem, as opposed to "filling" the inherited forms merely, an attempt to coordinate the picture or image with thought moving almost contrapuntally in response. What is wanted is the coordination of the neutral reportage of the picture and the passionate, singular voice of the poet.

While such desire is clear enough in these first poems, there is little accomplishment. An exception is the title poem, the only one that Bronk kept from this collection to appear in the later *Light And Dark* (though the line arrangement is quite different and less satisfactory than what appears in the Elizabeth Press edition). As Gibbon remarks in his *Memoirs,* the writer knows better than anybody else what he has done. And we can easily concur with Bronk's judgement. For while the other poems demonstrate a kindling of consciousness generally and some skill in craft matters, this one does it. It does get at the desired coordination.

> This is my father photographed with friends, when he was young.
> Unsettled on the steps of a wooden porch, and the one
> who lived there elegant beside him. They and the others
> hopefully casual in the face of the deciding camera,
> the judgments of which are unfeeling but can be swayed.
> And I, as in some later picture of myself,
> look for a person identified beyond doubt, and knowing that he
> is none of the ones that he is not, yet still unsure,
> under the features composed and trusting, who is there.
> As if the decision were long and legal when handed down,
> hard to be read and truly rendered in such a case.
> And hard, in the face, to find our usual pitiful ends.
> God sweeten the bitter judgments of our lives. We wish so much.

It is almost a sonnet. The rhythm is that gravely regular, the vocabulary conversational and formal and entwined in its syntax, the two-part division of attention from the reported photograph to the poet himself, and to his "enlarging" consideration of the photograph. What is distinctive is the voice that breaks out, abrupt, in the last two lines. You can detect a voice in the other lines, but it is just voice, any voice beyond Muzak noise flow, the museum's transistor voice wanting to tell you something instructive about Matisse, but not about itself or what he/she/it thinks about Matisse.

The voice of the last two lines is distinct from the modulation that precedes it because judgement is given. A choice has been made, and so we are made aware, in a way that is made all the more evident by its contrast with the reportage and representation that went before it, that a mind is present. What particular choice is almost, but not quite, irrelevant. We are so taken by this sudden violation of "aesthetic distance" that it almost doesn't matter. For here is someone who would speak directly and intensely: there's some feeling here that goes deeper than the nervous sensitivity of first collections. What this mind and its voice choose is not happy. It suggests that we don't count all that much, that our own lives, and not some exterior tribunal, judge us so, and that our god-wishing is part of only wishing instead of doing. The voice is bleak, skeptical, and we don't care: like a torso turned in the air, a voice comes out of this poem to speak to us.

I find that voice singular, recognizably separate from the standard, appropriate poet discourse that precedes it in the poem and from the voicings of the past that Eliot would call tradition. It is like hearing Ray Charles in the local church choir and in Palestrina's choir. There is another voice, however, which haunts the early poems. Consider:

> Her last notes turned again to meet the first,
> enclosing space whose entry hearing held
> since her first notes began. Whatever her words
> whatever that was she sang, speaking of change,
> the flight of time, of our mortality,
> the flowing turmoil space in which we move,
> she said the moment shaped was more than these.
> Her singing took the flight and held it still.
>
> (from "Her Singing")

And:

> She measured to the hour its solitude.
> She was the single artificer of the world

In which she sang. And when she sang, the sea,
Whatever self it had, became the self
That was her song, for she was the maker. Then we,
As we beheld her striding there alone,
Knew that there never was a world for her
Except the one she sang and, singing, made.

(from "The Idea of Order at Key West")

The first could have been a rejected companion stanza for the second; they are that close. The closeness, and its instances are numerous if not always so obvious throughout Bronk's early poems, is proof of intention. It's difficult to sound so precisely like someone else by chance over a period of time.

The voice behind Bronk's voice is Wallace Stevens. Faced with such close identification, we need not ask why it was done. For the motivation must be experienced similarly by each young poet in the realization of his or her own voice's lack. But what did Bronk gain by its assumption, and how truly complete was it? Gain cancels lack: a voice is given, and with it come a sense of organization that is not so utterly dependent on inherited form systems, a tonal range that is connected with a range of attitude and subject matter, a set of values. Stevens' voice can be characterized as august and senatorial. He writes a loose iambic line in a variety of stanza formations; his attitude is aloof, patrician, occasionally clownish. His subject matter remains constant throughout all his poems: a constant meditation on the relation of the imagination and reality.

Whether he consciously proposed it as a problem or not, it is Stevens who realized that such ongoing activity could free him from the necessity of writing discrete lyrics with discrete subjects and all their attendant difficulties of a new start/stop each time. Further, he realized that continuing meditation on the same theme, which stated in itself would quickly turn to argument and then to prose, required a symbol structure for even the possibility of lasting elaboration and variation. The root idea, then, must be what the mathematicians term "elegant," as elegant as the theme for Bach's *Art of the Fugue*. It is: poetry properly occurs when the imagination and reality are in right relation. This allows for an immediate richness. There is the literal poetry by virtue of something that bears resemblance by its sound and shape to usual poetry, and there is the symbolic pure poetry always sought after and only occasionally achieved within the literal.

Throughout Stevens' poetry green is an indicator for the pure poetry. Symbolically: green = yellow, color of sun-reality and associated with the tropic South (see "Yellow Afternoon," the twenty-ninth stanza of "An Ordinary Evening in New Haven," the second stanza of "Esthétique du Mal"), *plus* blue, color of sky-imagination (see "The Man with the Blue Guitar," "Holiday in Reality," "Sea Surface Full of Clouds"). Thus Stevens can write of this unification, now in terms of related geographic and time symbols, in "Notes toward a Supreme Fiction":

> Morning and afternoon are clasped together
>
> And North and South are an intrinsic couple
> And sun and rain a plural, like two lovers
> That walk away as one in the greenest body.

But the pure poetry turns out to be a faint and volatile shadow made even more difficult to grasp because of its wrapping in flamboyant language. Often it does not appear at all because Stevens wishes to consider only one element of the amalgam or because the balance has been somehow upset. (It seems to be in the nature of each element to strive for and to presume independence of each other.) In fact, it is imperative for green not to become permanent in the poems. For if it were to do so, there would be no further need or interest in writing another poem.

I find myself writing about Stevens' use of symbols as if they were appliances that could be bought at the store. The truth of our experience as readers and writers, however, is that they are instances of a consistent but flexible and personal vocabulary consistently used within a recognizable range of variation. Stevens probably found them as we find them: as recurring parts of a vocabulary that in time cohere into not simply a list of favored terms but an entire language whose basis is personal, yet whose effect is the opposite of personal. Once the potential language is detected, it can begin to be spoken. There can be fluency beyond signification. Stevens' symbol language and his surface language—all those "whiroos / And scintillant sizzlings such as children like"—are important beyond their helping us understand Stevens because it is these things that are neither amplified nor adapted in Bronk's otherwise close identification.

In disregarding them, Bronk disregards much more. For as Northrop Frye has noticed, Stevens is a poet "for whom the theory and the practice of poetry were inseparable. His poetic vision is informed by a metaphysic; his metaphysic is informed by a theory of knowledge; his theory of knowledge is informed by a poetic vision." An instance of this continuation is Stevens' essay/poem "Three Academic Pieces," which deals theoretically with the levels of reality, the extent of resemblance, and the function of metaphor. This is followed by considerations of the same subjects in two poems that complete the series, "Someone Puts a Pineapple Together" and "Of Ideal Time and Choice."

The essay opens: "the accuracy of letters is an accuracy with respect to the structure of reality." Later, Stevens writes that the poet has his own meaning for reality; and *his* own meaning, as hinted by the Platonic "structure," is made explicit in another essay, "The Noble Rider and the Sound of Words." Here reality is *not* "that 'collection of solid, static objects extended in space' but the life that is lived in the scene that it composes; and so reality is not that external scene but the life that is lived in it. Reality is things as they are." The life that is lived in the external scene derives from our acts of perception, acts of composition, which are acts of the imagination. Stevens' reality is a quality following the arranging of perception. It is a quality possessed by "things as they are" *after* they have been positioned in a scene, a form, which can be a metaphor. You know something about apples: you see Cézanne's apples: you know something else about apples. It is not merely that the apples on your table are differently colored but that Cézanne's forms permit his apples to exist relatively free from the laws (expectations) of the usual-as-logical universe in which your apples exist. There has been a transformation. Things as they are tends to be how they aren't in the usual-as-logical universe.

The agent of transformation is the imagination, and its agent in poetry is metaphor. What identifies the imagination is its ability to perceive resemblances. Based on likeness, the value of resemblance in poetry is that it is the necessary first step in leading the reader to awareness of things-as-they-are reality. For if no resemblance from the exterior universe, which includes more than "nature," exists in the poem, there will be no consciousness greater than "this is a poem," which amounts to an outright denial of Stevens' conception of what the interpenetration of the imagination with reality through the forms/metaphors of the poem ought to achieve. It is like saying, and only saying, "this is a painting," when asked for an interpretation of Cézanne.

"This is a poem" denies Stevens's hope for poetry because it registers only poetry as artifice, external wordcraft. It does not pick up on resemblance as comparison or contrast and cannot partake of the "ideal," another term Stevens was forced to use to set off the quality of things-as-they-are-in-the-scene-they-compose reality from that other reality which, as with realist painters who are present illusionists of a past reality, may allow the engineers to get on with things, but which is no help for a truer seeing.

Returning to the first poem of "Three Academic Pieces," we find

> It is something on a table that he sees,
> The root of a form, as of this fruit, a fund,
> The angel at the center of this rind,
> This husk of Cuba, tufted emerald,
> Himself, may be, the irreducible X
> At the bottom of imagined artifice,
>
> Its inhabitant and elect expositor.

Stevens' angel identifies itself in a later poem, "Angel Surrounded by Paysans," where we're told, "I am the angel of reality," but it is an angel without ashen wing or tepid aureole. It is one of us, and: "Yet I am the necessary angel of earth, / Since, in my sight, you see the earth again." Angels are the highest divine representatives to approach human persons directly. Yet this angel is "of reality" and without the apparel of more "regular" angels. Furthermore, this angel is needed in order to see not heavenly regions but the earth *again*. What makes the earth re-visible is the poet himself.

My guess is that Stevens chose the figure because the angel is the most important translator to human persons as beings once intimate with the Creator of things, but who are now fallen away from that intimacy and require an intermediary. Stevens uses the myth aesthetically. Human persons-now are prevented from seeing the world by language, which no longer serves to point accurately and persuasively to the object, no longer allows us to see it, but only refers to other elements of the language, which act on it as modifiers. The poet—comprehender of the right relation of the imagination and reality—is the angel who works for renewed seeing. His own angel, it is the poet who is the "himself," "the irreducible X," and "the poem's inhabitant and elect expositor."

> It is as if there were three planets: the sun,
> The moon and the imagination, or say,
>
> Day, night and man and his endless effigies.

We can now begin to answer the questions of how much Bronk gained by assuming Stevens' voice and how complete the assumption was. Clearly, he got much more than the assured and fluent rhetoric of "The Idea of Order at Key West." For with the voice came Frye's circle of poetic vision-metaphysic-theory of knowledge-poetic vision. I doubt if Bronk— or any younger poet imitating an older master—was fully conscious of the implications of his choice. More likely, he took what he needed without paying too much attention to what else there might be. Influence is a practical, partial business. But inevitably, perhaps unconsciously and perhaps even against his will, the circle attendant to the voice must be included.

We should not be surprised that not all of the circle's elements are taken up. The most noticeable of these in the *Light And Dark* poems is the symbolism. Nor, with the possible exceptions of "Midsummer" and "Green as a Verity" in *The World, The Worldless,* does it appear in the latter work. Without Stevens' symbolism there is no chance (Bronk might say there was no felt need) for unifying the imagination with reality not only as they've been defined by Stevens, but also in their more general sense of the mind and the exterior universe. What we do find in this first book and what will become the darkening dogma of the later ones is the sense of irreparable division. So appearances at sunset, in "The Unsatisfied," suggest allegorical figures which at once are our "joy" and yet affirm what is exactly unattainable for us who are thus the "unsatisfied." Like those people in "At Tikal," who "imagined a world and it was as if it were there," we "build a kind of cage" to give shape to a world. "And oh, it is always a world and not the world."

This line, the last one in "At Tikal," brings us back to what attracts our attention to Bronk in the first place: the presence of a powerful, distinctive voice. And it is not Stevens' voice. Many lines in this poem could have been written by Stevens, who, however, could not have written this final, most crucial one from his unvarying position as elect expositor of his poems within his poems. He remains there because, unlike Bronk, a direct appeal is never made to his reader. Bronk constantly attempts to break out of his own constructions. Typically, his closing lines diminish the very careful reasoning that precedes them, the chamber music of that reasoning demolished with shouts and pleas made all the more urgent because they are not made to himself, but to ourselves. It is not easy to read William Bronk.

To come to that power, Bronk required Stevens' voice for the chamber music. It is no good shouting in an open field, and Stevens provides the furnished room for this passionate poetry to explode against. That it continues to explode throughout all of the books is due to the ignoring or flat rejection of the master's two-part symbolism. What remains will be the parts themselves, the sunset and the allegorical figures, which will be dealt with from every conceivable point of view and with a brooding meditative carefulness, but from which no unification emerges. The parts remain parts without pointing toward any inclusion that would hold them so that they become anything more than what they were to begin with.

To extend the figure a little: having chosen the room, Bronk has to live in it, even as he would kick it down. The explosions continue because Bronk has no alternative. With the voice came the metaphysic and the theory of knowledge, both of which depend on a symbol vocabulary for their elucidation and for their evasive "resolution." Without such vocabulary, having kept everything else, there can only be frustration and despair. "And oh, it is always a world and not the world."

Almost by default and out of defiance, that line becomes Bronk's own metaphysic and theory of knowledge. That is, the world suggested by music and poetry (the imagination, the mind) is more real than the supposed real world, but in the end it must be admitted that it isn't real either. That line, the terrible remnant of Stevens' circle, later becomes *The World, The Worldless* (New Directions, 1964), a book that has no parallel in American poetry of this century. It is an awesome achievement, one which the later books occasionally repeat in isolated poems without quite regaining its equilibrium between image and argument, between the hope for structures (worlds) given by the imagination and the despair at the realization that they are finally uninhabitable. Almost always the despairing realization does come. Yet the poems hold their aspect of hope that something can be known and consequently done, that the desirable and truly real world will be found, without their author slipping into a too-knowing Manichaean exercise. And the book will endure. All voices endure that are so passionate, so alertly intent in their pursuit of what we may as well call "the truth."

What follows is an exhibit of some of the resonant variousness with which these poems unceasingly return to their now located, never to be renounced proposition of the world, the worldless: that there is felt to be a desirable, real world; that what the mind's imagination apprehends turns out to be worlds—ourselves in fact reflected in the act of our own looking—without being that world; that we, then, are indeed the world-less. Let it begin with "Metonymy As An Approach To A Real World."

> Whether what we sense of this world
> is the what of this world only, or the what
> of which of several possible worlds
> —which what?—something of what we sense
> may be true, may be the world, what it is, what we sense.
> For the rest, a truce is possible, the tolerance
> of travelers, eating foreign foods, trying words
> that twist the tongue, to feel that time and place,
> not thinking that this is the real world.
>
> Conceded, that all the clocks tell local time;
> conceded, that "here" is anywhere we bound
> and fill a space; conceded, we make a world:
> is something caught there, contained there,
> something real, something which we can sense?
> Once in a city blocked and filled, I saw
> the light lie in the deep chasm of a street,
> palpable and blue, as though it had drifted in
> from say, the sea, a purity of space.

The convolutions of the opening five-line sentence show that Bronk is aware and confident of his theme from the start. The sentence in itself is a set of syntactic variations which could not have been done without a prior surety. There has to be something here, fixed, before there can be movement away from or against it. This first stanza is "reasonable." Something of what we sense *may* be true, and those other things that would violate our sense can be tolerated.

The second stanza formally reflects the first (two sentences, nine lines each), but it also contains Bronk's central, persistent question: "conceded, we make a world: / is something caught there, contained there, / something which we can sense?" We get an immediate response that will nevertheless not end the asking. For the response is curious. It carries a tone of testifying sincerity while its very terms undercut that sincerity (and the hope we share from that tone). What is more evanescent, less real, than light? It is not described in the language of quantum mechanics but *as though*, metonymy, the sign for the thing signified, a special case of metaphor. Certainly, a purity of space enhances our sense of the light. And yet where are we? What did this, made it palpable, was the mind's imagination, ourselves. So an approach, but no closer.

In this poem Bronk is so intent on his proposition that we follow him, the urgency of his voice (and not particularly the seriousness of his subject matter) pulling us along, the voice so compelling that we forget for a moment that there is considerable imagery, seeing, in the poem. The images are in tune with the urgent cadence. There are other poems whose titles boldly declare still other, continuing approaches to the proposition: "The World In Space and Time," "The Various Sizes of the World," "Aspects Of the World like Coral Reefs." These should not be taken as inevitable reduplications. There is always the feeling, which will gradually desert the later books, that something may be worked out so this voice might calm itself.

The "Aspects" poem demonstrates that the poet's intelligence allows for more than crazed bellowing. Here it's found that astronomy belies the evidence of our senses, so that "It is absurd to describe the world in sensible terms." With that line we prepare ourselves for a great roar of anguish that the sensed world and that other world of the mind cannot be got together. Instead:

> How good that even so, aspects of the world
> that are real, or seem to be real, should rise like reefs
> whose rough agglomerate smashes the sea.

It can be argued that the qualification "or seem to be real" still doesn't let go of the old argument amid the genial statement. But that is blind argument. The statement, which charms us after so much insistent self-debate, would lack all conviction if it issued from any context other than Bronk's ongoing proposition. Without that context, the sentiment is suspicious in itself and in showing the proposition to be merely good material, to be worked until other fashions are trotted by. Bronk stays within his circle, remnant of Stevens' circle, and gains strength and even eloquence from it. That he *must* stay there to keep those gains, and never stop the proposition's quizzing, is the price he pays.

Thus in "Virgin And Child With Music And Numbers," after the flat declaration

> We are not
> fulfilled. We cannot hope to be. No,
> we are held somewhere in the void of whole despair,
> enraptured, and only there does the world endure.

there comes: "Lady, sing to this Baby, even so." Even so: the phrase is repeated in each case for a reason. Even if the world or not *the* world but our notions of it all prove out wrong, show us up so that our satisfaction can exist only in always finding our assumptions wrong, perverse and mocking, the poet would have us yet act on these assumptions. Of course it is faith. As such, we read the poem as evidence of great tenderness not compromised by what went before these last lines but made all the more valued and genuine for them.

I would cite another exhibit, "For An Early Italian Musician," for its blend of strength and eloquence, the one a matter of having taken a position that will not be given up, despite the frustrations that any one position, like any single point of view, must eventually reveal; the other the result of that strength which encourages variation, which Bronk sustains throughout *The World, The Worldless.*

> Listening now to his music, how
> one wishes to have been the musician, and so
> to be beautiful forever as his music is,
> and he in it, who is now
> only his music, which is his world.
>
> How one always wishes for an end
> —to be complete.
>
> And there is also this:
> that one wishes to last, that one needs to make
> a world for survival, which cannot be done
> simply, or soon, but by a slow
> crystal on crystal accretion of a made
> world, a world made to last.
>
> One is nothing with no world.

He begins not with his proposition's argument but with an image which is still visual, sensed visually, despite originating in music. For the poem is taken up with what one imagines on hearing, say, a Corelli recorder sonata. And what is imagined does bring us back, though the connection is not arbitrary, to the argument.

What Bronk glimpses listening to this music is more an attribute of something than the thing itself. The attribute, wholeness, leads us to what it modifies and defines: a world. The musician is to be envied because his art secures him, now become its medium, in a definite world that is not really of his own making. There is the appearance, then, of an escape from subjectivity. In that world his music constructs, the musician is complete. As we perceive him, nothing is left out. He is subsumed within the music; he is completely defined by it (thus he has no name); he is the music. We are given two motives for finding his condition desirable: it is complete, and it is lasting (beauty being a value of the two).

Again we find ourselves operating in paradox. These are art qualities, not human ones. If they are to be possessed, the human is lost, caught up as the musician and Stevens' singer are caught. If we read the poem in the context of the entire book, there is an even greater, more devastating paradox. The poem's last line has a powerful, undeniable whip to it. One *is* nothing with no world. But the world conjured by the imagination's art takes away that fragile identity of self we wish to protect; and, ultimately, those conjurations are not real either.

It is a very beautiful and a very cruel poem. It has all the beautiful properties of art itself, complete and lasting, but we know from previous stages of the argument that what has been so seductively provided is a world, not the world. (The last line is careful to avoid using any article.) I think we would be justified now to protest that the dice are loaded, that the proposition is a not very well disguised catch-22 situation. There is a compelling reason, though, why we don't: Bronk himself doesn't seem to be aware of it. Nothing in the poems can be found to show he knows that the debate, so set up, can have no possible resolution. It is not too much to claim that Stevens' circle, incompletely translated as it had to be, gave Bronk the means for fluent and more than merely fluent speech at a time when he was practically mute. The discovery must have been exhilarating. But Bronk himself comes to see that, for all the variation—and the poems may be read as an ardent examination of the range's extent—there is no way out.

The last poem of the book, "The Outcry," ends:

> What I want to do is shout
> because we were all wrong, because the point

was not the point, because the world, or what
we took for the world, is breaking, breaking. We were wrong
and are not right. Break! Break! We are here!
What I want to do is shout! Break! Shout!

In lines before these Bronk claims his wanting to shout has nothing to do with either happiness or outrage. We can see why. Having come all this way, gone through the range of variation, we've ended up where we began, only more alive to the felt need to be in a world that is the world. So not happiness nor even outrage, but incredulous surprise. And we feel like joining the shouting. We are here, but there must be a way out of the empowering, but fatal, circle.

We remain here, which is not in the world as we might have assumed previously, but in the circle. Waiting for release, we must wonder why we allowed ourselves to be so bound at all. The answer, in the form of a quotation from Paul Klee in Stevens' essay "The Relations between Poetry and Painting," is an elaboration on what has already been given as Bronk's motivation for imitation. "But he is one chosen that today comes near to the secret places where original law fosters all evolution. And what artist would not establish himself there where the organic center of all movement in time and space—which he calls the mind or heart of creation—determines every function." Stevens is a little embarrassed by what he considers the sacerdotal jargon of the Klee quotation. He stands by it, however, because it's not too much to allow to those who "helped to create a new reality, a modern reality, since what has been created is nothing less."

And that reality is a reality of decreation

> in which our revelations are not the revelations of
> belief, but the precious portents of our own powers.
> The greatest truth we could hope to discover, in
> whatever field we discovered it, is that man's truth
> is the final resolution of everything. . . . and this is
> what gives them the validity and serious dignity
> that become them as among those that seek wisdom,
> seek understanding.

The Stevens quotations commemorate all of those efforts to be freed from the old illusory reality of the representational that we now sum up as modernism. For all his apologies for the high-flown tone, it is easy enough to understand why Stevens is adamant. By virtue of his circle he was enabled to position himself near Klee's center, no longer a mere commentator upon, no longer a mere illustrator of an already-established reality, but a creator of a reality which, partaking of the old reality and of his own imagination, is new, modern. No longer the romantic maudit exiled to the outer fringe, the poet now exists at the procreative and organic center, the position forgetting prose-taken generations would give over to static gods, the truth of that position returned to its own origin in human vision.

This is not "poesy" but wisdom and understanding. Or at least the seeking for them. The poet is once more a shaman and a researcher. Poetry is once more a vehicle for active thought which, if it celebrates anything, celebrates its own human thinkers. Who would not give up everything to be there?

Such eulogy goes too far. It's doubtful whether either Stevens or Bronk would be comfortable or even very much interested in the shaman-poet, though the researcher might be more acceptable. The desirable center has only indirectly to do with society or the tribe. Its function is to give the intelligence voice so that the prodigious search of appearance through metaphor may be given in turn a new seriousness and vitality. There may be understanding thus found that will be of use to the group, but our attention now is on the individual. Bronk and ourselves as his readers stay in the circle because without it there is no sign of existence. The voice signifies the mind which desires to identify itself as distinct from those of the past. It can do this only as the poet draws near to the "secret places." Through Stevens, Bronk is provided a voice, which is not Stevens' voice but eventually Bronk's own, distinct and recognizable, and he is provided with what I have called his proposition.

The assumption of another's voice to find one's own and then actually to find it is a great satisfaction. *The World, The Worldless* poems move with a precision and an assurance that we can barely hope for from the earlier work. These poems show their author's satisfaction and gratitude, so that there is some patience that no resolution to the proposition can be found. But, as they continue and still only increasingly subtle variations result, the voice grown louder and more insistent, the end is bewilderment, incredulity.

I have already offered an explanation as to why there in fact can never be resolution. What must be emphasized is that Bronk did achieve what all poets must achieve if they are to be anything more than Pound's "starters of crazes." He did get near the secret places, he did become the possessor of an individual voice, a more than "capable organ" for an intense and generous intelligence. "All poets" suggests union dues automatically paid. But very few poets ever write from the position of that achievement.

Curiously, the very magnitude of this achievement forces Bronk to make a most difficult decision. He has arrived, by assumption of the past and by his own considerable ability, at what seems the organic center, only to find that it isn't and that he is trapped within whatever it is. It is Faust's choice: either he breaks out and risks everything—however finally false and self-consuming it becomes—or he resides within, perversely demonstrating Gödel's Proof that a finite system may indeed have infinite application. It is a decision those concerned with last year's crazes will never have to worry about. Too much cannot be made of Bronk's achievement. Yet now, having so arrived, refusing to utilize the too-easy confessional crazes of his (and our) age, he is confronted with a decision whose potential for tragedy is much greater than its difficulty of execution.

He chose to reside within. The eventual consciousness of *The World, The Worldless* is a consciousness of this decision. Bronk may never have understood—or even been curious about—why his circle, after the initial transforming brilliance, became more and more a confinement rather than Stevens' heart of creation. Still there is no question that his circle, possessing its own darkening power, does exist. The poems that follow, in *The Empty Hands* (Elizabeth Press, 1969), in *That Tantalus* (Elizabeth Press, 1971), are not noticeably poorer for the choice. In fact, with tighter editing and the cohesiveness of a single volume, their treatment of the propositional calculus would be found even more varied and more starkly intense.

There are, too, poems that could not be predicted from the world/worldless poetics and as such are indications of a not yet wholly captive sensibility. One of these is "Something Like Tepees."

> Glances and recollections, letters of sorts
> is what we get from each other. Rose called.
>
> I had forgotten. Well, no I hadn't. I'd stopped
> expecting. We learn. Not much. Not finally.

We learn. That we aren't, as we thought we were, alone.
There are others here. All right. It isn't much.

Remember once. There was a time we meant
to make something like tepees, I out of you,

you from me, and live there, make it home
as though to make a house were what we meant.

Journeys do not end in lovers meeting.
Nor end. Sometimes we touch and touch again.

But the poet knows what he is doing; the titles are accurate. His hands are empty and, like Tantalus, he remains avid for a world that will never turn out to be the world. Thus, for all the moving tenderness of this poem, the majority are concerned with the unavoidable negative consequences of Bronk's proposition. The result, weirdly parallel with an increasing technical sophistication, is that the voice grows morose, ironic, cynical. The voice has enlarged its modulations while the hope dwindles.

In "Walking Around" the despair is all the more affecting for being held as implication within the images. The poem first considers our movements and reflects that the common-sense geometries—versions of the old supposed real world—are "vines / of belief, covering the structure of experience." Bronk urges us to refuse their claims, to realize that in our walking around, we are more like a spider making its web "to sensitize a space." The comparison is revealing. We begin to think of space as something defined by our movement, our existence become a resting on, arrested, tension.

The poem, though, is not content with that insight.

> What should we make of this,
> which is the structure of experience—walking around,
> walking around, nowhere, being like
> that explosion in silence, those nets of white inside
> the rot of trees, radiating everywhere?

The images are ruinous. We follow them, assenting to their description of our existence in space, perhaps even feeling some excitement because of their accuracy, only to find ourselves as caught as their maker. It is one thing to exist in illusion, but is it not worse to have woven webs that, after

having thought to combat illusion, only organize the destructive nothingness of that explosion in silence? As in "The Elms Dying—and my
friend, Lew Stillwell, dead," we find what is truly terrible is that not any
death diminishes the world. It and time, despite our preoccupation with
them as somehow standing between us and our desires' fulfillment, are
constant. The point is: "Always. We have it. That there is no / diminish-
ment. Never. Nothing. Help us. Help!"

There is an obvious progression from the incredulous shout of "The
Outcry," the last poem in *The World, The Worldless*, to this direct
pleading for help. I have called it a dark progress because all the brilliance of this poetry, warm and hard, eventually succumbs to the despair
of a mistranslated circle. As there are poems of moving tenderness and
rigorous precision, there is also a growing number of poems whose
syntax has become clotted with overblown rhetoric and dogmatic exposition, their metaphors/images shrunken in favor of near-prose philoso-
phizing. That they didn't succumb much sooner is due to the almost
inhuman determination of this singular poet, who, with no counterpart
among his contemporaries, most resembles Melville—D. H. Lawrence's
Melville, who "hated the world: was born hating it. But he was looking
for heaven. That is, choosingly. Choosingly, he was looking for paradise.
Unchoosingly, he was mad with hatred of the world."

Change "born" to "came to," change "heaven" and "paradise" to "the
real world," change "mad with hatred of the world" to "mad with hatred
for his circle, for himself gone vain and contemptuous." What we now
read is a poetry begun to choke and feed upon itself. This shouldn't be
confused with avant-garde gestures. It is something much older and more
serious; it is hubris. A poem title from the next book, *To Praise The Music*,
"Not To Be Satan Nor To Deal With Him" is not fanciful.

The entire progression moves before us in *To Praise The Music* (Elizabeth Press, 1972). There are poems here that equal or surpass anything
Bronk has written before. The title poem is one of them. It begins with
metaphors and images, now rarities, of the scene out-there of trees in late
winter, pausing self-consciously—"oh, it is all as if"—then continues
with something by way of affirmation: "but as if, yes, / as if they sang
songs, as if they praised. / Oh, I envy them. I know the songs." It is
difficult to imagine a more convincing affirmation.

The second stanza of this sonnet (all these poems are sonnets; the form is peculiarly suited to Bronk's proposition) is of a complexity to require full quotation.

> As if I know some other things besides.
> As if; but I don't know, not more
> than to say the trees know. The trees don't know
> and neither do I. What is it keeps me from praise?
> I praise. If only to say their songs,
> say yes to them, to praise the songs they sing.
> Envied music. I sing to praise their song.

He takes it all back. He doesn't know, and the trees don't know. The bravery (or effrontery) of his question is large. What keeps anyone from praising what they feel bound to recognize as unreal? His answer, then, carries not enough conviction. It is automatic and perhaps a little scornful. "I praise" = I believe, and he's insisted for some time that he doesn't, that he can't.

Still, he will say it, if only to be able to praise the songs the trees sing. The poem properly belongs to *The World, The Worldless* when he didn't quite know that, finally, his powerful circle wouldn't allow the affirmation of such praise which, after all, means *this is real*. Yet, having gone round and round it ourselves, we know. You can't sing to praise their songs unless you sing to praise them, to say they—the trees and their world out there—are real. You may, like Stevens, want to say their songs change how we perceive them, but that does not seek to deny their them/thereness reality. You can't have it both ways. This, then, is a sad poem. For surely Bronk must know what we have come to know through his poetry. It is a backward look to a former and consciously discarded innocence, and "I praise" will not ring true.

There are other such poems (see "Dos-A-Dos" and "The Ignorant Lust After Knowledge"), but they are overshadowed by too many that are halfgood, having a memorable last stanza that salvages some of the accumulating wreckage or, not even that, the circle's wreckage only. Nothing of consequence gets said in the first twelve lines of "Getting Us Straight," for instance, but then there are the last two: "We are the world. Nothing better for us. / Nothing but us. No explanations. Us." Those lines stand by themselves. They make a coda for the entire proposition and its dark resident that is nearly immutable and yet horribly vulnerable. You can disagree, but it won't matter. The hard sureness of their rhythm will have them stand.

There are other instances of this coda which cannot quite pull it off, however, when surrounded by poems such as "About Dynamism, Desire And Other Fictions."

> Also the Golden Age was a dark time
> if there was one. I think it is now and was not
> ever. It is dark now as it always was.
>
> The thing I wanted to tell you is how we propose
> a drama, sort of, a story of our lives
> which requires changes—sequences of time,
>
> such that once there was this or something else
> —dark, say, or the Golden Age, and then
> something happened and *this* came about.
>
> Well I don't think it did. What I want
> you to know is that nothing happened and nothing can,
> that stories are fictions, truth doesn't tell one,
>
> that the beautiful is that, nothing more,
> and enough, no story, nothing to do or tell.

The title is a giveaway to what began as intensity, became a resonant power, and now beckons to us as an almost depraved arrogance. It is all a fiction. And we know because Bronk tells us so. In these poems, and even more nakedly so in *The Meantime* and *Finding Losses* (Elizabeth Press, both 1976), he is always telling us how it really is. All the poems turn on this two-step: it looks like this or maybe this or even this, but it's really that.

It is a truism, but it still holds: poetry is showing, metaphor and image; prose is telling, exposition and analysis. What is distressing about this representative poem is that not only can it not even mount some illustrations for its argument (the circle turns and turns; we're back to the old illusionism), but it also isn't even an argument. It won't do to label this philosophy, which amounts to the violation of poetry, as the dithering of Santayana's *Three Philosophical Poets* makes redundantly clear (not to forget a like confusion in Stevens' essay "A Collect of Philosophy"). For what we get is dogma: this is how it is. A dogmatic voice is a tired voice in poetry, maybe even a dead one. There is no need for the persuasion of figures. And why should there be? He knows. Hubris.

Silence And Metaphor (Elizabeth Press, 1975) duplicates To Praise The Music. The introductory poem "Here is the silence" at first promises to be nothing more than a condensed version of the dark dogma. But there is more. Again, it is provided with a redeeming coda. Before we reach it, we're told that the silence is here and everywhere, that it has always been so, and that there is no time. Accordingly, there's no reason for expectation, for worrying about whether one ought to do one thing or another. While sound does not exist here, noise does.

What we hear "under the noise" is silence "final, always, wherever." All of this is given in two-line stanzas held together by very terse speaking. It is declamation, but the concision gives it a certain appeal. It could end well enough and predictably with "Silence is all." But there is one more stanza: "Grass, I thought to keep you, would have stayed; / and you, trees, water, gone too." The abstractions are momentarily forgotten, the world out there returned to. It is a quality of these codas that, as opposed to the typically aggressive, closely reasoned character of the poems' beginnings, they are voiced more personally, the rhetorical volume turned down, their speech given almost hesitantly as if forced against their writer's will.

This reverses the usual development from initial image to final judgement/statement. We come to realize it has to develop in this order— "prose" statement followed by bare reference to objects of the out-there world—because the circle and its poet's arrogance have consumed the world. Objects, and thus images, can exist only as memories before it was found how pointlessly relative everything is. The coda redeems all the willful loss (Bronk is his own conscious destroyer) until we come to a further realization. The coda makes a sad farewell to the world. It's gone. Whatever metaphors may appear in later poems will be written out of the silence, themselves "those nets of white inside / the rot of trees," out of the vacuum remaining after the world's explosion. The coda makes a sad farewell to a world not going but long gone. The tone would have us believe he has no choice, that the truth, the mind, or some other agent has forced the poet to agree to the exploding. But we know better. He is his own agent.

With the world already acknowledged lost, the Silence poems shrink to a uniform two four-line stanzas each, dwarf sonnets. Trying to bridge a void, the poems must tighten up to avoid falling in on themselves. Correspondingly, the voice must expand to fill even their reduced space. These poems are unavoidably all talk. The voice booms and roars along, making ever more elaborate shifts in its arguing, but it can enhance only itself in an emptiness.

> If this world were, I suppose it were much
> as we think it is. There are parts, of course, we have yet
> to work out—things no one knows for sure.
> Someone always comes up with something, though.
>
> We too: I suppose, if we were, that this
> is what we were. I like to read about
> the various claims, talk to people, see
> what might have been if we were,—if the world were.
>
> ("Hypotheses")

Everything's subjunctive. It lets the talk go on; we know the world is gone, impossible to believe any longer, but the talk at least continues on the basis of if. In the end, of course, it makes no difference. Still, it lets the voice talk on, splendid in the solipsistic silence that surrounds it.

The ghastliness of the paradox, that the voice itself would become the world it displaced and fitfully mourned, is no less for being plain to see (hear). So that:

> The abstractions are what is left, after we die
> of course, but before that, too. In a while
> if not now, it is all dismissed, dismissed.
> Not to say it didn't happen, it did
>
> in a sense, it happened, as one sets a stage
> and something happens, can be said to. On stage,
> we watch the abstractions, how they look, what
> they seem to be, their presence. They are there.
>
> ("What Goes, What Stays")

They, the abstractions, are what stays. Rather: not the abstractions so much as their originating mind, their orating voice. The abstractions are given to be the remorseless vectors of a destruction that the victimized poet would have preferred not happen, but which he is powerless to prevent. And it is a delusion. There are no such vectors in Bronk's circle and, if there were, their origin is in his vision, his theory of knowledge. These poems are so many mirrors that all reflect a universe of not three, but one planet, the sun-self, the egotistical sublime made a metaphysic.

All of Bronk's titles have been accurate. The last two, *The Meantime* and *Finding Losses,* are true to that practice. The sensed world having been displaced and dissolved, the voice having explored all the variations, the nothing that is left *is* but a mean time in which what one finds are losses, nothing compounding nothing. Given the relentless logic of his proposition, which is superior to that other ordinary logic, there is no alternative or evasion.

There is a certain courage involved. These poems were written over a considerable number of years. There was time for Bronk to reject the circle that forced him into a situation for which, as I believe the poems plainly show, he came to understand there could be no resolution. But he maintains his residence within, a proud figure among his own wreckage. Our admiration is checked by what supports that endurance, which is pride, the motive power for his all-consuming voice. Or as one of the *Losses* poems is titled: "Pride, Which Goes Not Only Before But Behind And Probably Sideways Too." Renunciation, other circles, Pound's penitent silence: they are all rejected by pride which, like the voice, grows to an almost hideous splendor.

There can be no surprise, then, to "Surprise Ending."

> Of course, in a sense we aren't anyone.
> No, more than a sense. But there isn't someone across
> the galaxy either, or no one we could talk
> to, ever. Oddly talk is what it's about.

There can be no confusing this dark arrogance with existential heroics.

> If there were a maker I'd praise the maker but
> I think there isn't one; making is ours.
> My random love sings at random. I
> (who am I?) sing nevertheless (to what?): I praise.
>
> ("The Random")

There can be no stopping pride's rush to hubris.

> 2. Blessed art thou, oh God, in thy impotence.
> If there is another way to live, as we wish
> there were, we would. What more were there?
> Love God. We are at one in this.
>
> ("He Praises Nescience and Impotence")

There isn't someone across the galaxy, as there is no one to talk to, because the maker and sole citizen of that universe is the poet's I-praising I, before whom the old God of those who mistakenly thought they lived in the world out there will be found impotent, His place taken by another. The idea of Him is spiritual; it emanates from the mind but is impotent nonetheless because it doesn't derive from *his* mind. (It belongs to the old spirituality of the out-there world; both are obliterated in his assumption.) And he would tease us with his question. Who is he? He is God. What does he sing to? Himself: I praise I till kingdom come.

We cannot read the frequent biblical references in Bronk's poetry in the usual ways. When he says that deprivation is to be driven out of the Eden garden, to be amazed "how far the unexpected world goes: / the opening out. It is hard to live here," we must remember that he drove himself out of that old world—now implicitly turned into the original paradise—that he constitutes the entire scope of that unexpected world of self. It *is* hard to live there because nothing else is there. The self, however aggrandized, can feed on the self only so long. "One is nothing with no world."

A sign of how hard it is to live there is the poems' gradual diminution. They are down to near-zero imagery and four lines each in *Finding Losses,* and what the future would seem to hold is an accelerated grimace into unmetaphoric silence. Almost from the beginning Bronk's poetry has been a holding action against the decay that came, became manifest, at the same time as the burst into powerful articulation with the assumption of Stevens' voice and circle. The dark progress of Bronk's poetry should not be confused with lazy literary sociology (senility attempting to imitate youthful success) or even with saying the same thing so often that its own sayer can't bear to say it again. That proposes the poet doesn't quite know what he's doing. William Bronk is a terribly knowing poet.

And yet, reading *The Meantime,* one is tempted to put aside all the steadily accumulating evidence of the decay. For even in its narrow circumstances the voice is compelling.

> Amazement is not too strong a word
> so I am amazed at the way the language survives
> other structures: we go on talking as if
> we had never lost all we come at last
> to lose, the time and place the language described,
> was part of, itself, the hypnotist who set
> his subjects in trance and movement and walked off stage,
> left them doing whatever it was they did
> and walked away to where, wherever it is
> there is nothing to do, nothing for them to do,
> nothing doing, where its own sound
> is all the language hears or listens to
> and talks and keeps on talking to the end.
>   ("The Increasing Abstraction Of Language")

Bronk is the hypnotist, and we are his willing subjects. The voice is so compelling that we are tempted to forgive him for including us, the "we," in what is utterly his vision, his world, alone. The "we" must be changed to "I." And then the terror of a dark, utterly dark nothingness is revealed by the stage lighting of his poetry. He is his own hypnotist, his own subject; there is nothing for him to do. There is nothing left to do but let the voice run its scales on and on, now and then permitting itself in what seems a moment of relaxed sympathy to forget itself and so one more subjunctive respite is taken, more distant overtones are explored, on and on until the voice can stand itself no longer.

In the end we come back to Stevens. "The imagination loses vitality as it ceases to adhere to what is real. When it adheres to the unreal and intensifies what is unreal, while its first effect may be extraordinary, that effect is the maximum effect it will ever have." The imagination for Stevens is the power of the mind over the possibilities of things. While the power and the possibilities continually strive against each other for dominance in his poetry, they are kept in a floating balance, the ideal symmetry of which can be managed only briefly and symbolically. Bronk assumes Stevens' voice to find his own, does find his own and brilliantly, but retains a mistaken version of his master's circle even after the mistake—the result of a necessarily partial assumption—would appear to be recognized out of pride. Reality changes from substance to subtlety. And the mind, through his extraordinary voice, intensifies itself to the exclusion of all else. The only light remaining is stage light. William Bronk is the dark angel of the power of the mind.

Zukofsky's "Mantis"

The question that matters for reading "Mantis" and Zukofsky's own twisting interpretation of his poem is: what form should that take? (The poem may be found in either the 1971 Norton edition of *All: The Collected Short Poems* or the 1991 Johns Hopkins University Press edition of the *Complete Short Poetry*.) "That" is five or six thoughts' reflection (pulse's witness) of what was happening without transitions, the actual twisting of many and diverse thoughts (the coincidence of the mantis lost in the subway, the growing oppression of the poor), the contents of "the simultaneous, / The diaphanous, historical / In one head." That is, what shape best fits or suits them? What shape do they in themselves define? Zukofsky's answer is the sestina with its repeated end words that wind the lines around themselves as continuously as the mind winds the sensorium's information.

It may be objected that this choice forgets to mention the villanelle, which, with only two rhymes and several repetitions of the first and third lines, would also allow for the suggestion of simultaneous winding motion. To this objection Zukofsky might reply that such repetition, after all, is static. The first and third lines are not twisting or weaving. They simply reappear throughout the poem, each time the words of the lines in identical order with their first occurrence. The end words of the first stanza in a sestina, in comparison, are in motion (transformation), which then forces the poem as a whole to be "moving." So "leaves," the end word for the first line of Zukofsky's sestina, occurs on the second line in the second stanza, on the fourth line in the third stanza, the fifth line of the fourth stanza, the third line of the fifth stanza, the sixth line of the sixth stanza, not repeating again in its first line position until the three-line coda stanza. Too, the use of the end words in other than end positions (e.g., "it" in the third stanza) carries the poem's motion even closer to the originating "thoughts' torsion."

Other repeating French forms—the rondeau or the rondel—might be mentioned. Yet they share the villanelle's static countermotion and, besides, almost always imply a playfulness that is out of keeping with the seriousness of the "poor's helplessness / The poor's separateness / Bringing self-disgust." That the sestina is in concert with the poet's seriousness is made clear by Karl Shapiro, a poet whose own practice obviously and radically differs from Zukofsky's, in his reflection on the form.

> The sestina seems not necessarily to be a mere curious exercise or virtuoso showpiece, but at least ideally to be a form designed to encourage and express a meditation or reverie upon certain thoughts or images. If such an obsessive vision or reverie-like impulse does not in fact exist or come into existence as the poem is written, the six key words will seem unmotivated and the whole poem will turn out to be an academic exercise. *The sestina would seem to require the poet's deepest love and conviction,* involve his deepest impressions as these take on a rather obsessive quality. (my italics)

The question remains whether Zukofsky actually fulfills the sestina shape "sincerely," that is, as a force and not wickerwork. The poem's source is the coincidence of Zukofsky seeing the mantis with begging eyes, which then flies at his chest as he stands at a subway station. In the act of seeing the mantis, the poet—without transitions—immediately has several thoughts' reflection, one on another, which connects the mantis' desperate situation with that of the poor.

The combination of his multiple reflection and his interest in stating the creature's ungainliness lead him to choose the sestina as a suitable form for this collective. The question may now be subdivided and rephrased: Is this situation and its attendant associations described, "written" with adequate care for detail? Is Zukofsky's complex emotion as reported in his interpretation—surprise, curiosity toward the creature, sadness toward the condition of the poor, outrage at those responsible for that condition, resolution to help the mantis and the poor—sufficiently objectified?

The poem's first stanza begins with a startled recognition of something that is totally out of place. Hence the surprised, exclamatory naming: Mantis! praying mantis! A logical sequence is then set up with "since" (logical and causal: since you have done this, I will do that). But the sequence is left seemingly incomplete in the first stanza. Since the leaves of the mantis's wings and terrified eyes beg the poet to take it up, "it," by line position, would seem to refer to the parenthetical thoughts' torsion. If this is the case, Zukofsky would be depicting the mantis as begging him to take up what he alone can be expected to be conscious of, the contents of his own forgetting and remembering head. Or, following the interpretation ("That this thoughts' torsion / Is really a sestina"), the mantis urges the poet to take up the sestina, to save it from the ravages of inattention or misuse.

Such readings are torturous and silly. I prefer "it" as referring back to the mantis itself, thoughts' torsion being a parallel (correlative, an aside as in drama) speech from Zukofsky's "conscience" as a distinct third-person voice saying within him, as an admonishment to himself, "Look, take it up, save it!" The logical-causal expectation aroused by "since" is met, though not in the anticipated orderly fashion.

Since the mantis begs *and* since the poet can't bear to look at it or to touch it, the mantis may be rescued by an anonymous nearby "You"— "You can." But no one sees "you"—the mantis—lost in the cars' drafts on the lit subway stone. There will be no rescue of "you" by a nonseeing (or caring) "You." The poet, alone, is forced to return, despite himself, to what he alone has apparently cared to see, the mantis. The distinction between upper case and lower case "you" returns in the third stanza with the "You" indicating the collective singular surrounding the mantis and the poet—the public crowd—while the "you" is once more the mantis, now being asked by the poet where the newsboy as representative of the crowd would put "him."

Another series of questions, in the second stanza, precedes this, which—from the poet to the mantis—serve to identify the mantis with the poor by their shared position (the stone) and, by extension, shared emotions of terror, being lost and "not seen" by those of the public crowd around them.

> The mantis, then,
> Is a small incident of one's physical vision
> Which is the poor's helplessness
> The poor's separateness.

The stanza ends with what Zukofsky's interpretation accurately describes as "pun, fact, banality." The shops' crowds—the public crowd(s)—are a jam and offer no food or any attention to the mantis or, by association, to the poor.

The first line of the third stanza returns to the multiple references of "it." What even the newsboy sees is "it" as the mantis *and* "No use, papers make money, makes stone, stone, / Banks." That is, even the crowd's representative is somehow aware that the economic system will not alter itself, that the poor will continue as they are. The newsboy says it, the mantis, is harmless, a painfully unconscious pun revealing his real nonsight in relation to the double reference of "it." Then "You?": are You, the crowd, harmless? And: where will he, its representative, put the mantis? For there are no safe places, as the spinning syntax of "here, here's" indicates in ending one thought and instantly turning to another in the smallest of spaces.

Here = the subway station. Here's news = perhaps the newsboy's papers; their characteristically inaccurate and superficial reporting, as opposed to the lover-poet's, *is* too poor to save the poor. They offer no information which their readers could reliably use as a basis for positive action. The poem's reader's own remembering head then recalls, from the second stanza, "the poor / . . . who rising from the news may trample you—." In their anger with the unreal or unreliable news, the poor may trample a mantis. There is no shelter for it or for any of the separate poor when "the times" have made the massed poor sightless in their rage with a condition that continues "steadying lost."

In the fourth stanza the poet overcomes his fear to allow the mantis to light upon his chest, an item of his shame and of the poor who laugh at his fright: shame at his noncaring for the creature itself and as an emblem of the separate poor (as opposed to the laughing mass). The mantis is described through three images: spectre, strawberry, a stone that (as a sign) "leads" lost children through the close paths left by men. What do these mythic images, compacted by alliteration, signify? Possibly, that the mantis as sign is part spiritual entity, part sweet and infrequently obtainable fruit. It is as a delicious fruit to the lost, a delightful succor, and a reminder as spirit that men, like thorns in the paths they leave, can kill, that other men are in fact dangerous.

Notice that "(once men)" in the fifth stanza's first line functions similarly to "(thoughts' torsion)"; while both are *in* the line, the parenthesis removes them from the line's development of the poem's larger, ongoing movement. These removals register the poet's onlooking consciousness of the composition process without greatly disturbing the lines' motion. The poet is *in* the poem as actor/speaker and as the reflective maker of the poem itself. If, according to myth, the mantis was killed by thorns that were once men, the poet asks who can possibly save "you" now, "what male love bring a fly, be lost / Within your mouth, prophetess, harmless to leaves / And hands, faked flower"? That is, not only who can save you—if not persons, as another mantis—, but also who, in view of your devouring love, could want to? These questions, though—as indicated by the dash following "flower" in the fourth line—are false. For the "myth is: dead, bones, it / Was assembled, apes wing in wind."

The answers to the poet's questions are given by himself back to the mantis that is told it will not be saved, will not be killed either by mythic thornmen, but *will* "die, touch, beg, of the poor." Zukofsky's use of "of the poor" is unclear, particularly with regard to "die" and "touch." Going back to the previous line, we see it is "on stone" that this will happen to the mantis. It will die on the subway platform's stone, die of the poor's inattention—caused by their despairing anger with the news of banks and money that is "beyond" them (and the inattention of the shops' public crowd, those with at least some money)—in spite of the mantis' being near enough to touch them, in spite of "her" begging eyes.

The first line of the sixth stanza connects back with the fifth by a number of close associations: "android" with "apes," "loving beggar" with "love" and "beg" from separate lines, "dive" with the likely outcome of apes winging in the wind, "poor" with—as printed—"poor" immediately above it on the preceding stanza's last line. The connections function beyond the formally desirable binding of the poem, which in itself is again only wickerwork, to what the poet now requests of the mantis: to attempt to restore the sight of the poor ("Save it!") by sacrificing itself before them. The connection between the two stanzas must hold if the sacrifice is to count for anything. If the mantis is to die of the inattention of the poor as given in the fifth stanza, then the poet's request really does ask sacrifice by the mantis.

In the interpretation's language, the mantis *can start* history. In exchange for such sacrifice, the poet affords the mantis a magical speech:

> Say, I am old as the glove, the moon, it
> Is my old shoe, yours, be free as the leaves.

Reading it, the reader's own however intuitional head remembers Zukofsky's "poets measure by means of words, whose effect as offshoot of nature may (or should) be that their strength of suggestion can never be accounted for completely." Perhaps the exchange is fair, as fair as it ever could be.

What the mantis gains is passionate oration, as

> speech, language, utterance, tongue moved for a time to sound; barring confusion as the push of *this* animalcule—as against *that*—curving a lobe of itself around food particle or dust; or a humane red showing thru a translucent film of cells of one life, or the sallow green of another—follicles hairing views—spectra. *Or they see* as eyelashes flicker; or come out one by one, air without hairs, *eyes—round, unfringed.* (my italics, last sentence only)

And to alter the direction of another statement—the preceding quotation is from *Bottom: On Shakespeare*—by Zukofsky, the mantis is given a measured order of words moving to a visual end, a product of the poet's love, that demonstrates loving compassion for the poor (from the mantis, from the poet) so that they may see with round, unfringed eyes. The poet's hope is that their restored sight, restored from the nonsight of the newspaper, will permit them to see themselves, each other, as they are, the separate individual poor. With that seeing, there is a chance of truly being saved, by each other, and not by the banks.

What remains after the joint exhortation of the mantis and the poet to the poor to be as free as the leaves is a three-line coda, which is the

> only thing that can sum up the
> jumble of order in the lines weaving
> "thoughts," pulsations, running commentary, one upon the other,

> itself a jumble of order
> as far as poetic
> sequence is concerned:
>
> > the mantis
> > the poor's strength
> > the new world.

As a summary, the coda is complexly addressed to the mantis and to the poor. The mantis is again urged to fly upon the poor, whose armies' strength will arise like leaves from a stone-on-stone accretion to build the new world "in your eyes."

> Fly, mantis, on the poor, arise like leaves
> The armies of the poor, strength: stone on stone
> And build the new world in your eyes, Save it!

I cite the coda entire to emphasize the complexity of the poet's appeal, especially the final "Save it!" The reader is thereby referred back to the third line of the first stanza, where "it" is read as a pronoun for the mantis. Now, in the coda, "it" may again refer to the mantis, which the poet wishes the new world-building armies of the poor to save, but there is the additional reference, gathered from the shared stone, of all the separate poor. The two references coexist in "it" somewhat separately. The point is that, while separate, both references are at once within "it": the saving is an interdependent act by the mantis and the arisen armies of the poor, who now see beyond the newspaper generalities to read particulars (individuals) and presumably act upon their vision. First the mantis saves the poor by forcing them to sight, which then permits them to see its own plight and to save it.

This paraphrase no more than prepares for questions of rhythm and style. While it, along with the poet's own interpretation, does indicate that Zukofsky faithfully attends to the shape of his several thoughts' torsion in choosing the sestina for the poem's form, it may be claimed that "Mantis" is merely another instance of inherited form writing. That is: if Zukofsky had been listening to himself and writing in accord with what he heard, why was he not content to let the poem's form (shape) reveal itself as it moved toward its own completion?

Zukofsky's interpretation, in response, makes it clear that he has listened, is conscious of himself, the equivalent of Charles Olson's breath-registering. As evidence:

> Thoughts'—two or three or five or
> Six thoughts' reflection (pulse's witness) of what was happening
> All immediate, not moved by any transition.

> Feeling this, what should be the form
> Which the ungainliness already suggested
> Should take?

And:

> Consider:
> "(thoughts' torsion)"
> la battaglia delli diversi pensieri . . .
> The actual twisting
> Of many and diverse thoughts

> What form should *that* take?

Typically, or so Olson would have us believe, the nonprojectivist or closed poet begins with the form and ends with a poem determined by the form. The actual subject, in effect, is the form itself. What closed poets express is themselves as possessors of literary acumen. They are illusionist reproducers of items of past—what may come to be known as tradition—writing. They can, after all, produce recognizable "literature."

Zukofsky, though, begins with his poem's originating thoughts (and even before them, with what his eyes see, i.e., "a small incident of one's physical vision"), reflects on what they define, and then proceeds to select the sestina, a form in accord with the cumulative shape or defini- tion of his many and diverse thoughts. His position is analogous to that of projectivist poets who find to their surprise (alarm?) that their listening directs them toward a sonnet. There is a certain degree of admirable courage in Zukofsky's resolve to stick with the sestina as "the only / Form that will include the most pertinent subject of our day— / The poor." Zukofsky *is* conscious, awake. For there is no demand that he cite the objection contained in Williams' "—Our world will not stand it, / the implications of a too regular form" in his interpretation.

As Olson comments from the context of his projective verse essay: "is it not the PLAY of the mind we are after, is not that that shows whether a mind is there at all?" Active and sympathetic consciousness, with respect to the seriousness of Zukofsky's subject, may be substituted for Olson's play. The point is that an audience does want to know a mind is there—as opposed to a form-filling, tradition-controlled automaton—as some indication of the poet's love and sincerity. That a mind is active in the poem's shape (surface) can be seen from Zukofsky's treatment of rhythm in "Mantis."

Given the poet's convoluted thoughts and a recalcitrantly convolute form, what should the sound-shape, the *bellezza,* be to fulfill and not just fill the sestina and the "pledge" of the sincere poet's love? It should participate in and be, in effect, a growing definition of that convolution. As such a definition and as the product of a pattern of stanzas rather than a single stanza arrangement, the poem's rhythm emerges from binary comparison. I read the first two lines as (hen)decasyllabic patterns.

> Mańtiś! | práyińg măntís! | sińce yóur | wińgs' leáves
> Ańd yóur | térrĭfĭed eýes, | pĭns, bŕight, | bláck ańd póor

The remainder of the lines in the first stanza may be read similarly, though with internal variation and a syllable count that varies from nine to twelve. The unitive rhythmic contour of the first stanza does sound convolute. The first two measures of the above lines are made up of short repeating duple coordinates that tend to sound more quickly, despite the stacatto effects in the second line, than the longer and more distinct sounds of both lines' latter two measures. These measures do not resolve the rapidity of the first two measures so much as they repeat them, but (generally) more gradually. This enlargement or gliding effect is achieved in the fourth line, for example, by the vowel sounds in "cannot touch,— You" and by the delaying/holding of punctuation.

Further reading shows that all six lines in the other five stanzas may also be read as hendecasyllabic patterns with a tendency for a faster-slower (many smaller vs. fewer longer) line-sound organization. The relevance of this sameness is that an even closer line analysis is necessary to decide how densely the rhythms of the lines and stanzas operate in relation with one another.

With their similar choppy alliterative effects, the second lines of the first three stanzas immediately present themselves as instances of close relation (pins-prop-prey-papers), but in place of an infinitely regressing analysis of each line's words, I shall examine only the end rhyme words, the *parola-rima,* and their reappearance at other points on the line. The end rhyme words in their first stanza order are leaves, poor, it, You-you, lost, stone. The occurrence of these words on different lines in later stanzas is controlled by Zukofsky's model, Dante's *rime petrose* sestina (itself based on Arnaut Daniel's *Lo ferm voler*), which follows a scheme known in medieval Latin treatises as *retrogradatio cruciata.*

By this scheme the sixth and last rhyme word of each stanza becomes the first of the next stanza, the fifth and fourth become the third and fifth, whereas the first, second, and third become the second, fourth, and sixth. The poet takes one from the end of the preceding stanza, then one from the beginning alternately. All the possible combinations are exhausted in six stanzas and the poem, as a mathematical unit, is complete. To that Dante adds a *congedo* of three lines in which he uses all six rhyme words, one at the end and one in the middle of each line. With the exception of "lost," Zukofsky's coda follows Dante's practice, including the connection between four of the rhyme words by assonance (poor, you, lost, stone in Zukofsky; *donna, ombra, petra, erba* in Dante).

Except for "leaves," all of Zukofsky's rhyme words appear at more than their predetermined end positions throughout the poem. Thus "poor" appears ten times (most emphatically in the coda, with two repetitions in three lines), "it" appears nine times, "you" and the related "your" appear twenty-one times, "lost" appears seven times, and "stone" appears ten times. The result is a heightened fugal complexity of very few words with the repeated rhyme words occurring as a constant "leaf around leaf" growing subject, their other line appearances acting as countersubjects and episodes caught up in and resonating, by repetition of exact and near-same sound equivalents, against the sounds made by nonrhyme words (voices).

Zukofsky's preoccupation with music, particularly that of Bach, is well known. But as Kenneth Cox has noticed, Zukofsky's work, including "Mantis," is not musical as that term is conventionally applied to poetry, which has more to do with imitative "sound effects" than anything else. For Zukofsky "is concerned for the pitch of vowel and duration of syllable which fit verse to be sung and it distinguishes song from declamation and declamation from recitative." The pitch of vowel and duration of syllable: "poor" in the first stanza ends with a series of rim-shot "sprung" monosyllabic words. There, in alliteration with the relatively closed sound of "pins," it is open—longer held, though not stressed—. Its pitch, coming after the crackling "bright, black," is descending, lower, suggesting that it is (as it in fact is) the most crucial element of the series.

"Poor" appears only once, the end rhyme for the fourth line in the second stanza, but is extended by earlier alliteration with "prop, prey" in line 2. "Papers" likewise carries the *p* sound in the third stanza. Here "poor," in the fifth line, again has lower pitch and comparatively longer syllable duration by the juxtapositioning of "too," ascending and open. In the sixth line, these qualities are played off against the expansive "too" with "Like all the separate poor *to* save the lost." "To" is the extreme opposite of "too," signifying the seeming paradox of the newspaper which in the blurring generality of its contents is inadequate for any particular problem or its solution in the case of the separate poor. The poor get poorer.

The close repetition (lines 2 and 3) in the fourth stanza creates a just-delayed trip-hammer effect that underscores the nonseeing of the poor. "Poor" is again at the climax of a serial movement in the next stanza: "On stone, / Mantis, you will die, touch, beg, of the poor." And again, with the anticipation made by close comma partition and the specifying prepositional phrase "of the . . . ," "poor" is low pitched and held. In this case, however, pitch and duration are virtual. What lowers and holds them is the ruthless meaning that all of these things will happen to the mantis as a result *of the poor.* In direct opposition (further stated by the lines' literal closeness), the first line of the sixth stanza has "poor" as the end-object of the dive of the mantis—now become a loving beggar— "*to the* poor." Thus the final line of the preceding stanza declares the mantis to be the victim of the poor's nonseeing inattention, and the very next line implores the mantis to sacrifice itself to the poor, to force them to see, as a loving beggar. The space constriction involved is not coincidental.

It may seem odd that the poet's voice, which heretofore in the poem is undeviatingly grim, suddenly becomes compassionate. Yet the change is of the nature of the act required. It would be "irrational," as love may be thought irrational when faced with the equations of individual gain, for the mantis to give itself to the poor. The immediacy of the change in the appearance of "poor" substantiates ("sounds") the genuine disinterest the poet would have the mantis embody (i.e., his own), as an urged idea.

"But the mantis *can start* / History." The coda maintains the prepositional focus upon "poor" through the poet's final urging. "On the poor" is a variation of "to the poor." Both are *for* the poor (directives to the mantis) as "of the poor" is not, a stage at which (strength) the sacrifice of the mantis is not needed. The second "of the poor" (the first was in the last line of the fifth stanza) is crucial. For while in both places there are indications of power, it is the poor's strength, which now sees, that will save the mantis.

In each of the coda's first two lines, "poor" lies precisely in the center of the line, stopped there by commas. The pitch and duration are quite similar, though usage/meaning developing out of syntax makes them utterly different. The first "poor" remains in need of the mantis' loving sacrifice. The second "poor" comes, presumably the effected result of that sacrifice, as armies whose strength will build a new world. "Poor" ranges throughout the poem, weaving the poem by sound and what might be called "position associations" with other words, the sound of the word never allowed to leave the reader's forgetting and remembering head, to come down twice, again and again, the central insistent subject of "Mantis."

What does this single word, watched and listened to through its changes, sound like? What, in the words of Robert Duncan, is the "hidden thing / revealed in its pulse and / durations"? It is a fugue, a principle, a process, one voice contrasting and joining with others. Or as Bach has written: "the parts of a fugue should behave like reasonable men in an orderly discussion." Yet the poet's voice in "Mantis" is anything but reasonable. How can such "voicing" be identified with fugue as defined by its great master? Before responding to that question, I would cite Zukofsky's own description of fugue as made in a discussion of *Pericles* in *Bottom: On Shakespeare.*

> And if that intellective portion of mind that is music can make poetry and prose interchangeable, because there is a note always to come back to a second time—sung to the scale the "subjects" of speech are so few and words only ring changes one on another, the differences perceived by their fictions are so slight music makes them few. Up, down, outwards—for even inversions and exact repetitions move on—are the melodic statement and hence the words' sense: or after syllables have been heard before in contiguity, they may also be augmented or diminished, or brought to crowd answer on subject in a great fugue.

There is no real discrepancy between Bach's understanding (and practice) of fugue and Zukofsky's. A reading of *"A,"* which cites Bach's definition, only serves to notice Zukofsky's continuing attentive sympathy for Bach's music which, in fact, is used as one of the poem's modes of organization. However casual that reading may be, it is impossible not to notice:

> What stirs is
>   his tracing a particular line,
> Tracings of lines
> Meeting by chance or design.
> With him *ornament,*
>   acquires
> A precision of appeal—
> Let no one think it
> Unnatural.

This appreciation of Bach's skill in renewing the use of the arabesque is followed a few pages later by the poet's account of his own work.

> This imagined music
> Traces the particular line
> Of lines meeting
>   by chance or design.

Bach's music and the poet's consciousness of his own art exist in shared words, shared so that, much later in *"A,"* Bach's quoted voice and Zukofsky's active composing voice become a single voice without trace of joinery:

> . . . old man and close lady
> as one August gust on another stop speaking
> in pretty ears: B's *Notenbuch* compiled by both:
> her copy has her initial no other signature:
> "between order and sensibility in its power at
> once to suggest all complexity and keep every
> form each form taking up the same theme":
> not by "association" it is *so* things come to
> me.

"Certainly," as Robert Creeley writes in his introduction to the 1967 Doubleday edition of *"A" 1–12,* "Zukofsky *hears* Bach."

Still, "Mantis" outrightly violates the reasonable and the orderly. And still again the sestina reveals itself as a mathematically unforgiving form, forcing those without great surety of technique to become its enthralled manipulators. The form *is* orderly. Here, though, lies the clue. For if a sonnet as an instance of received or inherited form may be said to be orderly, then the sestina is demonically so. Or as two of Dante's commentators, K. Forster and P. Boyde in *Dante's Lyric Poetry,* write with admirable brevity: "the form in itself renders an obsession." "Poor" in "Mantis" sounds an obsession with "the most pertinent subject of our day— / The poor—." But the ways in which "poor" is sounded—exact repetition, augmentation, diminution—*are* the ways of the fugue process. "Mantis" is a fugue, but speeded up, a film made blurred and jumbled by being run at more than usual speed, quarter notes transposed to eighths and sixteenths, without transitions.

The rhythm of "Mantis" does fulfill the shape chosen for the poet's torsioned thoughts, the relentless sestina experienced as fugal drive and not wickerwork. The realization grows, however, that the poet's emotion, no matter how apparently genuine, can never, despite the attractions of biography, be known beyond the necessary remove of the poem itself, a construction of language, with its own special tests for sincerity, style, and technique.

Style acts as a corrective, critical template of adjustment (judgement) upon patterns of expectation developing from the poet's word combinations. Its judgements, based on awareness of good continuation, are expressed as in or out of style. In the case of "Mantis," the governing style is the obsession of the sestina form in the right relation with the subject of the poor. It is accordingly never enough merely to exhibit one more contemporary reproduction of the form.

How a test of style for "Mantis" comes out depends on the functioning of individual words. For is is there that the patterns of expectation inhering in shape either contribute as "minor units of sincerity" or simply act as a form's required identifying place-holders. "Wind-up" in the second stanza, for instance, is curious, but not incomprehensibly arbitrary: a combination of wind's motion and that of mechanical toys can easily be "applied" to the mantis as insect and sharer of the terror of the lost poor who are controlled at will by the banks and newspapers. A part of the coda—" . . . arise like leaves / The armies of the poor . . . "—wrenches the syntactic expectation made by "Fly, mantis, on the poor . . . ," but such inversion is suitable for *la battaglia* and for additional stress upon the inextricably tied fate of the mantis and the poor. These instances appear to stand out in relief from the poem but then resolve themselves into its larger shape.

Less easily resolved are the three parentheses: (thoughts' torsion), (is it love your raised stomach prays?), and (once men). I have already pointed out that Zukofsky uses the parenthesis to remove or disengage his voice from the flow of the poem to comment upon it as an actor might use an aside. The involvement of audience in this comparison is not without interest, though any consideration is made difficult by the anonymity of the modern mass art patron audience (what is "out there" according to Stravinsky) and by the serious poet's own insulation from a dictating audience while in the act of composition. Who is Zukofsky talking to? Perhaps to himself: "While you're partly right you're all wrong— / I speak to myself most often" *("A"-12)*. Perhaps to anyone "out there."

The point remains that, for however momentary a time, the energy of the sestina is made to pause, then plunge on in its convolutions. The parentheses are delays, disruptions of the poem's musical shape. In measuring the disruption more precisely, it must be admitted that the parentheses are of some aid as landmarks in the otherwise blurring speed of the sestina. Their very aid uncovers their difficulty: that they are somehow outside the poem which does not possess the larger space of drama. A further distinction can be made between the parentheses themselves. "(Is it love's food your raised stomach prays?)" represents another level of the poet's voice *in* the poem, addressed to the mantis, whereas "(thoughts' torsion)" and "(once men)" are essentially exterior explanations.

Yet no satisfactory link can be found for "(thoughts' torsion)" and "it" of the same line, and the reader is forced to assume that the parenthetical torsion, though perhaps in a more impersonal manner, represents another level, distinct from the passionate voice level of most of the poem, even to the extent of interior admonishing "mind-voice" conscience. Likewise, "(once men)" may be taken as spoken by the poet; but it is spoken to neither the mantis nor to the poor—nor to the poet himself. Its lack of "local" direction is a sign for its explaining connection with "the paths men leave" and the mantis' death by thorns with the mythic explanation—Cadmus reversed—which helps in turn to connect with the later flat reference to "the myth."

Arguing for Dante's Donna Pietra as a symbol of a poetics, Leslie Fiedler has remarked that "if there is a 'true love' behind the *rime pietrose,* it is the love of Arnaut Daniel." I at first read this to refer to Daniel's own "real" romances in comparison with Fiedler's idée fixe description of Dante as a member of university homosexual society more concerned with finding a subject to justify a new style than with the unrelenting charm of any historical lady. A later reading is that whether Dante's sestina was written for an actual female or not, what *"Al poco giorno"* inescapably demonstrates is a love of language as embodied in the practice of Arnaut Daniel, *il miglior fabbro,* the best smith of language.

To repeat, the poet's emotion can never be directly warranted. Similarly, reversing analysis cannot be expected to lay bare anything like the full dynamics of the composition sequence. The emotion that can be indicated through analysis is love of language from the treatment of style and technique. There is at least the implication that, by virtue of his treatment, Zukofsky successfully objectifies his complex emotion toward the poor in "Mantis."

If the poet's personal love or compassionate emotion for the poor cannot be finally determined, it nonetheless can be inferred from his love of language, his consciousness of word combinations and their construction to the extent that, in Eric Mottram's phrase, "technique is mythicized." The poem is an emotional object made of words. The emotion is objectified—held for the inspection of others—if the poet has sufficient technique, the particular point-to-point realization of the shape to rhythm to style sequence. The undeniable obsession of Zukofsky's sestina, his "successful" consciousness and realization of technique, all these "facts of practice" ground the extensions I have made of his understanding of sincerity as the care for detail founded on love that sees with the eyes (with the justly coordinating mind), the "engenderer" of his composition sequence. Such care may come to exist for language well constructed, not pure, for language seen as an object of delight in the eyes of the sincere poet who desires to witness his love.

How to Do Things with Words

In *Film Noir* and in its predecessor *Corona,* the visual design of the page is important beyond usual concern for layout appearance. Each page of Bruce Andrews' work is *designed.* The pages of *Film Noir* have a specifically Mondrian look ("Broadway Boogie-Woogie") about them. This is produced by a geometric mix of sans serif bold-face capitals and serif lower case types. Because the capitals are so set off from the rest of the page, they tend to take on a coherence of their own, and the suspicion grows that they must make up some sort of code. But if there is such a code, I have not been able to break it.

This leads me to suggest that the rationale for Andrews' visual page design is in agreement with what I take to be the motivation of his work considered as a total effort: to have the reader come to a heightened experience of language. Consciously or not, there is a certain bravery involved in such enterprise. For it must mean that literature, however defined, will not result (nor should it be expected). These pages are both after and before literature. Like other instances of late modernist writing, they implicitly question whether literature as traditionally understood may or should continue to be done by the aware writer.

This heightened experience of language is achieved by teasing (the code-looking noncode), by irritation (promised syntactic structures that desert their promise, dissolving into still other latent structures without ever quite assuming a final fix), and most often by juxtapositioning in a variety of tensions aspects of language not typically found in the same or even remotely related spaces. "Aspects of language" may be considered fuzzy. More exactly, they can be individual words from individual "languages," phrases from privileged or professional vocabularies, phrases from ordinary (as seemingly "overheard") conversational usage, the names of persons, a variety of suggested speaking tones for all these, and, not least, puns.

When all of these are combined with graphic design on a single page, an effect of rich and rewarding complexity is achieved. In fact, so much of this is going on at the same time that quotation is difficult. It is like trying to point out single-note solos in the music of Cecil Taylor.

But for pun: "Contrary to metaphor staples fled from cardboard like a / flock of psoriasis before the cure." And from the same page, for phrases:

A <u>cockade of.</u>_____

A <u>rosette of.</u>____

A <u>niggertoe of.</u>____

If you can supply something for cockade, to complete the phrase, will it also be appropriate for rosette and niggertoe? And what new fourth thing do those three add up to?

For juxtaposition and tone: "The flower always / almond in person, baby." There is also a device I have not mentioned, the graphic enlargement and isolation of a single word on the page:

PHOSPHORUS

All of these instances have been taken from a single page of *Film Noir,* and they represent only a partial inventory for that page. Even partial quotation, which only approximates the shifting and several levels of juxtaposition present on each page, is sufficient to indicate Bruce Andrews' fine ear. For the ear (and eye) responsible for these pages is quite literally sophisticated.

There is the question, however, whether the bravery and sophistication of such writing, which—considered as a general approach—is shared by a number of poets in addition to Andrews, hasn't turned the analytic preparation that is modernism into a self-contained (and contented) style of its own. Whether such writing hasn't made an end out of what was originally proposed as a preparation. The problem of this act of translation is its resultant small range of possibility. It can force or encourage a more conscious experience of language; it can produce varieties of irony in the process. It is not clear that it can do anything else. Thus Clark Coolidge says he wants people to read words. That desire is an old one for the other arts in this century. Painters, musicians, and sculptors have been wanting people to see paint, to hear sound, and experience textures and the three-dimensionality of space for some time. The writing in *Film Noir* represents the translation of what is by now an only-too-well-documented desire in terms of poetry.

One would think poetry need not commit itself in such lock-step fashion to the well-worn strategies of this historical desire which, if pushed, could easily end in the disaster of conceptual art *(cogito ergo sum . . . artiste!).* Reading words as words is fine and perhaps always necessary. My objection is that language in the hands/vision of the poet is capable of much more. There is no need to repeat the development of the other arts, most of which have long since dropped the modernist program for the more unruly, unpredictable, but much larger realm of individual vision. Surely, Cézanne would agree there's little use in redoubting?

Turning means to ends produces mannerism. John Ashbery has become our most visible mannerist poet. His achievement is that he has been able to give some extension to modernist exercises so that they at least take on the appearance of usual poems on the page and whose tone seems appropriately (approximately) aesthetic. It is an intrepid achievement, though of an emperor's clothes nature. As indicated, *Film Noir* is itself intrepid without yet coming to Ashbery's assumption of invention. Before Bruce Andrews moves further in that direction, I would hope he might consider the difference between translation and transformation.

A Preface

What I wish to do this afternoon is to formulate a preface for my new book *Peace On Earth,* or rather for the first poem "Slow Song for Mark Rothko" of that book. Following the example of Henry James, I shall try to recover (for you and for myself) the attitudes with which I approached my materials, the laws and "old intentions" involved in the poem's composition.

When I look back at my notes and worksheets for the poem, I find my first interest was neither Rothko nor his paintings, but stained glass. I came to feel almost a hunger for the dense, complexly luminous colors shining within the giant black boxes of cathedrals. This hunger was for the colors themselves. It may also have been for the basic properties of stained glass as laid down by Suger, the abbot of St. Denis in the twelfth century: a bearer of holy images, intrinsically rich material resembling precious stones, a mystery because it glows without fire or heat. Like the composer Messiaen, I was dazzled by the colors of stained glass and moved by the presence of mystery, by—to combine Messiaen and Grosseteste—the power of the light residing in and shining through the glass as embodied spirit.

Allow me to mention two other elements closely related in my mind with stained glass. They are: Gregorian chant, the dense yet ultimately restful rhythms of which strike me as singularly close equivalents of stained glass, and the language of Meister Eckhart, the German speculative theologian. Because Eckhart continues to haunt my work and because his theology is truly complicated, I hesitate to attempt any sort of synopsis. It is, in any case, his language—not his system—which interests me.

Please be clear: I am no medievalist. My interest in these things, as in stained glass itself, proceeds from need. I can agree with Wallace Stevens that poetry is the scholar's art so long as it's understood that the research is motivated by one's own need. One goes, searches where one must to find the right materials and tools for the job at hand.

Another association was of course Rothko's paintings. It struck me that they were translations, faithful transformations of stained glass. Their colors are dense and complexly luminous. Their scale is such that, looking at them, we are made to feel taken in, absorbed into their light. The difference is the abstraction. The cathedral along with the specific figures and symbols of the Christian story are no longer present. Even the stars and little flower shapes are no more, so that it is light itself that is concentrated on, made to hover and to radiate in floating blocks of color.

The relation between stained glass and Rothko's painting was strengthened when I learned his method of working approximated the medieval methods for making glass. Medieval or Old glass, particularly the inner-glowing red, is the result of several thin laminations. The inner structure of all Old glass is made dense and complex by these laminations and by the impurities, air bubbles, and streaks within them. The Old glass is translucent, not transparent. According to Diane Waldman, in the catalogue for the Guggenheim Museum's 1978 retrospective of Rothko's work, he

> perfected a technique of dyeing . . . with his paint which enabled him to saturate the threads of his canvas with his medium so that pigment and canvas become one. By applying thin washes of paint, one over another, and often allowing some of the colors in the bottom layers to appear through the top coat of pigment, Rothko achieves the effect of a hidden light source. . . . Rothko creates a quality of inner light which seems to emanate from the very core of the work.

As I continued to think about the relation between glass and painting, I was further encouraged by Rothko's own statements. One of the most important of these is: "the people who weep before my pictures are having the same religious experience I had when I painted them. If you . . . are moved only by their color relationships, then you miss the point." And one other that is made use of in my poem: "I do not believe that there was ever a question of being abstract or representational. It is really a matter of ending this silence and solitude, of breathing and stretching one's arms again."

Very simply, I was and am now tremendously moved by this last statement. It seems to me to be true in its recognition of silence and solitude as the prevailing conditions of our lives and necessary in its call to bring those conditions to an end. I felt compelled to render homage to Rothko—for the value of his insight, for the example of his work—and I felt compelled to bring about that desired end in my own way.

As I moved closer to the composition of such a poem, it became clear that I would have to find ways to translate the qualities inhering not only in stained glass and Rothko's painting, but also those in Gregorian chant and Meister Eckhart. These qualities would have to come to exist in language as sound. It occurs to me that all my work, before and since this poem, involves translation or, more accurately, transformation to make the poem a "sound object."

Let me reconsider a single element of this transformation—the line. My friend and fellow poet Ted Pearson has warned me that composition involves more than making up one's mind about line length. While that's obviously so, I think it is also the case that, in William Carlos Williams' phrase, "a new line is a new measure." Change the line, and you change the vision. Thus, in talking about the line of "Slow Song For Mark Rothko," other more than strictly technical matters are at stake.

In my previous book, *Dodeka,* the line was short, almost nervously taut as in the music of Webern. By itself, this went against the horizontality of Rothko's paintings and of the overall rhythm of the chant. Trying out lines that were much longer than what I was used to, that made a closer approximation to the dimensions of Rothko's blocks, I first used single long sentences. These were no good because they tended to sag in the middle, were difficult to connect from one line to the next, and the sameness of their rhythm was dull. Eventually, I devised a line made up of several short "atomic" phrases, no one of them complete as with a sentence, but kept continually in motion toward completion.

I was encouraged in my formulation of line by the example of Steve Reich's music. In this music, specifically "Music for Mallet Instruments, Voices, and Organ," one hears music as a process. One hears the music compose itself. As Reich has written, "what I'm interested in is a compositional process and a sounding music that are one and the same thing. I don't know any secrets of structure that you can't hear. We all listen to the process together since it's quite audible, and one of the reasons it's audible is because it's happening extremely gradually." And: "listening to a gradual musical process, one can participate in a particularly liberating and impersonal kind of ritual. Focusing in on the musical process makes possible that shift of attention away from *he* and *she* and *you* and *me* outwards (or inwards) towards *it*."

I was encouraged because Reich's music demonstrated a coordination of form and content that not only seemed right in itself but also corresponded with my own efforts to construct a complex long line and with my desire to construct an entire poem which would be an opening out, something by way of an embrace. The line could be long, could have a sufficient shifting density if it were made as a gradual process of accretion, the phrase or larger stanza/sentence putting itself together gradually, though not necessarily at a steady oom-pah, marching-band pace. As I came to discover, such a poem would have to be read aloud to make sense. The reader would have to break the silence of the cold page. There could be a liberation of participation, an ending of the silence and solitude.

This did not mean that I attempted to work out a system to adapt Reich's music into language. It was simply an encouragement, an indication that such a conception of line and larger intention went together, that they were possible.

Now it might be asked whether this isn't terribly, maybe even incestuously, arty? My answer is that the work of Rothko and Reich exists for me as the ring of Blue Mountains surrounding this valley. They simply *are*. Their art exists in the same continuous reality, the same continuous *day* of those mountains. What is at stake is need. You find what you need, among the entire past and present universe, to get the job done. Your search in that universe of human objects and natural objects is guided by need. Had I not come upon Reich's music at this time, I nevertheless would have found it or something like it. You find, sooner or later, what you need and what the job of composition requires. The issue is not art or nonart for the materials of new art, but whether one is alert to all the possibilities of the entire universe.

What must be understood—and what distinguishes the writing of a poem from an engineering project—is that you find out the nature of the job (and thus the necessary materials and methods of working) as you go along. Robert Creeley: "I see *as* I write." In this way the poem is a true creation or invention and not simply a reproduction of what is already known. What keeps one searching is the depth and degree of one's need.

Encouraged by the example of Reich's music, I continued to work out language equivalents for the qualities of stained glass and Rothko's painting. Since the impurity of the glass as well as the subtle variegation within Rothko's color blocks were critical, I decided to introduce occasional separate, distinct or "disjointed" vocabularies within the body of the poem. This impurity/variegation would also be reflected in the irregular accretional rhythm of the line adding to itself as it went along and by the "soft" beginnings and endings of lines. This softness—done with prepositions and unstressed final syllables—would help keep each line and its larger stanza in a constant shifting motion. The lamination of the glass and the saturation of Rothko's several thin washes could be approximated by the line/stanza's gradual, but never quite complete, growth and by several versions or layers of a stanza, each one beginning with the same or similar language as the last.

Perhaps you are asking yourselves what has happened to the imagination's fabled freedom in all of this. Doesn't this, in fact, sound more like engineering than the sweet produce of inspiration and the muses? My answer is Stravinsky's answer in his *Poetics of Music*. "The more art is controlled, limited, worked over, the more it is free." In the lecture from which this is taken, Stravinsky explains that, even if he were asked to compose music in "this abyss of freedom," he would still not succumb to the dizziness that seizes him before "the virtuality of this infinitude." Instead, he will be reassured

> by the thought that I have 7 notes of the scale and its chromatic intervals at my disposal, that strong and weak accents are within my reach, and that in all of these I possess solid and concrete elements which offer me a field of experience just as vast as the upsetting and dizzy infinitude that had just frightened me. It is into this field that I shall sink my roots, fully convinced that the combinations which have at their disposal twelve sounds in each octave and all possible rhythmic varieties promise me riches that all the activity of human genius will never exhaust.

Without wanting to irritate the musicians among us, I would suggest that the English language possesses at least as many such riches. As a poet, it is, finally, the field of language into which I must sink my roots.

Stravinsky concludes: "the more constraints one imposes, the more one frees one's self of the chains that shackle the spirit." In my desire to transform the qualities of stained glass and Rothko's painting, I have willingly placed many impositions upon myself. Yet is is precisely these so-called impositions which allowed me, allowed and forced me to follow out, to continue the search instigated by my need so that there might be new rooms of language in which a radiant, complex light might dwell.

The Poem as a Woven Scarf

There can be no doubt. The question is how the poem is to be returned to enacted speech as a first consideration in composition and as a final, radical reality. How is the poem to be the voice's enactment of language, one interior calling out to another, so there may be presence and community?

There can be no staining or saturation of the silence without some sense of the poem as a definition of space. Language is the means of the definition, and the voice's enactment of language is the means of the staining within the definition.

My own definitions have grown larger over the years. The *Dodeka* poem (1977) is an example. It was written in strips or series of four-line poems. I had frames printed around each poem to compress the space immediately surrounding the lines, separating it off from the rest of the page. They were protected from their smallness and took on intensity. But it was difficult for them to contain any complex sound. To get such a sound—I had in mind the closing unison in organum, after which nothing else needs to be said—all the lines in a series were recombined, plaited together to make a large single poem which filled the space implied by the "points" of the tiny poems. The points along the bands of the series were converted to a single dense constellation. In this way, I was led to a definition of the poem that would be large enough to be or to suggest its own frame.

Large definitions commit one to a long line. The line is prevented from falling in on itself by a recurrent, but never exactly repeating, cadence. This cadence undergoes a continuous motion (transformation). It is not quite accurate to say it shifts in and out of phase unless the phase of the cadence is understood to have no set identity. It is always identifiable in its overlapping *motion* of addition and decay. While periodicity may be heard in this motion, the end of the poem is necessarily different from its beginning; the motion involves an actual journey. The range of possible motion is the range of the poet's voice. Its development is governed by the poet's breathing, what the voice can say or sing.

One of the functions of this unresting cadence is to defeat the silent reading eye. If not enacted by the voice, the cadence makes no sense. Its shifting motion only confuses and irritates the eye. The voice, though, finds its own punctuation in terms of what—as a phrase, then a coordination of phrases—can literally be spoken. Recurrence lends depth and density to the voice; it also gives the voice duration.

In the long poem "Peace On Earth" (1979), for instance, I found my voice tired and hardened because of a very deliberate cadence and the poem's length (it takes nearly an hour to read). Saturation was obtained at the cost of my becoming a drone. To keep the voice open so that its attack could continue to be light through prolonged recurrence, particles of a distinct vocabulary are fed into a space already defined by the poem's original language. The new vocabulary is like a foreign language. Moving throughout these contiguous vocabularies, the cadence produces cross-rhythms within itself, and the voice is reopened. As the voice becomes larger, more open, the vision found in the poem may become larger. "Peace On Earth" is meant to be more than one person's private response to the war in Vietnam.

I had thought density was the true goal. If the motion of the cadence made for a sufficient density, then the space would have to be saturated. The silence of the page and of the meeting room would be overcome. Everything would be inescapably penetrated with light, and found vision would become a present reality. But this is not desirable because it immobilizes. Complete saturation leaves no room to move.

The model ought not to be the ecstatically still saint, but the moved dancer. The dancer is encouraged to move by the gaps between the notes of music. The gaps are larger than the moments needed for the articulation of words. The dancer can move freely in the openness of the gaps. If there is no room to move, if there cannot be free response to the call, then it is hopeless to expect conversation. The gesture (embrace) toward community suffocates; vision turns into dogmatic dictation.

Thus I am drawn to the poem as a woven scarf with many openings through which light enters. It could be spread out, enlarged to a scarf of migrating birds in the sky. Yet however dense the weave and however enlarged the area, the poem must contain a perceptible pattern of openings, composed silences, within itself. The response is not itself composed, as in a church service. Its possibility is invited.

There are, to be sure, uncertainties. Who knows what the dancers will do? Who knows what those who had formerly been only auditors will say in those gaps? Nevertheless, they offer a chance which must be taken, a chance of response or torsion against which the poet may, in turn, respond and so enlarge the poem. This means the eyes will have to look up from the page, which no longer determines the final extent of the poem. It may grow larger, more complex than the originating words on the page. The presumption of being the only speaker, however self-effacing, will have to be put aside. Above all, there will have to be responsibility to a community which, in part, the poet has helped come into existence.

(The community may be limited, as a dialogue, to "aspects" of the self. It is difficult for this not to be despairing. Samuel Beckett: "the voice alone is company but not enough." Yet even bitter search is preferable to ceaseless ironic chatter.)

The found light may not lead back to splendor. One must accept the risk of finding a grey light or no light at all. The space may be saturated with darkness, a rose window of niemandsroses.

The poem I want to write is a densely woven scarf through which whatever light there is, whatever other voices there are, may enter.

On Working
with Dancers

It is difficult to speak and to move at the same time. It is more difficult to speak with articulation and to move with purpose at the same time.

I came to appreciate such difficulty while working in collaboration with Trina Collins, director of the modern dance company Danceteller. The collaboration proceeded unevenly. There was a great deal of preliminary conversation, but the sequence of activity was that I wrote a poem called "Dehiscence," and she then choreographed a dance around it.

"Around" because the dancers, and not myself, were to speak the poem in various recitative-like combinations as they moved in their dance. They were to become their own speakers, their own live sound system.

This meant my participation didn't end with the delivery of the text of the poem. The dancers found it unlike any poetry they were familiar with, and they were reluctant to begin until they had been given specific indications for rhythm and intonation. Another, but less easily satisfied, part of their reluctance was their desire for a meaning. How could they dance to something until they'd been told what it was about? Thus I ended up meeting frequently with the company to read the text aloud and to talk about its composition.

We also discussed other texts—Meister Eckhart's sermons, paintings by Rothko and O'Keefe, music of Messiaen—that had been of interest to me at the time. I was hesitant, however, to talk about meaning for a number of reasons. The poem was a development of an earlier one; it began where the other had left off. The new poem was written as a development of that end scene or vision. The meaning included the earlier poem. It was a process and as such had to be arrived at by going through it. Knowledge of what preceded the poem at hand might make one more comfortable, in terms of expectation, with the opening situation of this new dance text, but it would not necessarily explain what was to be done with it. From my point of view, the explaining, once begun, promised never to end.

Perhaps my hesitation was due to the suspicion that their desire for a meaning amounted to an evasion of process. And, further, that—like the texts for traditional ballet—it would be turned into a *pretext* for their dance. That is, once assured of a meaning they could only too easily forget or displace the words so that their dance became the "real" text. If the dancers were given a meaning, the process would be shrunken and immobilized. The text would become portable, if not altogether disposable.

Their desire was nonetheless understandable. They wanted something to dance *to*. The sooner it was given definition, the sooner they could get on with their dancing. If the words are not to be removed to a background music function (pre-text become post-text), however, the writer has to find a means of insisting that the words are read through completely before they're made to undergo translation. This is minimal, simply practical. The larger insistence is that the reading is never completed.

This—the practical—was accomplished for "Dehiscence" by its initial unfamiliarity and by the decision that the dancers would speak the poem as they moved. For there to be any performance, they had to pay attention to the words and to the measured durations of silence interwoven with them. Eventually, each dancer had to memorize the entire poem (twelve pages), even though no one dancer was assigned all the words. Not to do so would result in confusion. It *is* difficult to speak and to move at the same time if something like a balance of attention (tension) cannot be established.

The words and the silences were composed; they could only be done in certain ways. They also carried a deliberate implication of tone. The words were to be spoken in a humming manner—not declaiming, not whispering—along a scale deliberately limited to three or four tones. To project speech in this manner requires tensed muscles. Only certain kinds of movement are possible in the series of tensions that make up a dance with dancer-spoken words.

It would be wrong to claim that the poem governed the dance. What it did do was require continued attention (reading) in rehearsal and in performance. The level of this attention varied constantly but was always present. The poem came to exist in neither foreground nor background but in a moving center.

This seems to me a desirable position. It offers some possibility that the words will continue to be read (if not so intently by the dancers, then by their audience), that the process will continue to be gone through. In the end, which is performance, the text writer is seated with the audience. There's a certain usefulness in reading oneself from a distance. Projected by trained bodies and voices in special lighting, the vision can be examined minutely, in itself and in terms of the response of the other audience members (you watch them watch you). You can see and hear your text as never before.

Despite the applause (ironically, the nature of the "Dehiscence" poem made this inappropriate), it is also a very lonely experience. If the text writer desires community, and I do, then the writer will have to consider learning how to dance.

Louis Zukofsky: Songs of Degrees

I hope everybody would . . . just read the words. This activity is a kind of mathematics but more sensuous, and it has little to do with learning. It has something to do with structure. But I won't go into that aspect—simply say, the contingency of one poet reading another that way makes for a kind of friendship which is exempt from all the vicissitudes and changes and tempers that are involved in friendship.
—Louis Zukofsky, "For Wallace Stevens"

This essay is not written for T. S. Eliot's first twenty critics, nor for his "rare twenty-second" who has followed the career of Louis Zukofsky intelligently and who recognizes its consistency. Rather, and like Eliot's essay on the metric and poetry of Ezra Pound, it is for those who were perhaps made curious by the *New York Times* inverted headline for the poet's obituary (May 12, 1978)—"Of Objectivist School and Novelist / Louis Zukofsky, 74, a Major Poet"—and, being made curious, resolved to read something by this major poet whose name existed for them, if it existed at all, as a heard-about, but mostly exotic, unfamiliar reputation. This essay is for those who are reading Zukofsky for essentially the first time. It is a reading of a series of seven short poems, the "Songs of Degrees," and is something of an introduction to the poetics and poetry of Louis Zukofsky as a larger consistent whole.

We can begin, by indirection, with a statement Zukofsky made to me at the close of an exasperating interview. I had come as an admiring younger poet in hope of answers to long-thought-over questions about his writing and in the never quite to be admitted expectation that the much older poet might recognize what I felt to be a sympathy between my poems and his own. The answers were not to be forthcoming. What was—a flood of invective against the uncomprehending young and those of an older generation who presumed upon his friendship for favors—made anything like conversation impossible. I went away with the memory of a thin man bundled up in grey—overcoat, trousers, and muffler for fear of his hotel lobby's drafts—with dark eyebrows the size of caterpillars perched atop his glasses. There was also a parting statement that for him it all came down to a matter of song, it was only song that mattered.

It may be that the wrong questions were asked or, if not wrong, were asked inappropriately. Yet if only because I had heard it before, Zukofsky's parting statement remained in my mind. Where I had heard it was *A Test of Poetry* (1948). This anthology of poems, juxtaposed for comparison with only occasional and even then very terse commentary, was put together by Zukofsky, as his preface mildly states, "to suggest standards." The juxtapositions are arranged in three parts. The poems in parts I and II are presented anonymously to encourage readers to consider their relative merits without reference to authorship. The poems in part III are accredited for the convenience of historical explanation. All three parts are coordinated with each other under a "consideration" (e.g., measure), in an appended chronological chart. Thus, in part II, Skelton's "To Mistress Margaret Hussey" and Thomas Hardy's "Timing Her" are compared as poems "intended for dance tunes or written with dance tunes in mind." These two poems are further related, by the consideration of recurrence, with poems by Keats, Lord Herbert of Cherbury, and Lorine Niedecker in part I and with others by William Carlos Williams, Shakespeare, and e. e. cummings in part III. In part II Zukofsky has contributed notes and commentary which are not only terse but also to the point. For instance, after a comparison of lines from two prosaic and naive translations of *The Odyssey* by Thomas Hobbes and William Morris, we read this note: "the music of verse carries an emotional quality; when the music slackens, emotion dissipates, and the poetry is poor."

The first direct reference to song in *A Test of Poetry* occurs in the comment and note for a comparison of an excerpt from Chaucer's "Book of the Duchesse" with a translation of Villon by Rossetti and the sixteenth-century lyric "O Western Wind." The comment identifies the first and third as English examples of words written to be sung; the Rossetti translation is less singable because attention is diverted from utterance to a kind of ornate comparative process. The note extends the comment to law: simplicity of utterance and song go together. Further, song as musical, poetic form is "usually defined by a continuous and complete statement of the words."

Continuous and complete: the adjectives obtain for the fitting of words with music, a matter of ongoing correspondence, *and* for the words alone in their own interplay of sight, sound, and ideation. In this play, words are made to present themselves continually one after and in reaction to another, to make an emerging order that has no end of potential relation, though levels of completeness or closure may take on definition in this process that in the composing focus of the poet is comparable to the covalent bonding and rebonding of atomic particles. The etymological roots of words delimit the levels—the roots of words and their possibility, through proliferation of usage—of relation and combination. The idea of levels is perhaps too linear. Words may spread and entwine as roots; or, abstracted, they may be sensed as Riemannian spaces mapping into one another.

Song involves a simplicity of utterance so that its coordinate balance with music and among the words themselves is not overwhelmed, so that the statement is grasped in the real or imagined singing. The singing is over when the statement is complete. The statement is complete when the potential of chosen words, as separate but complex entities and as a single bonded final whole entity, has been "actualized." Given the possibility of infinite relation (and language may be our best model for infinity), this completeness of statement can only be intimated. Song is, after all, an art.

The next direct reference to song in the *Test* comes after a comparison of Ophelia's singing in *Hamlet* with that of Bosola, "the common bellman," in Webster's *Duchess of Malfi*. Her singing is cited as an instance of a song that will sing to music, but which must be declaimed or intoned. Both are found to achieve the effect of terror, but by different means: Shakespeare by the melody in the words, Webster by "the extravagant cumulativeness" of tolling sounds and melodramatic imagery. Ophelia's song will sing to a tune, yet this is not to be known by putting it to any literal music. Instead, its realization derives from a quality inhering in Shakespeare's language, the melody *in* the words. Zukofsky honors the ideal of words put in coordinate balance with music, yet a shift has taken place. Poetry is song; it properly conjoins words and music, but somehow they remain apart in our time.

Looking back from our time to Shakespeare, a poet such as Zukofsky recognizes song but must speak of it in terms of careful division. Hence what Webster has written is a song (with quotation marks) *and* a lyric (in italics). Twentieth-century poetry is lyric poetry. It tends not to sing to music, even though collaborations such as Elliott Carter's setting of John

Ashbery's "Syringa" continue to be attempted. For whatever reasons one might cite for the division, it has been the condition of poetry in English since Campion. In response, later poets have deliberately written a poetry, beginning perhaps as early as Spenser, which more and more internalizes musical qualities within language. The words of a Campion ayre are noticeable for an almost-homogenized smoothness. This is not a fault, however, because the music specifically composed for them by Campion can be counted on to provide what will be heard as a pleasingly complex texture in the ayre's total sung and played performance. The lyric poem represents an effort to supply a like complexity by means of language alone. When contemporary composers go about setting a contemporary poem, they typically find, as a consequence, that little room remains for their notes.

The Carter-Ashbery collaboration is a case in point. Carter's composition for mezzo-soprano, bass, and an ensemble of eleven players attempts to provide what is already present in the poem—articulation of what is in itself complexly articulate. This attempt is made even more complicated by the composer's additional setting of a collection of Greek texts to express a "subliminal background" for the poem. The result, double complexity on top of a further complexity, is unavoidably turgid. And when a supposedly simpler composer, Aaron Copland, sets the poems of a supposedly simpler poet, Emily Dickinson, for only piano and soprano, we still hear a not-unlike result.

We hear that result because a sufficient melody has been made to reside in the words, whatever the possibilities for more extended and complex melodies in instrumental music. Melody appears early in Zukofsky's poetics. In his introductory program essay for the 1931 objectivist number of *Poetry,* which he edited through the instigation of Ezra Pound, he writes: "in sincerity shapes appear concomitants, precursors of . . . completed sound or structure, *melody* or form. Writing occurs which is the detail, not mirage of seeing, of thinking with the things as they exist, and of directing them along a line of *melody.*" "Sincerity," the first of the two major terms that model the composition experience in Zukofsky's poetics, is the care for detail. The term may or may not derive from Pound's earlier translation of a Chinese ideogram, in *Ta Hsio: The Great Digest,* as sincerity, "the precise definition of the word, pictorially the sun's lance coming to rest on the precise spot verbally. The righthand half of this compound means: to perfect, bring to focus."

Sincerity for Zukofsky is an attitude or ethics, one of whose enactments is the poet's focusing precisely on details of the outside physical universe and on details of the universe of language, words. The attitude originates with the fundamental human desire to know. The active process originates with sense perception of the universe outside the poem and with sight in particular.

As Zukofsky, condensing and modifying a passage from Aristotle's *Metaphysics*, writes in book 12 of his long poem *"A":*

> All men by nature desire
> (It is put—but, in effect, *love*) to know
> We delight in our senses
> Aside from their usefulness
> They are loved for themselves—
> And most of all the sense of sight
> Brings to light differences
>   between things.

Without this delight-giving perception of differences, there can be no knowledge of detail—whether historic or contemporary, thing or event, singular or plural—and ultimately there can be no poem. Thus this same necessary perception must also be applied to words. "His ear is sincere," Zukofsky observes in a later essay, "A Statement For Poetry" (1950), "if his words convey his awareness of the range of differences and subtleties of duration."

Differences of duration are differences of sound. It is by giving careful attention to these and to the many other details of sound in the words that the poet proceeds in composition. How the details, including those of sight and the other senses, are to be combined is determined by their own growing, atomic suggestion of potential shapes or lines, the concomitants and precursors, of melody.

By definition a melody is a continuous movement that is always on its way. It is not the sum of its component sound details but is the progress of the moving line passing through the successive sounds. In Zukofsky's usage, however, melody is both the continuously moving line as it grows and defines itself in the concatenation of word sound detail, *and* it is the completed structure or form that is the culmination and the memory of that motion. It is both verb and noun, both the joining of the metal fish that flexes in the hand and the assembled fish left on the window sill. All of the care-engendered movement that leads to and constitutes melody, attitude and composing act, occurs from and in a condition of sincerity. The completed structure of melody occurs in a separate condition of objectification, the second major term of Zukofsky's poetics, which he also calls rested totality, "the apprehension satisfied completely as to the appearance of the art form as an object."

If the appearance of melody as object is experienced as satisfied apprehension, then that experience takes place in our minds as readers. In the French for attending a play, *j'assiste à une pièce*. The object is not the poem as printed text but a composite of our reading assistance, sounding and listening as we go, in response to the poem's evolving line of melody. Or: the object is not the composite but its result. Before our reading can provide any assistance, however, the poet has already focused upon the details of sense perception and of language to make a continuous and complete statement organized by the poet's own sounding and listening to the melody in the words. While some objectification may exist in a single word or line, our sense of rested totality as a complete structure would seem to require most if not all the words and lines of a poem.

We experience the poem's melody as a completely defined object, the fish on the window sill, when the singing comes to an end. If the poem's melody satisfies our sense of structure, if there can be something like agreement between the poet's first and our later listenings, then the experience may extend to a feeling of rest. This includes the poem's subject matter, which should not be thought restricted to literal objects. Once the melody line has completely defined itself, the subject can be felt to be known as completely as an object. The repetition of my sentence emphasizes their relation. The subject—its images and concepts—is inwound with and known through the melody.

To link relevant statements by Zukofsky: "the poet's image is not dissociable from the movement or the cadenced shape of the poem" (preface to An *"Objectivists" Anthology,* 1932); "the rhythm of every one of the *notes* of vowels, consonants, and diphthongs makes the 'concepts' " (letter to Cid Corman, 1957). Cadence and rhythm are manifestations of voice, real or imagined, singing the melody in the words.

Through it our prodigious search of appearance may be brought to rest.

All of this is given condensed demonstration in a poem from Zukofsky's *Anew* collection (1946).

> The lines of this new song are nothing
> But a tune making the nothing full
> Stonelike become more hard than silent
> The tune's image holding in the line.

The lines of this new song are "nothing" because the usual ground of poetry, sense perception, has been almost entirely excluded. Certainly, there is a growth of word-sound detail, but it *begins* in composition and not in the universe outside the poem. The poem begins abstract and becomes transparent. Reading it, we have the curious sensation of reading about its subject at the same time that the same subject, the song's melody or tune, constructs itself as an object. This construction proceeds as a continuous growing line of lines, each a complete sentence and each a self-contained rhythm, foursquare. The lines, though, are aware of themselves. Their completeness—as grammatical sense, rhythm, and "self-awareness"—is shared by all the other lines. The melody's structure or image of the tune will have to partake of their transparency and of their solidity: not an object, stone, but its quality made musical, "more hard than silent."

One of Zukofsky's favored definitions of poetry, following Pound again, is adapted from Dante's description of canzone as the completed action of writing words to be set to music. (It is the probable source for the earlier reference in *A Test of Poetry* to song as a continuous and complete statement of the words.) Poetry since Campion and Dowland has sought to complete the action of writing *in* writing. It has desired a sufficient music be made to reside in words, a sufficient structure be made to emerge from that internalized music. What distinguishes Zukofsky in the tradition of this effort is his extreme translation of its terms.

Previously, a poet might consider the possibility of the musical, but it was something added to or subtracted from a few standard forms. The music is microtonally "under" the standard forms and within the words from the beginning. From there it may define itself any number of ways consistent with its developing line, its emerging structure in the progress of composition. It acts both as a regulating guide, as in or out of tune, for composition and as a necessary, even primary component of a poem's meaning. It is a commonplace that twentieth-century poetry often tends to be about itself. In Zukofsky's translation, poetry becomes the real or imagined singing of the song that sings itself.

Zukofsky's poetry exists along a range of real and imagined song. It should be read and heard as such. Above all, it has to be understood that its meaning, like its melody, exists in the words, and that the two are inextricable. If you don't hear the melody line—in process or at rest—in a Zukofsky poem, then the meaning must remain elusive. The testimony of one of Zukofsky's most interested readers, William Carlos Williams, should not be lost: "it irritated me so that I could not read the works of this poet with anything like satisfaction . . . I didn't realize how close my attention to detail had to be to follow the really very simple language."

The "Songs of Degrees" series was written in the period 1953–1955 and published in *Some Time* (1956). All seven poems are valentines. The first consists of two sentences, both made with a minimum of words that, in the delicacy of their interplay, gently remind us their tone is more intimate than small.

> Hear, her
> Clear
> Mirror,
> Care
> His error.
> In her
> Care
> Is clear.

The first line syncopates its two words by initial sound and by punctuation. The closeness of the internal vowels attracts the ear to hear a likeness and in that act of closer attraction makes subtle distinctions at the same time. The second line of "clear" keeps the "ear-er" center and adds another sound. The third line, a single word again, preserves the center and contributes two more sound details. "Error," two lines later, catches "-or" and part of an earlier sound, "err-" with "her." The second sentence starts with one of the poem's few nonechoing words. All others appear in the first sentence.

"Her" follows "hear" as a close but distinct sound (tone quality and duration). "Clear" is also close, but distinct; its ideation requires isolation on the line. Later it will balance evenly with "care" in the first sentence's downward pull, then not so evenly, compressed, in the second sentence. It seems likely that "mirror" came by association with "clear" and by its sound linkage. "Care," as in caring too much, can only be a valentine's error. It is chosen to counterbalance "clear." The second sentence speeds up by condensing the terms of the first, counterpointing against the initially slower rhythm and maintaining a richness of statement at the same time. We may read it as care is clear in her, meaning not in error, or as in her care the unstated mirror is clear, blameless.

The poem moves by degrees of sameness and difference. The degrees are degrees of sound, details of consonance and dissonance which, in their approach to and temporary withholding of resolution, define a line of melody. This line is embodied in the syllable-to-syllable, word-to-word torsion on a line and in the downward alteration of slightly longer against shorter lines. The degrees operate horizontally and vertically. The relatively complex "problem" of the first sentence requires the release of the second as counterpoised construction of sound and as love's own resolution, the poet's feeling for "her." This melody line of complex problem—compact release is given in and through word sounds which also give the meaning—love—which a valentine, by definition, should offer. Yet there is no reference to love nor to any of the commercial trappings. As Zukofsky begins at a level of word-sound detail under that of standard forms, so his expression of feeling lies beneath stock formulations in order to emerge anew. This poem is a new love song. Or as Zukofsky writes in his *Test:* "cadence plus definite language equal the full meaning."

The second valentine poem takes the very same words as the first but combines them in still more various, fuguelike orders. This is the first stanza:

> Hear her
> (Clear mirror)
> Care.
> His error.
> In her care—
> Is clear.

The word-sound details function in all those ways found in the first poem, but differently. Now the first line's words connect by like and unlike sounds only to be swept together by imperative grammar urging the clear mirror to hear her care. And her care is "his error" of the third line. Her care (for him, her error) is clear. The words are the same; the sentiment is almost, but not quite, the same. Because of the realignment of word sound, the second sentence of the second stanza does not duplicate the meaning of the first poem's second sentence even though identical wording is used in each sentence.

The second stanza repeats the first poem in its word and line order. Its new placement within the larger poem forces a new reading. What comes after it is a new stanza length, five lines, using the unvarying tone-row words, but this time without any punctuation. As a result, the relative flow from line to line is quicker. The stanza's rhythm changes, and the meaning changes: the clear mirror is once more invoked to hear her, only this version has at least a double possibility of reference in its closing three lines. Each version has care as his error. Each differs in how she and her redeeming care are juxtaposed against him and his error. The theme (idea of the melody) of her loving errorlessness, of his subsequent need of her, is constant throughout. It is important that there be such evident constancy *and* such variation.

The third stanza's variation registers by a syntax making "Care his error" the subject qualified by "In her care" and completed as sentence expectation by "Is clear," acting as predicate. "Is clear," however, has no period. The flow hesitates and then moves through the page space separating the predicate from the next stanza, which is precisely double the length of the third. This variant has all its lines but one made up of single words. And so one more change in tempo (and meaning) is played. These leaner lines go slower, not faster, than their only slightly longer equivalents in the first three stanzas of this second valentine. We sense such a change because each word-line must be pronounced fully in enunciated isolation, each word its own syntax, its own cadence. Thus this stanza expands almost leisurely in contrast with what went before it. Does the meaning vary? Of course: this time care his error in her is simply clear.

Without end punctuation, the fourth stanza maintains the flow into the next and final variation made upon Zukofsky's constant theme. This variation moves slowest of all.

Hear
Her
Clear,
Mirror,
Care
His
Error in
Her—
Care
Is
Clear.

Again, all lines but one are single words. The stanza moves slowest of all because it contains the most lines, one more than the fourth. It's unlikely this difference would be noticed in less minutely arranged poetry. This stanza reflects the same order of stanza 4, with these exceptions: commas are placed after "Clear" and "Mirror" of lines 3 and 4; a dash occurs after "Her" of line 8; "Care Is Clear" spreads out over three lines instead of the two it takes up elsewhere in the poem.

Once more each word must be enunciated by itself, creating its own cadence. The commas direct us to read the first three lines as a command or supplication spoken to the mirror. The mirror is to hear her clear and so understand that care as error is *his* error though reflected, perhaps because of her own care, in her. At that point the dash prevents us from connecting "Her" with "Care," so that the final three lines apply to the situation generally: care is clear. Those lines conclude the poem with rhythmic snap and with emphatic affirmation of the poet's love. That is, the rhythmic contour of those lines resolves all the degrees of dissonance in their antecedents to a melody line that is felt as definitely as an object and at the same time resolves the worrying complication of error. This latter resolution—the rest or content of love reassured—occurs in and through the first.

To repeat, the presiding theme of her loving superiority or errorlessness, of his need for her loving care, is constant throughout. Nevertheless, this constancy is not merely repeated over and over. By virtue of Zukofsky's extremely finely focused technique, the total possible number of variations permitted by these few words emerges. A computer might produce a greater number, but the supreme art of these poems persuades us that we have indeed heard a completely "actualized" statement of the words and an equally complete statement of the poet's love for her, his valentine.

That very completeness, determined more by tracing and composing in accord with the words' inhering melody line through all its close changes than by an accumulation of "evidence," saves these valentines from the trivially occasional. As Williams writes with moving insight in his review of Zukofsky's *Anew:* "by knowing how to write Zukofsky has found it possible again to love. You cannot express anything unless you invent how to express it. A poem is . . . an adult release to knowledge." I would make the tracing, the attentive listening to and composition according to the melody in these few words equal "knowing how to write." For this knowledge gives the poet access to something other than even their considerable formal achievement.

Tracing and listening, Zukofsky composes his songs of close degrees, revealing in the process a "new" definition of love (care reflecting care) that is adult in its complexity. But we do no violence to his definition if, in contrast with the discursions of analysis, we hear it as "simple," simply and immediately given in the singing of the song.

Williams' insight, I believe, is the single most profound and most useful observation yet made about Zukofsky's work. Its profundity consists in the perception of the work's abiding motivation, its usefulness in that motivation's connection of the poetics and the poetry. We can designate it "love" if by that we understand reflective care. For it is care which is the more fundamental term than either sincerity or objectification. The four-line new song from *Anew* was curious because its care had by-passed sense perception of the external world to concentrate upon the details of language in the process of becoming a song. The song was exclusively about its own process of becoming song. Without our reading assistance, the composite poem as object in process must stay in its page space—claustral, unsounded, and incomplete—the poet's voice unacknowledged in his song. The poem cannot become a fully realized object, and we cannot participate in what, beyond the not incidental pleasure of its melody, may renew our own attention to the worlds of the total universe of human experience. *Care is clear* only if it exists in the words' composed melody line in the first place, to be reflected, returned, in a reader's loverlike close attention.

With longer lines and less immediately insistent word play, the third poem in the series proposes a very different melody line, a different set of changes.

> The birds are our friends—
> Jannequin's,
> The sun's.
> *The man is our friend?*
> *Our friend.*

Jannequin's birds take us back to Pound, who prints Gerhart Münch's violin transcription of Clement Jannequin's four-part chanson "Le Chant des oiseaux" as Canto LXXV in his *Pisan Cantos.* Pound's advocacy of Jannequin probably derives from the sheer pleasure of this imitative or descriptive music and from his conviction that it developed out of Provençal troubadour poetry. The derivation matters to Pound as evidence of a tradition's substantiation of one of the three ways he would have language charged with meaning, namely, melopoeia, inducing emotional correlations by the sound and rhythm of speech. The derivation matters to Zukofsky who, following Pound, defines songwriting as the tracing out of the melody within words.

Jannequin's birds take us back to Pound, too, because this third poem is a song of homage and friendship, another sort of valentine, for a poet the younger Zukofsky always kept in admiring, but not uncritical, focus. The final sentence of Zukofsky's *"Work/Sundown"* essay (published in 1948, the third year of Pound's confinement at St. Elizabeths Hospital, where he was held as "insane and mentally unfit for trial") is representative: "it will matter very little against his finest work overshadowed in his lifetime by the hell of Belsen which he overlooked." In the poem, friendship is witnessed without fuss when Zukofsky has *his* birds inquire if the man is our friend. The response, which I hear as a combination of the poet's voice with those of the birds, is *"Our friend."*

In ways similar to the radiant nodes or vortex clusters of the *Cantos,* the next seven stanzas make a rhyming weave of allusion and association taken from Old Testament sources. Significantly, the first of these is the *Book of Ezra.* Zukofsky's practice is to avoid merely relocating the biblical excerpts. The fact that he cites his precise sources in a footnote published with the poem indicates their function as a background or screen against which the lines of the poem are to be read in counterpoint.

There is a heard, literal melody of sound in the words, a literal melody line to which the poet's chosen words contribute in their progress through dissonance, and there is an ongoing melody of allusion and association of ideas sometimes outside, as hinted at in the poem, and sometimes within a direct interplay of concepts.

The screen consists, in the order of the footnote, of *Ezra* 1–6: rebuilding the Temple in Jerusalem and the Jews' relations with Persian kings (Cyrus, Artaxerxes, Darius) during the rebuilding; *I Chronicles* 6:31 and 15:16: David's hiring of singers and musicians to raise sounds of joy for the bringing of the holy ark and his appointment of those in charge of song service at the Temple after the ark rested there; *II Samuel* 23:4: a description of the just ruler ("he dawns on them like the morning, like rain that makes grass to sprout from the earth") and *Genesis* 23: Abraham's burial of Sarah in the cave of Machpelah.

Two stanzas will demonstrate Zukofsky's glancing play on and transformation of his sources.

> The sound in the Temple built after exile
> Is never worth the sound
> At the earth where no temple stood
> And on which no law of exile can fall.
>
> Blood flows; not hateful good,
> Not this measure is blood.
> Crabbed and lovely both is root.
> What is never imposes.

The sources are innocent of the insight of these stanzas: that earth sound—"what is"—is preferable to the calamity involved with the bloody history of the Temple, that a sufficient complexity—crabbed and lovely as the grass of *II Samuel*—is there as given for the attentive who presume no need for the imposition of external law.

If Pound enters more directly into the poem than the Jannequin association, it is in the character of David, described in the Old Testament as one concerned with singing and music and previously observed in the poem as one who "never chartered nor coddled his ground." But

> On this earth
> We will not—nor did the prophet much—
>   mention

David.

The birds sing:
The man is our friend,
Our friend.

The poem ends as it began, though even here there is subtle but mean-ingful variation in punctuation, with the sung testimony of the birds. And now it becomes clear why the opening set-off line appears within quotes. It is none other than the dash-enclosed phrase of the close. The technique is musical. A sliver of what might be called the exposition is presented only later to be picked up, integrated into its whole expression, one refraction of what we now hear as the poem's sonatalike order.

There is the atomic sort of melody-line accretion within that order also, but I want to return to this other, Poundian music of allusion and associa-tion. For this song may also be considered as a motet in which the tenor line is made up of Old Testament excerpts, more hinted at than heard, with Zukofsky's lines the superimposed second voice that is audible. It is an unobtrusive song of friendship for an older poet who had long ago written his own "Song of the Degrees" (*Lustra,* 1915), reminding him without rancour that the writing (singing)—and not the David–political man aspect—was the basis of his homage. The point of the poem's sources could hardly have been lost on Pound.

After the interval of "Happiest February," a capriccio on the valentine theme ("Many more happy Valentines. / How many? . . . As many as many"), there is another poem of friendship and homage for an older contemporary master:

William
Carlos
Williams
alive!

As those opening lines announce, this one has an altogether different rhythm and tone. Each reflects the characteristic practice of its honored "subject." Accordingly, the lines for Williams are clipped, the address direct, the diction more relaxed and conversational.

> Thinking of
> Billy
>
> The kid
> shoots
> to kill . . .

These lines celebrate that side of Williams which insisted "I remain only a half educated barbarian" in a letter to Zukofsky, the side demanding no ideas but in things, and "Pah! / It is unclean / which is not straight to the mark—" (from "Young Love," a poem in *Spring and All*, Zukofsky's favorite of all Williams' books).

But there are other sides to "the invariant Bill Williams," one of which Zukofsky had noted several years before in his essay "American Poetry 1920–1930." "The criticism of dialecticians inclined to think of Wm Carlos Williams as a mountain goat butting among crags has never stopped to analyze the metaphysical concept behind his improvisations. But it is a definite metaphysical concept: the thought is the thing which, in turn, produces the thought." The mountain goat has a mind, however he might argue to the contrary, capable of metaphysical conception. This, "the expanse / of his / *mind*," is handled in equal measure with the rough and ready side. And the poem moves in a free gaiety, the gaiety of Williams' "Trees," that is unusual for Zukofsky. What might be called a phenomenological description of the mind's expanse in action is preceded by what sounds like a scat singer's improvisation on his subject's name.

> reach
> C
> a cove—
> call it
> Carlos:
>
> smell W
> double U
>
> two W's,
> ravine and
> runnel

C's cluster all separate and yet together, kept together by a remembering, quick reflecting organization (line) of word sound. W's/double U's are put in pun motion only to constitute images, objects, gorge and gutter. The sound, improvised on the sound and shape of Williams' name, suggests another, "later" organization of tangible object. These sink high in a high fog which lifts to reveal "the other world."

We have gone from a landscape given objectification through Zukof-sky's improvisation to this other world which we can read as the external scene apprehended by sight, the world known as distinct from and outside ourselves, the world out *there*. The sequence may or may not matter. Whichever comes first—inside (self, language, mind) or outside (nature, world, eyes)—the desirability of their coordination remains the crucial point.

This coordination, itself a metaphysical concept, is no accident. It may be relevant for Williams' poetry, but it is absolutely essential for Zukof-sky's. The necessity of eyes-with-mind is nothing less than the fundamental principle of his poetics. *Bottom: On Shakespeare* (1963), its most extensive expression, weaves itself around the single theme that Shake-speare's text favors the clear physical eye against the erring brain. Zukofsky's found theme in Shakespeare would not appear to favor coordination. Consider, however, his attempt to locate the mind's proper function in the dialogue with his son in the "Definition" section of *Bottom*. There he glosses the proportion of Shakespeare's definition of love—love is to reason as the eyes are to the mind—as "when reason judges with eyes, love and mind are one." His son asks if his father's Shakespeare isn't just a cracked record playing one point over and over as the arithmetical substitution for the proportion would have to be 1 : 1 : : 1 : 1. Zukofsky replies that the proportion may have different enactments in different plays, as extremes of the characters always equal their dramatic means. "But from the desirable view of the perfection of character the characters are happy only when their eyes judge for equable equals. Then because they look with their eyes they love reasonably."

The father-son dialogue continues over seventy pages and almost the entire Shakespeare canon. Its summary, in the phrase Zukofsky uses for what he calls his Shakespeare theme in *"A"-13*, is: *Love sees*. It sees because its nature, perhaps larger than the compositional condition of sincerity, includes the desire for knowledge and the care for detail in both inside and outside worlds. It sees because the mind, when motivated by love, can coordinate the eyes' information with itself and with the entire sensorium, using its powers of abstraction or reason only for love's purpose of intensifying perception.

Or as Zukofsky adapts Spinoza in *"A"-12:*

> Since no one cares about anything he does not love
> And love is pleasure that dwells on its cause
> He who loves keeps what he loves:
> An image inwreathed with many things
> That may flourish, that draws cause
> To light up.

Shakespeare's definition of love (and Spinoza's), his "theme," are of course Zukofsky's own definition and theme. They increase the terms of his poetics and suggest a metaphysics, but without contradicting our earlier understanding of love as care reflecting care, nor its central position for all his writing. We begin with delight in knowing things through their perceived differences, and we end with an inwreathed (coordinate) image (poem) that makes those things flourish, light up. And thus they may give even more delight, be even more loved, because they have been apprehended with a greater intensity of perception.

The relation of this coordination to the musical aspect of the poetics is elegantly condensed in a diagram of proportion that appears in *"A"-12.*

$$\int_{-1}^{1} \int \quad \begin{array}{l} \text{sound} \\ \text{story—eyes : thing thought} \end{array}$$

This diagram—a variation of an earlier one that places music at the top of the violin sound hole shape (or superior position for the same shape as the mathematical sign for a definite integral) and speech at the bottom or inferior position—is the diagram of the simple as single (complex) whole of poetry in its presentation as song. There are two necessary coordinations: of eyes with mind at the lower limit, of eyes-mind with musical sound at the upper limit. The agent or device of both, as with that of sense perception and language in composition, is the poet's sense of a growing melody line in the words. All of the elements in the diagram for Zukofsky's poetics may have different enactments in different poems, but they are all one-to-one to each other in proportion because their coordination contributes to the oneness present in the singing of the song.

Returning to the poem, we follow the direction Zukofsky gives to Williams' sight moving on the *there* world and on "the same word," which is "mind."

> the sight
> *moves*—
>
> open—
>
> soothes
>
> smoothes
> over
>
> the
> same word
>
> that
> may have,
> to touch,
>
> two faces—
> the heart
> sees into—
>
> of one
> sound

The speech line is the line made by the sight's movement. The other, melody line manifests itself as always in the movement of word sound, specifically the vowel progression: moves, open, soothes, smoothes, over, word, to, touch, two, into, one, sound.

O is an open vowel. The line of this persistent vowel is literally a line, an unornamented vertical, in the straight accelerating drop of all the individual lines. The drop encourages speed, but the vowel also binds sight and mind in its motion of rapid changes of close degrees. The value of the vowels alters just perceptibly in those changes that still preserve something of a continuous core identity. The vowel is not the only element so involved. The initial *s*'s in their own progression make another core woven together with the vowel changes as a counterstrand. One sound is open, the other is a closed sibilant; both are one—their dissonance resolved—in the song's coordination. This last "one sound" can be only the direction of movement for Williams' sight and mind in the poem.

When analysis opens the mind's two faces, we read functions: as seat of abstracting reason, as coordinator of eyes' information. The figure is not made an absolute. For mind to establish contact, touch more than its own abstractions, it needs such functions. However the directness is achieved, both faces are merged in the other figure of the heart, which is at once the valentine, love's organ, and the true vital center with the unique capability to see "into." The faces are further merged in what the song's melody resolves to one sound. That is: the faces, like the speech and music limits of Zukofsky's diagram, become one with the heart in the unity of love as care-centered song. This unity or coordination, which he proposes as the goal of his poetics, is acknowledged by the poem's example or at the least by the implication of its example as existing "there," too, in the poetry of Williams.

Like the sonata order of Pound's homage, the poem comes back to Williams as "the kid" who is now torn and shot. The rationale for returning to this half barbarian side is unification as formal expectation (musically, recapitulation, eventual return to the opening home key), and as a younger poet's expression of care for a beloved precursor. Care is always technical and personal in Zukofsky. The poem is always a musical object and "an emotional object defined . . . by its technique and the poet's conviction or mastery with which these beliefs are expressed." Consequently, to follow up on the definition quoted from his *Test*, "only objectified emotion endures." The enduring emotion of all the poems in this series is love, not as one static thing, but as a continuing statement in its various degrees.

Zukofsky is a fast but gentle gunslinger. The shot comes so quickly it sounds like water. And it is with still more coordinating play, with the story line ideation of water and with a rippling mixture of vowel sounds, that this second poem of friendship ends. The play had begun with "purls," connecting the shooting's water sound with a high voice, in contrast with the previous high fog, that should undoubtedly be taken as Williams' own voice as master poet.

The heightened, elevated voice then becomes low, another modulation, as water moving with different, altering speeds down one stream.

> a
> high
> voice
>
> as with
> a lien
> on
> the sky
>
> that becomes
>
> low now
> frankly
>
> water—
>
> called also—
>
> softly—
>
> a kill.

The statement of the poem is continuous and complete. Vowels and other particles of articulation combine as cores (chords). Character as given name and assumed personae (wild man and lofty poet) appear in sonata order with the themes of the desirable coordination of eyes-mind and with the other theme of Zukofsky's frank and courteous affection for Williams. Both are instances of *Love sees*.

Sight and the mind and water reappear in "A wish," the sixth poem of the series. This time the combination is met in the external scene of Brooklyn—specifically the East River—and, perpendicular to the river, Clark Street, along which the poet goes to work (in the English Department of the Polytechnic Institute of Brooklyn where Zukofsky taught from 1947 to 1966).

> Looking down at the water
> three blocks away at Clark Street
> if but once a day,
>   my valentines,

> but day after day
> my mind going to work
>
> with eyes on the water
> tries me with a prayer,
>   my sweet,
> that my wish wear our look
> well, care for our days:
>   to long life!

It is the mind, "with eyes on the water," which encourages Zukofsky's prayer. The prayer is a consequence of the mind functioning in accord with the eyes, which direct its attention to the example of water, the "natural symbol" for that active coordination which we hear, finally, as the developing melody line in both this poem and the one for Williams. Or, keeping alert to the rather unmusical reportage of the first two lines: going to work, the poet glances at the river and at the same moment his mind urges him to prayer. Neither reading has to cancel out the other. The syntax of "my mind going to work / with eyes on the water" permits us to read both usual event in the external scene and the eyes-mind heard oneness desired by the technical and personal love-centered poetics.

The river, which is definitely out there, is also the river of song's coordinate melody. As Zukofsky writes in *"A"-12,*

> River, since a song does not turn back
>   to speak to
> Everyone of its order, but will run on
> In the words after the sun on
> The singer stops shining

I have written that the mind motivates his prayer, but Zukofsky's word is "tries." As with the syntax, we can read the verb in two ways—the first, according to its general sense, as a testing; the second, taken from carpentry, as bringing a piece of timber to a perfectly smooth surface by repeatedly testing it and planing off any roughness. What prompts this second specialized reading is the Williams poem in which sight "smoothes" and "soothes" the word, which is the mind expressed as two faces or functions kept together by a sound—the described voice of Williams and the melody of the poem—moving like water.

Eyes-mind *tests*—requires sincere attentive care for the details of language and of the external scene, of the inside and outside worlds; *smoothes*—coordinates those details according to the part-to-part, part-to-whole limits as required by the growing line of melody; *soothes*—offers "our look," that of love between Zukofsky and his wife, their care reflecting care, as a condition almost of grace to all the poet's valentines (assisting readers in addition to those—his wife and son, his friends and older masters—named in the poems) over a long lifetime. And the mode of this action, composition process and offered gift, is flowing song.

But there is more to the prayer of "A wish."

> So the song be for good
> and that time a new's written
> the water flow on,
> as there now, it be a completion
> to wharves below, a street
> away.

Made from an attitude of sincerity, the song is "for good," for the extension of that condition as the ethical translation of love beyond the private experience of the poet in composition and beyond the encircling embrace of husband and wife. This is how time is made new. The song's complete statement of the words brackets the content of a time, either as a duration of moments or as an entire experience. The achieved artifice of the poem as song, its melody, gives us the sense of being able to hold that content as we might hold a quartz crystal in our hands. We feel we can know the crystal definitely and completely. Knowing it in this way, we are released from glazed-over perpetual uncertainty to return to all that exists outside the song's brackets with quickened attention.

It could be said that we are prepared to love the content of "all that" again, to see it again. Yes, this is objectification, but we have extended that condition also. It still entails our assisting participation as readers. Now, however, we see that it makes for another sort of completion: not the completely satisfied apprehension of the poem as an art object, but—following that apprehension—our conscious, "heightened" conscious return to unbracketed duration and experience. This is much better. Zukofsky activates love as technical care and personal emotion to return us, finally, to a fully human existence which must include the possibility of tragedy, something the television and radio promise to seal off but without being able to make themselves more than perishable vehicles for escape. They cozen us into a knowing ignorance.

Zukofsky's means for this activation is the voice, the same means of "mass communication," but used with measurably greater skill and with nonpredatory intent for intensified perception, his own and ours as his readers. His work, nevertheless, appears like most poetry since Campion as a printed text and is probably read, like most poetry since then, in silence. This is a serious problem for a poetry conceived as song. Its writer has to hope that his care has been sufficient to convey to the silent reader some sense of musical structure as embodied in the cadence of an imagined voice.

Zukofsky is not unaware of the problem.

> *Can*
> The design
> Of the fugue
> Be transferred
> To poetry?

To reword the question: can the contrapuntal process of the fugue, in which a subject or melody must be capable of polyphonic development and must be amendable to simultaneous combinations with itself (stretto) and with other melodies or countersubjects, can this most involved of voice-based musical structures be transformed to obtain for the process of poems? The question, taken from *"A"-6*, should not be understood to mean that the fugue is necessarily the most desirable form for poetry. It *is* the extreme expression, as fugue is the extreme or upper limit of what can be heard as song, of the abiding question for all of Zukofsky's writing: can musical form obtain for poems?

One answer, in the affirmative, appears in the second half of "A wish."

> A way—
>
> *a good sprag memory*
> so the boy profits lively.
> It would make sense. As if there now
> that time brightens a page—

> stretched as by Providence—
> of a mind that
> in the Latin of Parson Evans—
> telling the boy the vocative
> *Remember, William, is "caret"*—
> Shakespeare went before
> to touch Bach who taught
> his choir boys Latin
> in the while
> proved by the fugue
>
> *Look, where his master comes;*
> *'tis a playing-day,*
> *I see.*
>
> See I, day-playing
> a 'tis;
> comes master his
> where,
> Look.

"A way" plays on the preceding "a street / away" and refers to how the conditions of Zukofsky's prayer may be accomplished. The single dash after "A way" indicates that the lines which follow are to be read as demonstration of that way. The first of these is actually a speech by the Welsh parson Sir Hugh Evans to Mrs. Page in Shakespeare's *Merry Wives of Windsor* (4.1). It would make sense that a good sprag memory is a way to the care that can achieve the renewal of time. For only it can bring together Shakespeare and Bach, words and music, the compelling excellence of whose art in creating complete structures as though in a continuous present, "as if there now," that, outside of art, could be brought about only by the time-stretching of Providence. It is Zukofsky's own good memory which recalls the parson instructing his pupil William that the vocative, the case of direct address (and of cadence), is *caret,* the Latin for "is wanting." I would like to think the care-*caret* rhyme, in such a minutely attentive poetry, is not incidental. The prayer, then, will be accomplished by care addressing itself directly to language and to others as Shakespeare and Bach continue to address us.

As Mistress Quickly comments on the Latin term: "that's a good root." The term may even surpass its pun. For without care as root there is insubstantial motive and insufficient ground for good memory, which in turn fosters the action of care reflecting care. That this is the case is "proved" by the mirror canon or retrograde motion of the poem's last two stanzas. This motion is a particular device of fugue process. The lines involved are taken from a speech by Mrs. Page with reference to the schoolmaster Parson.

Their reference also applies to Zukofsky's acknowledged masters, Shakespeare and Bach who, like Pound and Williams, supply him with models (that also become subjects) as to how he should go about his own play, that is, fugually, writing in an order of words that are made to remember themselves in their development toward a bracketed, but ultimately releasing, structure or melody. What Zukofsky has chosen to find in his models, in Schoenberg's description of what he learned from Bach, is "the art of producing everything from one thing." So the answer is yes: the design of the fugue can and, in fact, ought to be transferred to a poetry defined as song. For the process of fugue is nothing other than the extreme formal instance of that one thing, care reflecting care.

As the question of fugue transfer to poetry or the possibility of musical structure generally occurs throughout all of Zukofsky's work, we should expect that there are other answers besides the modest retrograde flourish of "A wish." The most conclusive of these is *Celia's L.Z. Masque,* the twenty-fourth and final book of *"A."* Originally published (1972) as a separate volume of over two hundred pages, the poem is printed in a five-part score: music, thought, drama, story, and poem. The music is Handel's *Pièces pour le Clavecin.* The other four parts (voices) are taken from previous publications by Zukofsky: thought = *Prepositions,* a collection of critical essays (1967); drama = *Arise, arise,* a play (1973); story = "It Was," a short story from the *Ferdinand* volume (1968), and poem = the preceding books of *"A"* itself, begun in 1928 and brought round to this final book some forty years later.

As the title of *"A"-24* indicates, its actual composer is Celia Zukofsky, the poet's wife. How this came about is explained in her remarks at a commemorative evening held for the poet on April 18, 1979, at the PEN American Center.

> To prove it [that he was writing one thing all his life] to him, I thought that I would just arrange this as I saw fit. I used the one play that he did, *Arise, arise* as the central theme—and then above it, I had two voices and then

there were two below. When I was all through, I thought I would amuse him with it and showed it to him. Whereupon he said, "That's fine. This will be 'A'-24." I thought it was rather silly, but he insisted and he put his name to it so it became "A"-24.

It may be surprising that such a fastidious poet would not merely concur with but would insist upon the adoption of someone else's arrangement of "himself" for the conclusion of his poem "of a life / —and a time." For another poet it might seem nothing less than the ultimate traduction.

There are several reasons why this is not the case for Zukofsky. First, we recall the presiding theme of her loving errorlessness: his need for her care and its evolution to a revealed definition of love as reflective care. Obviously, she, as the *she* of these poems, is much more significant than "someone else." True, she is not specifically identified as the poet's wife in those poems. Yet even the most casual reading of Zukofsky cannot fail to notice that the work consistently appeals to and gives honor to one woman above all others:

> Blest
> Ardent
> Celia
>   unhurt and
> Happy.

Done as a literary equivalent to musical practice, the BACH motive of this quotation, which ends "A"-12 and which, generalized to any reference to Bach or his music, recurs throughout all of "A" and many of the shorter poems. It is not joined with Celia's name by chance. Like that motive, she is a constant.

The association of Bach with fugue composition, as we are reminded by "A way," suggests a second reason for Zukofsky's insistence. What we are made to hear in this masque for voices and Handel's music, the regularity of which serves to throw the words into greater relief, is precisely the work in its recurrence—that is, a fugue. The form of "A"-24, then, is a faithful realization of the form inherent in the other, previous books of the poem and, as we hear, in all of Zukofsky's writing. More than a realization (the form can hardly be said to have had only potential existence before), it is a dramatization, a rearranged enactment of the writing as a larger consistent whole.

There can be no question about the extent and consistency of Zukof-sky's writing, which encompasses all the genres ("speeds" of language would be more accurate) in addition to literary criticism and translation. Yet its active completion, and perhaps most persuasive demonstration, occurs with a wife's attentive rereading and rearrangement, his extraordi-nary care reflected by hers. A third reason is that her composition allows Zukofsky to efface himself as a presiding, directive ego in the poem. As pointed out to me by Robert Creeley, Zukofsky takes leave or melds as a poet with his materials—emphasized by an extreme density of language that tends to cover the voice—in *"A"-23,* written some six years after Celia's completion of the final book. The exit is explicit:

> You spoke
> for me of *my* cell,
> I'll not work its silence
> and peace again—now anybody's
> sloth to stretch in, psalter
> and breviary: ashes, I a
> breviary better lug stone.

The melding is no less explicit in the poet's anticipating summing up of the poem, looking both backward and forward, which now subsumes his presence to become part of a complex landscape:

> music, thought, drama, story, poem
> parks' sunburst—animals, grace notes—
> z-sited path are but us.

The words thus become primary in *"A"-24.* These acts are explicit and deliberate so that the words may become not *autonomous,* which is not possible and probably not really desirable, but *available* to take part more freely in their own informing music, which then becomes a gift, material for the use of others. Of course this release of language is a matter of degree. It is unlikely, having gone through the more than five hundred pages of *"A"* that lead up to book 24, that one would forget where the words came from. Nonetheless, the intention, like the poet's original care for the words' selection and combination, remains clear.

This intention distinguishes *"A"* from its two companion long poems written in this century—Pound's *Cantos* and Williams' *Paterson.* Despite the moving humility of the final *Drafts and Fragments*—"To confess wrong without losing rightness: / Charity I have had sometimes, / I cannot make it flow thru"—and despite the inclusive declaration that "We know nothing and can know nothing / but / the dance, to dance to a measure" in *Book 5,* their authors never seem able to let go of the poems as *their* poems. We must continue to deal with them, with the vicissitudes and tempers of their personalities, to get to the words. (This may be why, like Charles Olson's *Maximus,* both poems end in fragments. The voice is forced to carry on as long as its possessor can draw breath, the act of which, in turn, seems to depend on the voice's exercise.) *"A"-24,* however, opens the entire poem, the entire work, out into an available whole structure. In the terminology of the structuralists, it produces its own *vraisemblabisation.* Considered with the leave-taking of book 23, it also saves the work from itself, from satisfying only too well the inward inclination of its aesthetic—technically the fugue, personally the family.

It reiterates, further, what Eliot has called the highest possible achievement of the poet as poet: to pass on one's own language more highly developed, more refined, and more precise than it was before one wrote in it. We can suspect that it is our own ears, and not the language, which are developed and refined in reading a poet such as Zukofsky without denying his achievement. Not least Celia Zukofsky's arrangement remembers the one thing underlying all the words of a shared life and time: *the heart became the sentence aloud.*

The scale of "their song" in *"A"-24* does not discredit what we have learned in reading the smaller songs of degrees which, after all, partake of the same one thing as motivation. This particular transfer of fugue process is but the extreme formal expression of care. Long or short, it may have similarly complete expressions without the benefit of preexistent musical forms. Certainly, the other poems of "Songs of Degrees" utilize fugue process, whether or not their use can be tagged with its specific devices. That is to say, there can be new lines of melody, new measures which still observe the constant principles of musical, cadenced structure.

The seventh and last poem in the series, "March first," begins with small leaves "making a hell / of a noise" as children in conflict with their parents.

> Littlest children fight with their fathers,
> The mothers are distracted or
>   stark mad

Rehearsing with them—
Tiniest green and teemingest teen—
Reciting
"We are the generations of leaves."

Our first response has to be that the poet must have become tired or lost interest in the series. Instead of the close degrees of fugal work in the other poems, we find a skit or what a musicologist might call a free fantasy on the sound of the leaves. This is a reversal of procedure, literally a re-hear-sing. "March first" begins with a sound, found in the outside world rather than grown in composition, and proceeds to act it out, to furnish a scenario for the actors, who are themselves furnished by metaphor (leaf noise = fighting children) to make an image not of, but from, the tune. As Zukofsky has the uncle character in his novel *Ferdinand* remark: "the tune still has insuperable balance. . . . We don't know how much until we hear the words acted in the scene for which the sounds were meant." Then, through the song that tiniest green and teemingest teen recite at the end of their scenario, the poem reverses itself once more.

Previously, the complete melody of a song was realized in the reflection of its reader's careful attention. It could take on that completeness of structure, objectification, only as an imagined music. But "We are the generations of leaves," as demonstrated by the quotation marks, is a song that sings itself. It doesn't need our assistance, even though we have to reread it to hear it sing.

In his "Ezra Pound" essay (1932), Zukofsky lists three musics to be found in the *Cantos:* (1) the music of the words themselves, (2) the music produced by the juxtaposition of word against word, line against line, entire canto against canto, (3) the suggested music of all the *Cantos* at once. The purpose of "March first," which is only casually fugal, is clear when considered as an instance of this second music. It is a coda for the series, a different though no less conscious sort of leave-taking than in *"A"-23,* a relaxation and release from the variously dense music, microtonal row to sonata-ordered vortex, of the first six poems of "Songs of Degrees."

The suggested music of all of the poems in the series is a fugue made to move in a number of rhythms and pitches that are deliberately intimate in their range of degrees. As Zukofsky writes in *"A"-13,* the understanding of this actual and suggested music of adult complexity is not to be had by the manipulation of eight definitions and seven axioms, but by "only the image of a voice: *Love you.*" This image of voice is the same as the variously enacted image in the "Songs of Degrees" and in *"A"-24*. Converted to an object, it becomes a valentine.

The valentine returns us to the abiding motivation, the one thing, the single theme, the persistent fugue subject of the series and of all of Zukofsky's work as a larger consistent whole. While we hear the valentine simply and immediately as a statement of love in the singing of the songs, its nature is complexly adult: care reflecting care. The care is technical and personal. It begins with the poet's love of the knowledge of things in their difference, with his sincere care for the details of the physical universe and of the universe of language. Through his coordination of eyes with mind he is able to compose a song whose order proceeds as a developing line originating from and directed in its development by the melody in the words.

If his composition has been done with adequate care, then a continuous and complete statement of the words comes about that in its suggestion—as form or structure—and in our own careful attention as readers gives us the sense that we know objects, a metal fish or quartz crystal in our hands. With that knowledge comes, in turn, a sense of rest. We are taken out of the flux, however momentarily; time has been made new. Whatever its intonation or enactment at a given moment, the valentine holds, like the "simple" subject of Bach's *Art of the Fugue,* throughout all the complex music inwreathed and flourishing around it in the poetry of Louis Zukofsky. And all of that music comes down to a matter of song. If we are to get that image, we must first hear it.

I have tried, unsuccessfully, to honor Zukofsky's hope that a reading of his work would content itself with just the words. This essay, in any case, has had little to do with scholarship. It does have something to do with structure. That is: there can be none, neither satisfying art object nor revivified consciousness of our lives outside art, unless the immaculate care of this poetry find reflection ("desire until all be bright") in our reading. The product of structure, the art object, the poem, assumes its ultimate justification, beyond even the craft satisfactions of an object well made, when the internalized music of the words opens out into a sufficient and available structure; when it offers a path through the space, the landscape of language it composes not merely for our appreciation but also for active use. Care, then use are the lessons to be learned. Otherwise, reading serves only to distract us from perception. Writing is made to turn against its own intention.

The poetry of Louis Zukofsky is a rare instance of the highest achievement in recent writing. The work of others may attain that level, but few, if any, have offered it as a deliberate gift, as a material released for future use. As such, it contains imperatives (care and use) that are not to be met by anything less than sincere (close) attention. Those who would read the work and accept the gift may remind those who waver of William Carlos Williams' hard questions: "what are you gonna do? Deny love?"

Play and the Poetry of Susan Howe

Play, first and last, is the sovereign principle of composition and the source of all our closest attention to poetry. Lacking the significant play of language, poetry becomes a stale consideration of style and attitude, something merely to be studied by means of chronology and paraphrase for some vaguely defined cultural benefit. Lacking significant play, poetry becomes merely the dim reflection of such study. It is the quality of play, its range and depth, which determines the quality of the poetry. For play, in being most truly representative of the dynamic nature of language, is also most truly representative of the human.

The poetry of Susan Howe's *Pythagorean Silence* is exceptional for its forthright recognition of play. As she writes in a poem which serves as the preface to her book:

> we that were wood
> when that a wide wood was
> In a physical Universe playing with
> words
> Bark be my limbs my hair be leaf
> Bride be my bow my lyre my quiver

Unlike the turn-of-the century symbolist writers or their descendants among the so-called language poets of the present, Susan Howe situates herself in this world, a world known and experienced through the senses, where she will proceed to play with words, known and experienced rather differently, as the essential act of the poet. Her poetry, then, will be neither a slavish reporting of sensation nor an exercise in solipsism. In Stevens' terms, there will be a jar in the process of being formed (or its form being apprehended), but it will not be forgotten that it takes place in Tennessee. If only as a resistance, a kind of gravity, the place may make a contribution to the process of the play. The physical universe will be given a role.

The preface poem indicates what kinds of play we can expect to find. They are: (1) various arrangements of words on the page, typography and spacing, to suggest alterations of voicing and meaning; (2) vocabulary shifts which suggest similar alterations; (3) related to both 1 and 2, assumption of dramatic or rhetorical roles; (4) sound devices such as deliberately heavy alliteration and rhyme, particularly as they occur in riddles and children's games; (5) wit, punning, the interplay of concepts. And although the last two lines of the preface poem only sound as if they were from Wyatt or Sidney translating Sappho, we will also find allusion and quotation.

None of these is new. What *is* new and valuable in Susan Howe's poetry is the direct declaration of play as the center of the poem and her ability to concentrate all of its means and intensities into the poem's ongoing composition. Her poetry gives pleasure in its play and produces meaning of human significance.

Pythagorean Silence consists of three sections. The first of the three, *"Pearl Harbor,"* develops around the poet's memory of a childhood visit with her father to the zoo in Buffalo, New York, on the December day that Pearl Harbor was bombed. The section is a meditation or brooding on this experience and on elements that, outside the immediate circumstance, she brings to bear through association. On the section's opening page, for example, a character (SHE) whispers that Herod had all the little baby children murdered. This leads to Rachel weeping for *her* children and, on the next page, to an extended awareness arrived at through Rachel.

R
(her cry
silences
whole
vocabularies
of *names*
for
things

This not-to-be-predicted awareness—that language is a fundamentally human vehicle for human needs, not a crude software inventory system—is achieved out of, ultimately almost outside of, the poet's original experience. Thus she is not reduced to the embarrassment that purely personal writing, the confessional, has become in our time, whatever its emotional extremity or traditional technical expertise.

As a meditation on personal experience, the section does not follow the contour of theme and variation. A meditation of this sort, like Hamlet's soliloquizing, is a continual search for theme. Its formal construction also rules out such development. Each page of the section contains a separate poem. The page is the organizing unit or frame for Susan Howe's poetry. In this first section, as in the last, each poem is composed in relation to the available space of a single page. Her meditation is literally acted out. Her own speaker voice is always present but can be displaced by other voices. There are no transitions. What keeps the sequence of page-to-page and scene-to-scene juxtaposition from seeming utterly arbitrary, untransformed cut-up, is the constant presence of her speaker voice and a sharing of terms and roles which recur, never exactly the same, throughout the section. The snow in which one is told to lie down on page 10 is and is not the same snow in which the HE and SHE characters meet on the first page. Like Noh drama, the essentially static motion of juxtaposition encourages the growth of increasingly refined play of all kinds within the space of each page unit. The static motion emphasizes the sense of boundaries. Without boundaries there can be little play.

The difficulties of such writing are considerable. Above all, the poet must stay true to the ongoing, even restless, nature of her meditation, and she must still find a way for her playing with words to matter beyond the relative skill of its own incidental activity. The child may only desire that play, any play, will never end. The adult reader has to ask for something more. In turn, the poet has the right to ask that reader to play along with the play of the poem with more than simply a willing suspension of disbelief.

With these difficulties in mind, it's of interest to consider the final page of this section. It begins with shadows seated at a kitchen table. They have been made shadows by a black cloud of war hanging over the landscape generally and by the shadow of a clock in the kitchen. The clock on this and previous pages suggests a countdown for approaching doom as the unavoidable end of war. The cause of war, here mentioned directly for the first time, is "the fist of fame." War has turned homes into fortresses. When their doors are opened, couples "buried in epochs of armor" exhibit themselves as having failed to prolong human life.

With language reminiscent of Ophelia, the poet informs us that the words of the couples are "weeds wrapped around my head." A withering of roses and the approach of darkness follow. There is a sense of things coming to an end as Ophelia came to her end. The words of the couples threaten to drag the poet down or to keep her life in a condition of drowning because they were used, per Rachel, in a fundamentally wrong way. They were used as things, armor, to protect the fame-craving self and actually to wage war. The words of the couples also threaten the poet purely as a long litany of defeat, a long-standing reminder of the failure to overcome war.

The poet does not portray herself as undergoing death, but she does conclude the section with a "dying" question: "Body and Soul / will we ever leave childhood together?" Properly, the question can have no final answer. This is not an evasion of responsibility. Remaining true to the principle of play, Susan Howe presents us with a question which has a large seriousness, is dramatically satisfying in its very largeness, and which must go on echoing in her readers' heads. The tension in the question is as moving as the poet's balancing of antagonistic demands is impressively accomplished.

There are seventeen numbered parts in the second section. As if to demonstrate an independence from the single-page format of "Pearl Harbor," most of these are over a page long. More important, the poet seems to have discovered her own voice, her given breadth of cadence. The earlier character voices of the scenes are now replaced by a single speaker voice with a regular line-length and stanza pattern. The line tends to be a long phrase that doesn't quite become a complete sentence. The stanza is made up of one long phrasal line and another half its length. The voice is varied by parenthesis, spacing within the line, single lines— sometimes of one word only—set between the regular two-line stanzas. We hear a definite voice range, within which there is full articulation (play). There can't be as many quick-change surprises as before, but there can be more power.

Further, there is more power because the poet has found a home key (not a theme) in the figure of Pythagoras. Clothed in white and so associated with the snow and ice landscape of the opening section, he is an expression of play at its deepest level, wonder and mystery. To think about Pythagoras is to attempt to deal with "odds of images," a handful of fragmentary attributions—golden thigh, theorem of geometry, mathematical relationships of the musical intervals, dietary stipulations, cult leader—which force the mind into play. Pythagoras grounds Susan Howe's play as an extension of her *"Pearl Harbor"* experience in the physical universe, a ground which while itself mysterious, encourages her voice to increasingly powerful play, wider and deeper because of even more definite boundaries, without turning her into the expositor of a single theme or the reteller of recostumed historical fiction.

Part no. 10, for instance, begins with reference to music and connects it with the idea of the dead couples isolated in their armor and fortresses.

> Each sequent separate musician
> (harmony
>
> a passion)
> across a deep divided deprivation
>
> (enchantment   captivity
> a paradise-prison)
>
> seems to hear a voice walking in the
> garden
>
> who seems to say
> I am master of myself and of the
>
> Universe

The idea is of separation, a loss of language as an exchange of interiors. The couples tried to protect the self and at the same time to aggrandize its claims. The musicians, whom I read as any artist or maker, are no better, whatever the possibility for a concord of their passions.

Each musician is situated in a deep divided deprivation as the effect of his or her art, which in its desire for enchantment promotes the twisted mishearing in the Genesis garden. Adam becomes his own lord and master of the universe. Each Adamic musician hears what the ego-driven self wants to hear, and there is no conversation. This is a private version of the war of the "engaged" couples. The end effect—isolation—is the same because, as stated earlier in the first section, rapture is always connected with rupture. Or, as in the preceding no. 9 of the second section, the musician is "rapt away to darkness." Rapture of the private self is no better than more public war (insightfully defined in this section as "mechanical necessitarianism"). Both must end in darkness.

The poet moves from the Pythagorean motif of music to reflection on the seemingly inescapable dark isolation in which even art, insofar as it's eager for enchantment, imprisons the supposedly unwarlike maker. This becomes a reflection on the nature of language.

> Ever tolling absence homeward   Words
> toil their way forward
> a true world
> fictively constructed

These stanzas recall Heidegger's discussion of Trakl's "A Winter Evening" poem in his "Language" essay. It may be that Susan Howe was drawn to it by the similarity of many of the details in her poem and Trakl's (from the first stanza of "A Winter Evening": "Window with falling snow is arrayed, / Long tolls the vesper bell, / The house is provided well").

In that essay, language is found to be neither expression nor even an activity of man. Rather, as Heidegger never tires of reiterating, *language speaks* as a kind of thing in itself. And its speaking involves naming. This naming is a calling rather than a handing out of titles or terms of classification. The naming calls and brings closer what it calls. "But the call does not wrest what it calls away from the remoteness in which it is kept by the calling there." The calling of language calls here into presence and there into absence. What is called is present in the language of the poem, though not necessarily in the reader's living room. The poem, as a formalization of the calling, provides a place of arrival for the two.

In Heidegger's summary: "the snowfall brings men under the sky that is darkening into night. The tolling of the evening bell brings them, as mortals, before the divine. House and table join mortals to the earth." All of these are gathered together by naming. The things called are given their existence as things in the language of the poem, and in their gathering we are given a world. We are given a home in the world by the speaking of language in the poem.

In *Pythagorean Silence,* Trakl's details are adopted, and portions of the vocabulary of Heidegger's understanding of language are taken over (played with). The absence Howe's words toll is a house as shelter or home, a sense of being at home in the world. The words are forever tolling in order for there to be a home. It is just this which, because of their mistaking names for things, the armored couples and separate musicians so conspicuously lack. The poet's words call forth absence, and out of the calling together of both presence and absence—Heidegger's mortals and the divine, Stevens's nothing that's not there and the nothing that is—a "true world" is constructed. It is true because it contains the physical universe *and* the realm of Pythagoras. In this realm, to collect at random from throughout all the second section of the poem, are the soul, Lucifer, theology's secret book, secrets and secrecy in general, dreams, King Arthur in the grey dawn, the Castle Perilous.

The realm of Pythagoras is made up of all such things or personages, actually spirits, who would not exist had they not been named by words in the calling of language (motivated by human need); it is the realm of words only. The construction of this true world is fictive because it has existence only within the poem. Thus there occurs, just before the quoted toiling and true world stanzas, the following: "Those passages as myth   in Myth / remain a fiction." Finally, at the close of part no. 10 we're told that perspectives perish with ourselves: "end of a house stretching its walls / away." When we through whom language speaks depart, the true world of the poem, physical universe plus myth and fiction, must likewise depart. The image, returning to and transforming Trakl's house, is strange and affecting. There can be no more play when the bounding walls, lines of perspective, of the house of language have stretched away.

Let the one part stand for the whole of the second section. For while there is constant and frequently startling play ("ideas gems games dodges") in all the parts, no. 10 fairly indicates the direction of Susan Howe's unresting meditation. Prosed, it goes something like this. We live properly in the true world in which we are given a home with its promise of shelter and family by the selfless speaking of language in the poem. In the interests of self-protection and "property" along with private rapture, however, we attempt to use and so necessarily misspeak language. The consequence, on all levels, is war. Perhaps because of this there is a certain sorrow always at the edge of all this poet's gaiety of language. She seems to share Hölderlin's sense that we live in a destitute time, a time when the evening of the world's age is declining toward its final night.

The serious question lurking everywhere in this poem is, how, having been dispossessed of our proper home by never-ceasing war, are we to go on living? But there is no answer. What is left the poet with "Poverty my mother and Possession / my father" is the wandering of a blind wisdom; Gloucester has no way and therefore wants no eyes (or whys). Wandering is a joyless, straited sort of play, but it is not playing the fool to sorrow.

Blind wisdom, though, is made feminine in the conclusion of this section: "We hear her walking in her room." The poet's voice contains and speaks through many other voices in this poem while remaining recognizably female. Therefore, it is the figure of Ophelia, not Gloucester, which we found at the close of the first section and which is returned to in the third and final section of the poem. In fourteen parts of a single page each and without a title, this third section reviews and comments on the "progress" of the poet's "elegaic Meditation," her movement "in solitary symbols through shadowy / surmises."

The problem is how to bring the play to an end. By its nature play does demand an ending, but an ending that doesn't traduce the poet's playing with words into sententious summary, nonplay. Susan Howe more than solves the problem by recapitulating and even further accelerating the play of her poem by throwing words—those which either already appeared in the sections or which share some association with them—out of their previous arrangements into new grids or patterns in which each word is suddenly atomic and free.

timid	satyr	vesper	winnow	
snow	chastity	berry-blood (secrecy)		
rosemary	poplar	holm-oak	juniper	
holly	casket	cud		

She arrives at this solution by remaining true to play as principle. That is, she puts the words on wheels—wheel of fortune and centrifuge—as the end of a chain of association that began with

Spinners and spinsters
riddles engulf
cobwebs mimic rings in rain
(chains).

The effect is one of saturation, space filled, the stacking up and spewing out of shredded finales in a symphony.

If there's triumph, there is also sorrow. The quoted grid reminds us of Ophelia's mad singing of herbs and flowers. It is to Ophelia that the poem's last line refers: "weeds shiver and my clothes spread wide." The poet's figure, her chosen voice to speak through, is Ophelia's. In my fascination with the never-failing skill of play in this poem, I have perhaps not sufficiently emphasized its darkness. From the first section to the end, we encounter a world not unlike that of Shostakovich's late quartets, a world declining toward its enduring night. For all the fireworks of her playing with words, Susan Howe's vision is of a world in which men and women have been made shadows by their own inability to let things be and so live out from under the black cloud of war. The world of *Pythagorean Silence* is both true and terrible.

I have written that the adult reader has to ask for something more than the sheer maintenance of play, however skillful in itself. Susan Howe's vision is that something. In *Pythagorean Silence* she has written a poem of rare power, both brilliant and dark. She has played with words for keeps. We cannot ask for more.

Of the Power
of the Word

Is anything more exciting and more
dangerous for the poet than his relation
to words?
—Heidegger

Poetics allows the poet to stand outside the poem. In that position it can
be determined not only how well the job has been done, but the basis for
the act of composition itself may also be investigated and the future
direction of the work, necessarily intwined with that investigation, decided upon. Poetics allows the poet to stand outside the poem with
something like the active engagement and responsibility of composition.
In this allowance, perhaps addressed to no one other than oneself, to a
doubting friend, or to anyone who would pause in walking through the
park, reticent or ardent, poetics remains conversation.

The poetics of a major poet, however, does not simply invite us to join
the conversation. Rather, it forces us to reconsider our own poetics. We
are forced to reconsider the nature and value of craft, the underlying basis
of composition, and the future of the poem. The poetics of a major poet
throws everything into question.

Robert Duncan is such a poet, a "big poet," in Charles Olson's description. His bigness, like that of Olson, reflects the degree to which he
would put everything concerning poetry in doubt. Good, even interesting
poets work within their generation's understanding, within the assumptions of that understanding of what the poem should be. Good poets
consider this question essentially once, as young poets, and work thereafter within the answer established at large by their contemporaries.
Major poets continue to consider not only the past or present generation's
answer, in reaction; they continue to consider all answers and their
assumptions. They open up the range of what the poem might be; they
keep the poem's range of possible definition open. By putting everything

in doubt, major poets make the poem always possible. We are called on—at times commanded—by major poets to respond. We must either respond—even to the point of interruption—or go down in their wake. And our response should be in kind. Let our questions bestow honor on one such poet and keep up our end of the conversation.

I take as the text for my questions a single passage from Duncan's *Truth & Life of Myth* essay.

> Speaking of a thing I call upon its name, and the Name takes over from me the story I would tell, if I let the dimmest realization of that power enter here. But the myth we are telling is the myth of the power of the Word. The Word, as we refer to It, undoes all the bounds of semantics we would draw in Its creative need to realize Its true Self. It takes over. Its desire would take over and seem to put out or to drown the individual reality—lonely invisible and consumed flame in the roaring light of the Sun—but Its creativity moves in all the realities and can only realize Itself in the Flesh, in the incarnation of concrete and mortal Form.

First sentence: words are two things, or fulfill two functions. They are the means by which things are summoned, brought to conscious definition, a kind of counting, and they are things in themselves. As names, they enable the speaker to call things not present into awareness for the purpose of telling the speaker's story; they aid the storytelling but are subservient to it. With words as names our attention is given to what is said to be there, what is said to happen in the story. Words as names give the poet an apparent power over things, a power to move things about in the interests of his or her story. As things in themselves, they are empowered to dictate their story to the speaker. They transform the poet as speaker to the bespoken. The story becomes an account of words. They are the actors in their own story which the speaker reproduces.

It would seem that both functions can be active simultaneously or that the poet can be aware of both simultaneously. The Homeric singer invokes the muse and is at the same time responsible for the word-to-word order in the moving line of his song. The poem, by extension, is a balancing, a maintenance of tension between the two. The word as name of a thing encourages accounting and manipulation (plot). It does not acknowledge the intrinsic properties of the word. It acknowledges form only insofar as that can be brought about by the list and its elaborations. The word as Name has a power capable of making our relation to the physical world tenuous, complicating our sense of any center, frustrating the communication of emotion or of action in response to such communication. The word as Name reduces men and women to isolate respondents without means of a like energy or offsetting response. It's desirable, to say the least, to find a balance between the upper- and lower-case word.

Second sentence: myth means story. The essay's headnotes build up a composite definition that corroborates and expands this meaning. Myth is the making of a sound (Liddell and Scott); myth is the development from such interjectional utterance to narrative, the plot of the *dromenon* or ritual action (Jane Harrison); myth is an expansion of empirical reality (Ernst Cassirer); myth, when a real event may be the enactment of a myth, is the truth of the fact and not the other way around (Kathleen Raine). The headnotes prepare for the essay's opening definition of myth as the story told of what cannot be told, of what cannot be revealed or known.

This would seem to give us myth as spiritual story. I write "seem" because the not-there is hardly an exclusive property of the spiritual. Myth, in Duncan's definition, can be either spiritual story or the story of absent empirical reality, real events or facts. The two can also be combined, interpenetrated. What is told is not simply the power of the Word but also *the story* of the Word's power. The reality of the word in itself and its ability to transform the speaker to bespoken, to "take over," is confirmed. Yet this is only a story, one among others. There could be other stories, other myths which we might relate at some other time.

Third sentence: an indication of the Word's power is that it somehow transcends the limitations human speakers would impose upon it by their definitions (bounds of semantics). This power is demonstrated in the story we (are made to?) tell. The motivation for its demonstration is need: the Word needs to realize Its true Self. This Self is apparently understood by that which is other than, if not antagonistic to, the impositions of the speaker's intended story (as the nature of the Word's need may be taken as other than the need of its speaker). As to how the Word can have such need in the first place, that's subsumed in the declaration of Self. If the word is granted an intrinsic existence (Name as opposed to the name of a thing), then it may be thought to have a self and thus a need to maintain that identity. Having a self creates need.

Another way to conceive of the word's self is as its ultimate etymological root, a sound. This develops from our sense of the self as somehow inside us, distinct from the outer body, an interior, the essential as opposed to the accidental. The word is spoken, and the self as root is carried, sounded, within our speech. Once this occurs, the word enters an endless branching process, which properly had its beginnings long before our usage, by way of its combination with other words and the speaking of others which continues to carry or recall and yet also deviate from the root. The process is creative in that the root is parent to the branching out to include other words and usages. The self as root, despite the ongoing nature of this process, is not lost but is further manifested. Each time the word is spoken, the root is sounded, carried and displayed.

Root reminds us of plants and flowers. A flower may contain its own seeds; it may be self-seeding. The speaker is true to the word's self so long as he or she attends to its root sound. That attendance gives the speaker a source of melody line and inclusive form. In speech the self as root is planted, blossoms, and in the natural decay of sound is replanted as seed waiting to bloom once again in "returned speech" by others who respond. The entire anthology depends upon a single root. The word is felt to have power, but only as it is sounded in our telling.

Last sentence: the desire of the word is its need to realize its "true" self, which may be understood as an interior etymological root which, as a usage and a sound, is always being manifested whenever the word is spoken. If the speaker becomes increasingly aware of the word as a thing in itself, there's the feeling of having become a passive vehicle, a subject courier for the word's story. The realization of the word's self means a corresponding obscuring of the speaker's self.

"To put out or to drown." This is given in the subjunctive by Duncan because the word's self-realization is active in "all the realities" and merely seems to obscure the individual speaker. For this realization can take place only in the flesh, in the resonating human interior. The closing terms of this last sentence bring into play specifically Christ-story associations. The myth of the word that Duncan would have us tell is any word in itself and the word as Christ incarnate, the Logos. The myth of the power of the word, as with the opening definition of myth itself, is given a playing ambivalence. It is any word, the Logos, or both at once.

There is much in Duncan's sentences that is disturbing. While the Aristotelian may object that there can't be an action without an actor to begin with and thus to speak of the word's need to realize itself is beside the point, anyone engaged in composition will readily admit, I think, that words are experienced both as the names of things and as things in themselves. In fact, composition makes us keenly aware of the latter; ordinary usage, which seeks to convert language into something else, does not. This is not a matter of theory. Whatever the nature of a chosen form, inherited or found, the poet quickly discovers the need to stay awake to the words' history of usage and sounds if the poem is to attain its form in any active way.

Readily enough we move from our experience of the form-aiding potential of the word to the upper-case absolute power of the word. The ease of the move is betrayed by the elaborate figure of the extinguished individual reality in the description of the word's desire to realize its true self. I'm aware that the figure derives from the story we have supposedly chosen to tell about the power of the word. Yet it is not simply one among equally possible others. This is particularly so when it's entangled with the Christ story, the old old story of Jesus and his love that has been told to the exclusion of others since the "beginning" of time. One way of reading the work of our fathers, the modernists, and of their fathers, the romantics, is as a struggle against the hegemony of any single story, any single vision, which is also a single definition of what the poem can be.

Duncan's poetics prompts us to consider the range of our choices, if any, and by what means that range can be assured, if it can be assured, in the face of the word's power.

Choice is available when the speaker has a story to tell. How and where is a story to be found? The most common solution has been to retell an already-existing story, to find what we would tell in what has already been told. As Duncan notes, this recognizes mythology as poets' lore. The problem is that, while we are given something to say, it is necessarily derivative, secondary, and inessential. One story displaces another only to repeat it. This process works to undermine the reality of our own lives in poetry in its suggestion that we exist only as we re-produce or represent the images of previous stories. We are made parts of a consuming process of repetition through our appropriation of the past. We are made readers and rereaders. And the more we read, the more we feel the need to read still more.

The poet, who is first a reader, makes no original discovery in reading. Instead, the poet becomes only more aware of the spider-web connected-ness of his or her sources and of the innumerable ghostly speakers still beyond them. At best, our displacements might operate as clever enough variations on previously laid-down themes. But what is finally repeated is an absence. The search for the originating source of an experience in language—in effect, for its first telling—is honorable, but futile. It only serves to expose the arbitrariness of the enterprise. The first recorded usage is all too obviously not the first. And if it is not the first, then there can be only a repeating of what is already a reproduction.

It may be, as Stevens writes, that "there was a myth before the myth began, / Venerable and articulate and complete." But what precedes both ourselves and the myth before myth is "a muddy centre." That center, the physical universe, is silent. When we would make our way back to the myth before myth, it leads us there, to silence and absence. (Even Heidegger, who attempts to establish an ontology for language, Saying instead of Being, is forced to propose a place of arrival created by the calling of naming. Called forth in the calling, this "place" is a "presence *sheltered in absence*.") The center is silent, presence is absent. Words, which we would trace back past the myths to the center as a final nontextual, nonlinguistic reference, are its representations. Words are carriers of absence.

The first *muthos,* conjectured in the Jane Harrison headnote, is relevant. What did this utterance interject with? It could only be silence. Duncan's opening definition of myth—which can be taken as a definition of the poem—emphasizes the *not-there*. The definition suggests there could be other stories about other things. It would say that, whatever their seeming subjects, they are also always "about" something else.

Earlier I sought to conceive of the word's self as its ultimate etymological root, a sound. I speculated how that root is engendered through our speaking. The implied ethics were that the poet should try to remain true to the word's self by attending to its root sound. Such attentive speaking was to encourage the root to blossom and, in the decay of sound, to bloom repeatedly in the returned speech of others. I would have the entire anthology depend on a single root.

All of this may be so. Yet it strikes me now as dangerous in its invention. For that root is attached to the center. What, consequently, it attaches all its related words and their speakers to is that same center, its silence and absence. Per Celan, its flowers are niemandsroses. The danger is that we forget this attachment, its final reference. Caught up in composition, aware of the care of our predecessors, we forget the reference, and we are tempted to formulate laws based on our stories. The expectation grows that there ought to be a primal storyteller, a primal creative agency responsible for all our smaller, individual stories. We will believe in this agency, try to divine its will and put ourselves in right relation to it. The idea of a range of choices becomes fruitless. It is dangerous to forget that the little boy and girl lost are found, given parents, only *within* Blake's songs.

This leads to a further question of whether it's possible for the poet to observe a condition of silence and remain a poet, active in the use of language and even interested in what his or her voice sounds like.

The answer is yes, and a catalogue of techniques of resolution might be drawn up. What we would have is the history of what we are learning to call postmodernism. But let us consider the answer contained in Duncan's poetics. Perhaps surprisingly, what I would draw from the passage in *Truth & Life of Myth* is also in the affirmative. Yet it is distinct from the typical postmodern resolution. That is based on ellipsis, collage of disparate vocabularies, contradictory or suspended syntaxes put in juxtaposition, cancellation, or erasure. These techniques acknowledge silence through the contrived failure or frustration of statement. (Whether these techniques, which would forcibly induce silence in the poem by way of failure or frustration, are actually sympathetic with a poetry concerned with the recognition of a silent center, of silence as the final reference, is a good question.)

It might be asked how they differ from what we find in old "poetry is a destructive force" modern poetry. Modernism struggles against what is perceived as univocal authoritative statement to open up a range or field of choices, which the postmodernist inherits as one available choice, a way in itself of speaking—not to fragment a previous symbolic whole, but to speak directly in fragments. The techniques should probably not be considered as inherently different. How the poet is able to come upon them is: postmodern poets inherit the choice of nonstatement as a way of speaking. Their voice(s) can sound like it isn't there. This is not to be confused with what we hear in Robert Duncan's poetry and poetics. That voice is radically present, nonstop, insistent to the point of irritation for the reader accustomed to both modernist and postmodernist not-saying. It is the voice of a believer for whom *none* of the gods—and *none* of the words—is dead.

What makes me answer yes for Duncan is not his use of taking-out techniques (he would want to bring everything in), nor, clearly, his voice.

What makes me answer yes is play. Previously, I noted a playing ambivalence in Duncan's definition of myth and in his telling of the power of the word. If we object, disturbed by the weaving of poetics in terms of the spiritual (and the reverse), disturbed by our sense that such power is threatening and might very well take over, his likely reply would be that *it is the myth that's being told now.* Others can be told which, given one's ability to realize form, to listen to each sound in turn, would be just as true or actual, just as compelling.

Assuming that all the stories of all the words may have such potential, then none need dominate over any other or its speaker. Like a *bricoleur* child, Duncan would play with all the words, tell all the myths. And in this constant smiling (not simply "positive") play, in which everything is make-believe and at the same time declared *to be* with all the resources of the skilled adult voice, operative upon us here and now, the silence is nonetheless observed. For the playing with each sound of each word, each possible story, means the "distractability" of all. To make the poem a ground for play does not deny the muddy center as its foundation.

In the fairy tales of George MacDonald, the older a man is, the younger he is. MacDonald's old man of the fire is to be truly identified as a child. Robert Duncan is a major poet, a poet with fire, by virtue of the constancy of his smiling play. We learn from his poetics that we need not deny the power of the word, as we need not deny the silent center, for fear of our realization as speakers and poets. We learn that our choices are governed not so much by incidental technique as by a willingness to listen to the root-self-sound of every word and that, therefore, the range of our choices is as limited or limitless as the number of words themselves.

George Oppen and the Anthologies

Having recently returned to George Oppen's *Collected Poems* and having been moved once again by them, I find myself confronted by a question I had not anticipated and for which there may be no ready answer. The question is: why aren't the poems better represented in the anthologies most often used by college classes and carried by most bookstores, the anthologies that for whatever reason have managed to stay in print? A quick check of current editions of *Contemporary American Poetry,* ed. A. Poulin; *The Norton Anthology of Poetry* (both the committee-edited volume and the specifically *Modern Poetry,* ed. Richard Ellmann and Robert O'Clair); *The New Pocket Anthology of American Verse,* ed. Oscar Williams and Hyman Sobiloff; and *The Voice That Is Great Within Us: American Poetry of the Twentieth Century,* ed. Hayden Carruth, turns up no representation at all. There is not a single Oppen poem in any of them. It is as though the poems never existed. While I have talked with Carruth, who simply stated that when he put his together he was familiar only with the early books and that he hadn't derived much pleasure from them, I have no acquaintance with the other editors nor with their selection procedures. What follows, then, is something of a speculation.

I wish to base my speculation on "Ballad," a poem from *Of Being Numerous.* The poem's physical dimensions are appropriate for an anthology format; it comes from an acclaimed volume (Pulitzer Prize, 1969). Further, its title refers to a recognizable verse form, something that suggests the possibility of ongoing tradition and thus of historical comparison, possibilities an anthology might be thought to encourage. If these external reasons would seem to qualify the poem for inclusion in an anthology, then it follows that we must look at "content" as a rationale for its exclusion.

The poem begins: "Astrolabes and lexicons / Once in the great houses—." These are instruments of measure for the natural world and for language. The nature of each and, together, their relation concerns every poet. Every poem represents a decision made about the two and their relation. The beginning lines might seem nostalgic. They imply that in the unspecified past, unspecified except for not being the present, these instruments may have been common enough property, if limited to the dwellers of the great houses. They also imply that neither that past nor its instruments are available in the present. The question that hinges on this further implication is how one is to live in a time when the great houses are at best relics or uninhabited museums.

The unsurprising and inescapable answer is that people must devise instruments as they can. They must either locate past examples or improvise their own from whatever comes to hand. There is always the risk that past examples will not function in a new present, that the improvisations will somehow not be adequate. The poet is hardly exempt from this risk. Hence the dash at the end of the second line is not incidental. I read it as a lingering punctuation, a lingering over something that might be considered remarkable in history, when once the instruments were available and functional, the equivalent for which must be come upon in what we feel to be the very different conditions of the present. My inclination is to regard the lingering not as nostalgic but as hesitant, a hesitancy in recognition of the difficulty or even impossibility of the task.

These beginning lines are put in a kind of suspension from the rest of the poem by the dash, as well as by their distinct vocabulary and self-contained syntax, so that they become an epigraph or headnote for it. The poem then proceeds as a narrative of the poet and his wife meeting "by chance" a poor lobsterman on Swan's Island, where he was born, and of being driven over the island in an old car by him. There is comment in passing on the lobsterman: "A well-spoken man / Hardly real / As he knew in those rough fields." Attention is given to things of the island, lobster pots and their gear, and then comes something unexpected, breaking up the inventory.

> The rocks outlived the classicists,
> The rocks and the lobstermen's huts

> And the sights of the island
> The ledges in the rough sea seen from the road

What's unexpected is the word "classicists." Its associations with books and study, above all with "culture," remind us of the beginning epigraph lines. Whether they are the owners or not, Jeffersonian aristocrats, the classicists are the likely occupants of the libraries of the great houses. Or if not the occupants, then the contributors to the libraries, the recorders through their books of what has been found admirable and significant in human history.

The great houses at least aspire to contain, if not actively demonstrate, those "records" which can, cumulatively, be considered as an index of what human thought is capable of. This enlargement is justified by the double sense of great houses as admirable, costly structures (as described in "Guest Room" from *This In Which*) and as, say, the house of Atreus, a noble family whose actions are "great" in their effect upon others. The classicists are charged with keeping the memory alive in us of that capability which, per the instruments, is one fundamentally of measure. As these instruments and the great houses, structures and families, are not now readily found, so the items of the natural world, the rocks of the island, have outlived the recorders of admirable human thought. The natural world is triumphant, a dominant ongoing present in comparison with the ever-receding past of the classicists. The lobstermen's huts are not great houses, and the lobsterman himself is hardly real in the presence of the rough fields.

One is reminded of the following from no. 26 of the collection's title poem:

> The power of the mind, the
> Power and weight
> Of the mind which
> Is not enough, it is nothing
>
> Against the natural world,
> Behemoth, white whale, beast
> They will say and less than beast,
> The fatal rock
>
> Which is the world—

The figure comes from Melville, but the thought differs from his Ishmaelean notion of survival in a treacherous white world, a survival made possible by the deliberate creation of a fictional space through language. The difference is one of degree. In Melville the deliberate fiction of fiction is called attention to—the contradictory placement of "The Town-Ho's Story" in the middle of *Moby-Dick,* the contradictory hinting of the narrator in *Pierre,* the contradictory evidence produced at the end in "Benito Cereno" and *Billy Budd*—if indirectly and for more crucial reasons than its recent glib emphasis (metafiction) whereby it becomes merely another technique to be studied by creative writing classes.

In Oppen there is an attempt to use language without subversion of statement and to know the world even as the persistent and perhaps irrevocable difficulties of either are readily acknowledged. Rather than set up structures only to collapse them by internal contradiction or ironic subversion, Oppen builds what might be called tentative structures that remain tentative. His poems betray no confidence in a final outcome, but the voice that emerges from them has a tone which suggests, however intransigent the difficulties, one might still attempt to use language "constructively" and to come to knowledge (measure) of the world.

Yet there is little interest in fiction-making per se, if only because the results are unsatisfactory even when "successful." Why concern yourself with fictions when measure obtains only problematically at best? Thus the dissatisfaction, in "Solution" from *The Materials,* with the puzzle, a polychrome "fiction" which completely covers the table without a gap or hole. "The puzzle is complete / Now in its red and green and brown." Even given completion according to its logic of artifice, the puzzle fails to satisfy because it is so patently a reductive covering of the world. There are more than three colors; there are sordid cellars and bare foundations. In Oppen there is still the attempt to use language, to measure the world, even as there is the awareness that the "fatal rock" has been and will continue to be the abiding present and presence of our lives. Far better than Ozymandias, the world mocks every completed puzzle. A shared element in the vision of both Melville and Oppen is this final fatality of the natural world. In view of this final fatality, the term that Oppen supplies in equation with "the human condition" is "precariousness." That the island's rocks have outlived the classicists is but one more instance of the world's fatal power, a power that, in motion, is most often manifested by the sea in Oppen's poetry. The rocks' longevity is the passive equivalent to the sea's terrific and measureless motion. Lived out in the motile presence of this power, our lives can only be precarious.

It is at this point that another hesitation occurs in the poem. For, after moving from the rocks to the sights of the island, Oppen also mentions the island's harbor and post office. These are products of human effort, not belonging to the set of the "outliving" natural world. The harbor may lose its defining contour, the post office fade and eventually fall. The hesitation is registered immediately thereafter: "Difficult to know what one means / —to be serious and know what one means—." The simply exterior is not automatically superior, outliving. One's eye may move easily enough among the sights of the island as among a group of fundamentally like objects, but the mind, finally powerless as it may be, knows that the harbor and post office, while definitely enough there, may well not be there as the rocks and the ledges will continue to be.

The order of the poem suggests that this difficulty, suddenly come upon, is something of a surprise. The mind, not simply the coordinator of the eyes' information, apparently does do something. Perhaps more is involved than a temporary unsuspected contradiction of the poet's assumptions. The problem is how to indicate this something. For the moment I think it can be considered a question of integration and not a fundamental contradiction. That is, the rocks still outlive the classicists. The question is just what sort of life does the mind have? What value, within the larger life of the natural world?

It's put somewhat differently in no. 36 from "Of Being Numerous."

> Tho the world
> Is the obvious, the seen
> And unforeseeable,
> That which one cannot
> Not see
>
> Which the first eyes
> Saw—
>
> For us
> Also each
> Man or woman
> Near is
> Knowledge

There is the possibility of human knowledge; we can learn from each other, but what we learn occurs in a larger context which, because it is to be seen equally by all and because, relative to our lifetime, it endures beyond us, is superior to the knowledge we would try to gain and to accumulate. We can visit other islands and we can learn from our visits, but what we learn must remain provisional against the outliving constancy of the larger context. What defines the islands is the sea. (Cf. "*The sea that made us / islands*" from "Coastal Strip," in *The Materials.*) The world is not to be defined by islandness, but by the surrounding constant sea. The sea is the world revealed in its motive power. The precariousness of our condition results from our having to live with the sea. It is precarious because of the power of the sea and because of its sheer largeness. The world, finally, cannot be seen as held, bracketed by our understanding.

The poem hesitates, but no outright answer to the almost accidentally come-upon dilemma is offered. This is one of the distinguishing features of George Oppen's poetry. It could be called phenomenological. Yet its combination of reportage and active, unrehearsed meditation on that reportage keep it from being confused with Husserlian projects or for that matter with the flat ironic tone assumed by much postmodernist writing. Perhaps it is this bare combination of reportage and active thought in process, as opposed to the rhetorical finish of most verse, the "commonwealth of parlance," that accounts for Oppen's nonexistence in the anthologies.

In a sense, this is understandable. The typical anthology piece has to stand on its own, self-reflexive, not need a reading context beyond what can fit in a footnote or two at the bottom of the page. The poem which at every point radiates process, often in a jagged hesitating manner, frustrates expectations fed on "finished" verse. Such a poem necessarily reminds the reader that the anthology piece, by itself, may not be enough, that much more reading may be required, that there are compositions which will not fit neatly on a page or two, and that, even if their lines will fit, their thought won't. Whether an anthology editor would be happy to include work which by its nature throws into question the presumed utility of this form of publication is to be doubted. Whether a flower of process will be included in the garland of finished blossoms is to be doubted. Expressed critically, Oppen's poetry is a continual, if quiet, opposition to the whole conception of rhetorical completion characterized by the closed field of New Criticism which, despite the ferment of deconstruction, remains the pervasive attitude—expectation and methodology—of our time.

As complication, this opposition is very quiet. It makes no flourish of challenge (an aspect of ceremony and a recognition of the governing attitude, New Critical or not). In fact, it is an opposition that often comes in the guise of the most old-fashioned of nineteenth-century conventions, the capital letter at the beginning of each line, and of our own century, the phonetic spelling of certain words.

The poem hesitates but moves on. What follows appears, atomistically, to have almost nothing to do with what comes before or after: "An island / Has a public quality." My first inclination was to skip over these lines, something their very flatness encourages. On rereading, the key term seems to be "public." By it I think Oppen intends what is exterior and available for inspection by all. This shifts attention away from a time-centered categorization by which, because they are both older and more enduring, the rocks are felt to be superior to the mortal classicists. Those physical things, harbor and post office, which have some connection with the human are somewhat superior to the rocks (the world). This, however, occurs more as a comment in passing, an aside, rather than as a conclusive answer. It is kept within the meditative movement of the poem, the tentative voice in the poem.

The poem moves on. The wife of the lobsterman, wearing a soft dress "such as poor women wear," rides along with them. She tells the Oppens two things. One is that they (the visitors) must have come "from God"; the other is that more than anything else she likes to visit other islands. Oppen doesn't comment upon her statements, and it is up to us to make what we can of them. In a sense, if only because the poet has chosen to quote them, they can be regarded as parts of his own discourse. I wish to concentrate on the second of the two.

Why should anyone want to visit other islands? The desire, first of all, implies that at some time one has or presently lives on an island of one's own. Islandness, per the "Coastal Strip" poem, is part of the precarious human condition. There is a paradox involved. One visits other islands to relieve the isolation of one's own. Yet visiting them can only promote a heightened feeling, "pluralized," of isolation. To use Oppen's word, perhaps more knowledge of the "public" is gained, but the knowledge is much the same in each case. That is, in the flat, broken phrase of a poem from *Myth of the Blaze*, "knowledge is / loneliness." The rocks outlive the classicists. The world will outlast us, will outlast the instruments we construct in an effort to come to an understanding of the world. The argument isn't with the mind's existence (or, as in philosophy, with the existence of other minds) nor even with the values, supposedly inscribed by the "classics," associated with it. There is no argument. As the flatness of Oppen's diction suggests, this is simply and irremediably how it is.

There is a paradox involved in the visiting of the other islands. The apparent motivation is to alleviate one's feeling of isolation and to add to one's knowledge. What is encountered is just the opposite: the feeling of isolation increases, and the knowledge comes to be a knowledge of its own provisionality. This explains Oppen's frequent reference to "shipwreck." The reference appears as early as "From Disaster" *(The Materials)* and as late as "Two Romance Poems" *(Myth of the Blaze).* It is particularly concentrated in *Of Being Numerous,* where it occurs as the "bright light of shipwreck." Later, this is often abbreviated to "light," whereby it haunts the poetry with its paradoxical, positive and negative at once, associations. (Cf. "One had not thought / To be afraid / Not of shadow but of light" from "But So As By Fire," in *Seascape: Needle's Eye.*)

Shipwreck results from collision with the world in its power. The abbreviation of the phrase to "light" indicates more a condition or effect than a literal event. If anything, this has to be a greater cause for fear than any event which, however catastrophic, can only happen once. There is light because of the understanding, inescapable, the collision forces upon the mind of the power of the world. The moment of the mind's understanding is the moment of collision. And once the moment has taken place (not that it is to be reduced to a single occurrence), it colors as a constant and complex condition every other moment of consciousness.

The paradox is that the light of understanding occurs precisely when the "darkness" of the fatal rock is encountered. (Cf. "It is the nature / Of the world: / It is as dark as radar" from "A Narrative," in *This In Which.*) In terms of isolation and knowledge, the visiting of other islands is an instance of shipwreck. The visiting increases the feeling of isolation.

> The absolute singular
> The unearthly bonds
> Of the singular
> Which is the bright light of shipwreck.
>
> (no. 9 from "Of Being Numerous")

While there can be knowledge gained from other persons as islands, it compels the mind, if not exactly to an increasement, to acknowledge its finite and provisional nature. It is the "virtue of the mind" to cause "to see" ("Guest Room"), and what is seen is the power of the world against which human life is a precarious balancing that will eventually come to shipwreck. The idea of the numerous as a saving response to shipwreck is an illusion. Multiplication, the people for the singular person, doesn't alter our experience in the world. If anything, the idea, as in the form of cities, disguises and compounds the wreckage. (Cf. ". . . over the city / Is the bright light of shipwreck," from no. 19, "Of Being Numerous.") Thus there is a brooding apocalyptic harmonic in the "constructive" voice of this poetry.

I had thought the ideal would be to live "responsively" with the world, to recognize its fatal nature and, like Ishmael, to float on the margin of what was disaster for others. Now I doubt if the vision of George Oppen's poetry allows for any such ideal or "right" behavior. However carefully one lives, however skillful in precarious balancing, *there will be shipwreck* if there is any consciousness at all.

The poem ends quietly with the statements of the lobsterman's wife. The second of the two, about liking to visit other islands more than anything else, is not enclosed by quotation marks and ends the poem with an ellipsis. The lack of enclosure is a gentle appropriation so that the words become the poet's own. I take the ellipsis to indicate, not that the woman had more to say than is reported by the poet, but rather that there are implications beyond her speech, perhaps implications she can hardly know. (The opening lines of "A Kind of Garden," in *Of Being Numerous,* may apply to her.) The appropriation is not plagiarism but an act of unassuming identification. Knowing full well what the woman is apparently unaware of—the inevitability of shipwreck with its increase of isolation and an increasing sense of knowledge as strictly provisional— the poet still chooses to be identified with those who, "innocent" or not, must undergo this inevitable, inevitably tragic experience, which is not limited to the last scene of the last act. Ishmael floats free on the margin of shipwreck, a spectator. Oppen, knowing the nature of the event and its cause, which is consciousness itself, chooses to join those caught up in the whirlpool. Surely, it is noble to do this.

Historically, Oppen's achievement is to have extended imagist-objectivist poetics to a vision. A poetics which emphasizes the visual and cadential image based on close attention to the particular is transformed into an encompassing vision by an awareness of its own limitations. The

more and more scrupulous exercise of attention produces further isolation and knowledge that more and more knows itself to be provisional. It
is these quietly encountered and acknowledged paradoxes—paradoxes
which should not be confused with those of Donne, bright particular star
of New Criticism, which depend for their puzzlelike brilliance on a
ground of unquestioned orthodox belief—that, collectively, give Oppen's
vision depth, complexity, and nobility. The last comes from his decision
not to be superior to his vision of human experience in the world but to be
part of it.

I have not chosen to base my speculation on "Ballad" because it is a
personal favorite nor because I consider it to be an indispensable key to
Oppen's poetry as a whole. The choice of the poem was somewhat
arbitrarily based on the publicity surrounding the *Of Being Numerous*
book and the fact that, "physically," the poem was not unlike those found
in the *Norton* and other anthologies. But Oppen's poems are not to be
found in these anthologies. It seems clear at this point that their nonexistence there has little to do with their author's public reputation or with
their gross morphology.

What, then, are the other reasons? One could be Oppen's disregard for
the conventions of punctuation or his penchant for conjoining lines
without warning. Unlike e. e. cummings, the poems do not end up as
vehicles for fairly conventional sentiments but with unconventional
wrappings. Another could be his disregard for some poetic devices
(rhyme, meter) while retaining certain conventions (capitals at the beginning of lines). This brings us back to the poem's title. In its versification
appendix, the third-edition *Norton* defines the ballad stanza as consisting
of four lines in which lines of iambic tetrameter alternate with those of
iambic trimeter, rhyming *a b c b* or *a b a b*. "Sir Patrick Spens," "The
Rime of the Ancient Mariner," and Emily Dickinson's "I taste a liquor
never brewed" are given as examples. Oppen's poem is not written in this
stanzaic form, and it does not sound like any of the examples. According
to the *Norton,* the poem can't be a ballad; and, by inference, its author is
guilty of duplicity.

If the poem can't be a "regular" ballad, what kind can it be? It could be,
like a Berrigan sonnet, an un- or antiversion of the form. Yet the poem
doesn't deliberately mock the form, nor does it completely ignore at least
some poetic conventions. If it is a ballad, then it must be one of "essence," concerned only with what is most essential to the form. And what
is most essential to the ballad form is song. If we look to Zukofsky's *Test*

Of Poetry, where the consideration of song is demonstrated primarily by ballads in all three of its parts, we find song "as musical, poetic form" defined as "a continuous and complete statement of the words." This statement has to do with the meaning and sound of the words. If there is nothing more to be said, if a melody line (cadence) has taken on adequate definition, then there is song which, further, comes *from* the words. (Cf. ". . . the cadence the verse / and the music essential" from "The Light-houses," a poem dedicated by Oppen to Zukofsky, *Myth of the Blaze.*)

To this definition might be added the expectations of rendition. That is, the ballad belongs to folk tradition and is to be sung in an unstudied manner, something that probably wouldn't be performed as such in the great houses. The song of "Ballad" is the statement developed from its beginning two lines and presented as a "story" in the others. In its relative lack of punctuation it is literally continuous, and it is complete in terms of action (the visit to Swan's Island) and vision (the world, people in the world, their fate). As for rendition, the voice that emerges from the poem is conversational, even plain, ready to disturb the flow of its story with an admission of difficulty. To cite Zukofsky again, "simplicity of utterance and song go together."

All of this is consciously apprehended in "Song, The Winds of Down-hill" from *Seascape: Needle's Eye.*

"out of poverty
to begin

again"   impoverished

of tone of pose that common
wealth

of parlance   Who
so poor the words

would   with   and   take on substantial

meaning   handholds   footholds

to dig in one's heels   sliding

hands and heels beyond the residential
lots   the plots   it is a poem

which may be sung
may well be sung

The poverty is an impoverishment not simply of accumulated literary tradition but also, specifically, of imagist-objectivist poetics. The poem represents, as does Oppen's poetry as a whole, a radical (if quiet) stripping away to reach the essential poem, the essential song.

Perhaps we arrive here at the root cause for the absence of his poetry from the anthologies. (It should be noted that it has appeared in several anthologies, some of which have had reasonably wide distribution, e.g., *The New Naked Poetry,* ed. Berg and Mezey; and *America a Prophecy,* ed. Rothenberg and Quasha. None of these, however, has had the sustained distribution—and the sustained influence—of those anthologies enumerated in my opening paragraph.) In an utterly quiet, utterly unassuming way, George Oppen has taken his imagist-objectivist inheritance and stripped it to the essentials to emerge with a distinguishable voice and with a "complete" vision. As an accomplishment, this bears comparison with that of his contemporary Zukofsky, who is represented in all the enumerated volumes with the exception of the Poulin, and with that of their common master, Pound, who has become a centerpiece of nearly all anthologies.

Zukofsky and Pound, in different but analogous ways, attempt to come to vision by expansion, proliferation of the image. Oppen, alone, consistently accomplishes what he would refer to as clarity by a stripping down that at the same time opens out and takes on depth. It takes time to read such poetry, and it takes time to comprehend an "ars povera" that is deliberate, conscious, and still "art," song. It is a requirement that Oppen himself is not unaware of: "one man could not understand me because I was saying / simple things; it seemed to him that nothing was being / said" (from "Route," *Of Being Numerous). Nothing is being said* unless there is understanding of the calculated impoverishment that has been undergone and unless the voice that nevertheless emerges from that impoverishment is heard in its quiet nobility. Whatever their selection procedures may be, the anthology editors have neither understood nor heard.

Let me come back to the time required by this poetry. It is a familiar chestnut that work of substance can be returned to without exhaustion. In the case of George Oppen's poetry, I would want to say it applies with a surprising accuracy. I have read it since the late 1960s, I have heard him read it, I have had conversation and correspondence with him about it. I have also done the sort of rereading that reviewing demands. Like the lyrics of Wyatt and Reznikoff running through his mind, Oppen's poetry runs through my own. Yet none of this reduces the requirement of time, the requirement of close attention to the particulars of his poetry, even its admitted difficulties, in order to hear the voice and perceive the vision.

Writing this, which may well repeat some of what I have written about his poetry in the past, has surprised me. For I thought I knew the work and find that I do not. For this reason it has moved me even as I have to wonder at what further readings will reveal. This is written as an indication that the required time and attention are not to be resolved by research into sources and influences but by thinking itself, the unrelenting effort along the "thought-paths" of Heidegger's description. It is not written, however, to exonerate those who haven't made the effort, who haven't been willing to follow the "handholds" and "footholds" to arrive at the substantial meaning and song of this poetry.

Again, I have no knowledge of the selection procedures. Yet, surprised and moved as I find myself, the conviction grows that the anthology editors have neither understood nor heard because they have not thought long or hard enough with the poetry of George Oppen. In his case they haven't been willing or able to stir beyond the customary lots and plots of past poetry. An anthology represents what is supposed to be worth keeping. My claim is that the poetry of George Oppen is eminently worth keeping because of its unique technical accomplishment and because of the vision—deep, complex, noble—made possible by that accomplishment. My hope is that the poetry of George Oppen will appear in the anthologies of influence before it is too late for its own influence to be felt in our time.

Call Me Isabel,
Call Me Pierre

Know how to read? you *must*
Before you can write.

—la Marquise de Boufflers
(trans. Ezra Pound)

Anyone who has read Melville's *Pierre* with attention has to wonder how Charles Olson, one of Melville's most passionate readers, could so misread this book, which more and more reveals its author as startlingly "contemporary" in his awareness of the relation of reading and writing. The question is why Olson should so misread. There is the further question of the significance of this misreading for those who come after Olson and who would write, who would concern themselves with staying in the play of language.

The answer to the first question begins before either *Pierre* or *Moby-Dick* with "Hawthorne and His Mosses, by a Virginian Spending His Summer in Vermont." Published in the *Literary World* for August 17 and 24, 1850, the review was written by Melville after the first version of *Moby-Dick* and before the version we now read. It is an invaluable document. Olson recognizes its importance and puts it to extensive use in *Call Me Ishmael: A Study of Melville.* For Olson the subject of the review is Hawthorne, Shakespeare, and Herman Melville. It is also "a document of Melville's right and perceptions, his declaration of the freedom of a man to fail." The review points Olson to Shakespeare (it was Olson who located the set of plays owned and read by Melville, the set wherein he found what he describes as the rough notes for the composition of *Moby-Dick* on the flyleaf of the last volume). In "American Shiloh," a subsection of part II, the Shakespeare references in the review are emphasized. They concentrate on Melville's contentions that we live in a world of lies, that such a world necessitates the telling of the truth covertly, that Shakespeare gives "those occasional flashings-forth of the intuitive Truth" to be spoken from the mouths of his dark characters. This leads Olson, later in the "Man, to man" section, to how Shakespeare reflects Melville's disillusion with the treacherous world. He finds this especially in *Timon*. The section ends with Olson connecting Melville's own disappointed friendships with Hawthorne and Jack Chase and Timon's "dream of friendship." The claim is made that Melville uses the blasted hero as a symbol through his books. This can take the form of another Ishmael of solitude or, with regard to *Pierre,* "as disillusion itself, man undone by goodness."

Let the inventory of *Call Me Ishmael* stop here. There is no argument that Olson fails to make perceptive connections between the review and *Moby-Dick*. What he does fail to do, which will lead inextricably to later misreading, is to understand the deliberately fictional nature of the review itself.

Not content to call attention to Shakespeare's indirect revelation of truth, Melville employs a like approach in the review. Thus he gives himself as "a Virginian Spending His Summer in Vermont." Aside perhaps from a question of personal modesty, the motivation is clear: not only is Melville telling the truth about Shakespeare and Hawthorne, he is also telling the truth which "he craftily says, or sometimes insinuates the things which we feel to be so terrifically true, that it were all but madness for any good man, in his own proper character, to utter, or even hint of them." The "he" of this quotation from the review is Shakespeare. It can apply as well to Melville, to his use of fictional strategy here and in the work to follow.

When we read through the review for a more exact sense of this terrible truth, we find that it has to do with the spiritual, the negatively spiritual, the blackness of darkness. This is the truth which lurks in Hawthorne's stories with their "mystical blackness" and "touch of Puritanic gloom" and which is behind Lear's speaking the sane madness of vital truth. I take that speaking to occur particularly in Lear's speeches in act 3, scene 4: "Unaccommodated man is no more but such a poor, / bare, forked animal, as thou art." The human being in Lear's speeches emerges as a bare animal, made to seem even more so because of presumptions about family and social community, a poor animal alone and at the mercy of a hostile physical universe. Or as Isabel writes to Pierre: "I felt that all good, harmless men and women were human things, placed at cross-purposes, in a world of snakes and lightnings, in a world of horrible and inscrutable inhumanities." The truth and the strategy go together. If you're persuaded of the fundamentally inimical character of the world, all snakes and lightnings, a character that manifests itself as the constant background of darkness for human affairs, a character that runs counter to any of the nineteenth-century "positive" orthodoxies, then you will have to find an indirect way to say it. "The names of all fine authors are fictitious ones."

Olson misses out on this connection. He does not notice the deliberate employment of the fiction of fiction. It is, after all, the Virginian author's fictitious country cousin, Cherry, who convinces him to read Hawthorne's *Mosses* rather than Dwight's *Travels in New England,* a conventional ("real") travel guide of the times. The first is preferred to the second because it includes the dark spiritual background along with the reporting of character and external locale. It is this spiritual background of mystical blackness, the "infinite obscure of his background" which, as Melville is quick to claim, is the same background to be found in Shakespeare. Less terrible, but yet another indication of Melville's employment of the fiction of fiction is the expression of the rights of American authors, as opposed to the British, to the appreciation of American readers put in the mouth of the Virginian's hot-headed Carolina cousin.

Perhaps distracted by his discovery of Melville's set of Shakespeare and Melville's markings, by a desire to be the first reader of a more original text (i.e., Melville's rough notes), Olson misses this connection. The miss, despite such insights as the identification of Pip as Shakespearean fool, causes him to misread both *Moby-Dick* and *Pierre*. Space, for instance, is crucial to Melville, but it's fictional space, Coleridge's "mental space," made up, not finally dependent upon the Pacific or anything else "out there" in the geographies of guidebooks.

Before going to how this misconnection works out in the two novels, a note should be made of the references to Spenser in the review. Not really developed in Melville's writing until "The Encantadas," the references are nonetheless important. They occur in Melville's remarks on Hawthorne's "Select Party," which he finds "the sweetest and sublimest thing that has been written since Spenser wrote." He goes on to claim parity with Spenser for Hawthorne and to argue that Spenser in his own day was considered as Hawthorne in his, a gentle and harmless man. The relation is hardly coincidental. Melville was interested in Spenser for essentially the same reason as Shakespeare and Hawthorne: all deal with darkness, with men and their actions against a spiritual background of darkness.

His interest involves him with questions of how this apprehension of the universe may be presented and how one, as a citizen, may survive.

In addition to the attraction of a like-minded worldview, Melville's interest is predicated on need: in the work of these writers were the answers to both questions. These answers have all to do with the symbolic capability of language. In *The Faerie Queene,* described by Spenser as "a dark conceit," they take on the form of allegory. To give body to the invisible realm, as Isabel MacCaffrey notes in the introduction to her *Spenser's Allegory: The Anatomy of Imagination,* is the particular task of allegory. MacCaffrey's argument is that Spenser's allegory is a model of the mind's life in the world. To cite only one passage from a later chapter: "Spenser's allegory is designed to demonstrate the darkness of our situation . . . the demonstration proceeds by introducing us to a fictive world whose enigmatic surface darkly reflects the everyday darkness in which we grope. It also provides us with clues . . . for penetrating that surface. The result is a model for us in learning to fathom our own lives." Despite their differences, Shakespeare, Spenser, and Hawthorne are made "correspondents" in providing Melville with models of how the threatening universe may be represented and survived through the symbolic capabilities of language. It is language which should be the focus of our attention in reading Melville, language that is symbolic, "fictional," for a purpose.

Consider the epilogue of *Moby-Dick.* It begins with a quotation from the Book of Job: "And I only am escaped alone to tell thee." The quotation is the formulaic line that concludes each of four reports of disaster to Job's property and family (1:14–19). Melville doesn't need the reference to establish Ishmael's aloneness, a condition given by the Old Testament context for his own name (Gen. 16:12: "And he will be a wild man; his hand will be against every man . . . ") from the beginning. What it does do is throw into relief that Ishmael is the *Pequod*'s sole survivor, that the voyage has been a terminal disaster for everyone else except him, and that the mode of his survival has *not* been the unquestioning faith and worship of Job.

Ishmael's explanation of how he survived is at the same time an explanation of his position as narrator, as symbolic language user who triumphs despite the dangers of the white world. Ishmael floats "on the margin" of the sinking ship "in full sight of it" and is thus able to be part and apart from it. As given in the fiction of the epilogue, he is able to float and then to seize the coffin life-buoy until discovered by the devious-cruising *Rachel* on the second day. What he manages to avoid is the vortex created by the sinking *Pequod,* the final destruction of Ahab's fiery hunt. We're told that by the time Ishmael reaches the vortex it has subsided into a creamy pool.

> When I reached it, it had subsided to a creamy pool. Round and round, then, and ever contracting towards the button-like black bubble at the axis of that slowly wheeling circle, like another Ixion I did revolve. Till, gaining that vital centre, the black bubble upward burst; and now, liberated by reason of its cunning spring, and, owing to its great buoyancy, rising with great force, the coffin life-buoy shot lengthwise from the sea, fell over, and floated by my side.

The concentration and manipulation of symbolic language is fascinating. The creamy pool takes us back to the "Whiteness of the Whale" chapter. There it is the whiteness of the whale that above all things appalls Ishmael. To strip one of Melville's most complex chapters to its bare bones, it has to be asked why whiteness so frightens Ishmael, that is, why it is "the most meaning symbol of spiritual things," "the very veil of the Christian's Deity," and the "intensifying agent" in things the most appalling to mankind.

There are three main reasons. (1) Its indefiniteness suggests the heartless voids and immensities of the universe (and forces us to recognize our comparative insignificance). (2) Whiteness is the visible absence of color and at the same time the concrete of all colors. Thus white is the "colorless, all-color of atheism," the hue of pre-form Chaos, the most fundamental condition of all, the beginning of beginnings. (3) The "other theory" of the natural philosophers is that all the colors of the natural world are imparted by the colorations of light, "so that all deified Nature absolutely paints like the harlot whose allurements cover nothing but the charnel-house within." When we think further about this, "the palsied universe lies before us a leper." Those who would attempt to find the truth through the study of exterior physical nature are wretched infidels who, like wilful travellers in Lapland, refuse to wear colored protective glasses. The result has to be blindness and destruction, products of "the monumental white shroud that wraps all the prospect."

The vortex motion of the creamy pool is the essential motion of a destructive white universe (a contributing or coordinate part of which is the *Pequod*'s wilful captain). At the axis of this motion is its seemingly impossible opposite, the "button-like black bubble." We can go no further than the bubble. It is the concentrated inside-out symbol of the terror of whiteness. When we confront it, we confront the essential product of whiteness, of the white whale that generated the black foam which blinded the captain of the *Samuel Enderby,* of Moby-Dick as perceived by Ahab as whiteness out of blackness, that same blackness of darkness.

The epilogue, which runs to only 262 words, is a catalogue of fictional devices. Besides the Job quotation and the reference to his own internally explicated color symbolism, there is the allusion by Ishmael to himself as another Ixion. It is appropriate for both his circling motion and for his status as a "celebrated sinner," as Ixion is described, a wild man who would go against, however covertly, all Christian orthodoxies, the orthodoxies ruling his day and that of his author. But the allusion holds only so far. Ishmael is superior to Ixion in that his ability as a narrator, a conscious fiction-maker, places him outside the control of a Zeus-Fate weaver. (Cf. Ishmael in "The Mat-maker" chapter; it is the narrator who is able to perceive the weave of chance, free will, and necessity and who will conduct himself accordingly.) It is Ishmael who can concentrate all the malignancy of the white world into a bubble and burst it. The very arbitrariness of the sudden reappearance of the coffin-buoy (coffin for Queequeg who can't read or write, buoy for Ishmael who can) only emphasizes the power of the narrator, who has full comprehension of the scene and remains safely on the margin, who controls the plot's sequence of development. The fictionality of Ishmael's situation is also heightened by the *Tempest*-like dream quality of the description of the time Ishmael spends floating unmolested—"the unharming sharks, they glided by as if with padlocks on their mouths"—in the very medium of the threatening universe.

What the *Rachel* found was only "another orphan" who happens to be the only orphan who survives. He survives to refer to the tale of Moby Dick dismissively in the middle of the novel, in "The Town-Ho's Story," contra "real" time and conventional plot sequence, where, per his own fictional double, Steelkilt, who can calmly look on the whale's destruction of Radney and think "his own thoughts," because he is able to utilize the symbolic capabilities of language.

Consider, for comparison, some of the Ishmael statements in *Call Me Ishmael*. The first is closer to the fictionality found in the Hawthorne review than might be expected. "Ishmael is fictive," writes Olson in opposition to those who would make a flat autobiographical equation between narrator and author, *and* "he is a chorus through whom Ahab's tragedy is seen, by whom what is black and what is white magic is made clear." Olson goes on to comment that, unless Ishmael's choric function is recognized, some of the vision of the book is lost. The *"Moby-Dick Manuscript"* section of part II, in which these comments are to be found, ends with the statement that Ishmael, by telling the story and tragedy of the crew, creates the *Moby-Dick* universe in which the Ahab-world is included. The choric identification, made on the basis of Melville's jotting "Eschylus Tragedies" in the same place as his "notes" for the novel, is of interest. If by choric is meant simply the peripheral, then there can be little question as to its relevance for a narrator who survives by floating on the margin of the scene.

But more than location is involved. However extensive the list of functions performed by the chorus of Aeschylus, the identification with the community is primary. Within that identification and as evidence for it are the *gnōmai,* the aphoristic wise sayings or maxims. They predominate in those lines given to the chorus throughout Aeschylus because they're technically useful and because they represent the wisdom of the community. As Rosenmeyer comments in his *Art of Aeschylus,* "Relying on a maxim is refuelling at the source." The source of the *gnōmai* is the community. This may explain why Olson doesn't develop this identification further. However seemingly marginal he may be—"passive" is Olson's word for him—Ishmael, the wild man who would rebel against the king of the cannibals and who would identify the terror of whiteness with the very veil of the Christian's deity, is anything but the dutiful representative of cultural tradition and community.

It can be agreed that the Ahab-world is included within the *Moby-Dick* universe. It is much more the case, though, that one white and whole universe is presented in the novel, the same universe for all, whatever their awareness of its nature. The blackness of darkness perceived and projected by Ahab is the inversion of that whiteness, of its appalling terror met head-on by an appallingly self-conscious hubris. Ahab is the human dramatic equivalent of the black button. Yet we do not truly engage Olson in these Ishmael statements. Earlier, the vision of *Moby-Dick* was mentioned. The key to that vision, according to Olson, "is space, and its feeding on man."

There are several "space statements" in *Call Me Ishmael*. In many ways the most indicative of these is the first, the true opening of the book. "I take SPACE to be the central fact to man born in America, from Folsom cave to now. I spell it large because it comes large here. Large, and without mercy." This is an American Studies space, a spirit of place space, an external reality however generalized, a great reality measured in terms of external reality. Space as a large, aggressively motile thing is Olson's central understanding and claim. Thus, for him, the dimensions of *Moby-Dick* are the result of Melville's experience of space. And space is not an abstraction, but "the body of Melville's experience." Space, which has a stubborn way of sticking to Americans, "is the exterior fact."

This identification of space in Melville as an exterior reality is a fundamental misreading. Not only does it praise Melville for what he isn't (a writer primarily concerned with depicting the external scene), but it also confuses a vital connection. This concerns the declaration of rivalry with the elements of external nature as the way to acquire the lost dimension of space *and* to disclose paternity. Such rivalry is Ahab's approach, and it results in disaster for himself and the crew. It does not so result for Ishmael, who can assume the bowsman's position without jeopardy and who avoids entanglements with Ahab's fate. Ishmael survives because, as narrator, he is capable of creating an alternative space, the result of linguistic and symbolic manipulation. If he discloses his paternity, it is by way of implication, "hints" made possible by language and not by direct confrontation with the external universe.

Moby-Dick—which begins with an etymology supplied by a late, consumptive usher to a grammar school and extracts concerning whales supplied by a sub-sub librarian, and which ends with an epilogue that has been found to be a veritable catalogue of fictional devices for all its brevity—is a profoundly literary book. In it Melville thought he had conceived a means for the human being as an aware language-user to survive and more than survive in a white and threatening world. The critique of this possibility was not long in coming. Before the final proof sheets for the whale book had been corrected, to follow Leon Howard's biography, he had begun writing *Pierre*.

Melville's critique of his narrator's fictional space and the possibility of survival and relatively free action in a merciless universe it seemed to provide focuses on the intertwined process of reading and writing. Indeed, it is not too much to say that the abiding subject of *Pierre* is reading and writing. This subject is addressed everywhere in the novel, but especially so in the characters of Isabel and Pierre. Isabel is set up by Melville as a test case for examining why anyone would consciously learn to read and write on their own volition, a learning that is undergone well past the age of childhood and without parental guidance or schooling institutions. She is as near a tabula rasa as is humanly plausible. Brought up as an orphan who has no recollection or knowledge of her parents ("I never knew a mortal mother"), she explains to Pierre that she learned to read and later to write specifically to establish the identity of her father. "No other purpose but that only one, did I have in learning then to read."

The occasion for her motivation is a handkerchief left by her father, who is known to her at this point only as the "kind gentleman" who sometimes visits her. Scanning the significantly white handkerchief closely, she finds a small line of fine faded yellowish writing in the middle. Later, she folds the handkerchief so that the writing is "invisibly buried in the heart of it," and opening it is "like opening a book." She then induces the farm woman who has taken her in to teach her the alphabet and spelling. Thereupon she deciphers the talismanic word "Glendinning." She connects it by sound with "gentleman," the generic term used to identify her father, on the basis of the same syllable count and initial letter. Her conclusion—and no other grounds than these are given for it—is: "yes, it must mean *my father.*"

Somehow persuaded of her father's death (the kind gentleman comes no longer to visit), Isabel does not act upon her discovery until a later encounter with Pierre, who, in a like sudden manner, she concludes must be her brother. This latter surmise leads her to write to Pierre, a letter which in turn leads to their meeting and eventual "fictitious" marriage. We see what Isabel gains from learning to read and write, namely, a brother and an assurance through him of her father's identity—and hence her own. What may not be so evident is what she loses.

First of all, she loses what Olson would call her own truth. Shortly after explaining about the handkerchief to Pierre, she exclaims—in response to his insistent questions about how a guitar now in her possession was once at Saddle Meadows, his own ancestral home—"better, a million times, and far sweeter are mysteries than surmises: though the mystery be unfathomable, it is still the unfathomableness of fullness; but the surmise, that is but shallow and unmeaning emptiness." When she held herself in perfect patience, not acting upon her paternal discovery, she existed at least within the boundaries of such fullness, still safe from the empty life and suicidal death that become her fate once she makes contact with Pierre. We do not have to guess at the nature of her postreading, but precontact, existence. It does not partake of the bower of bliss; she admits to not being able to identify that thing "which is called happiness," nor even to being interested in it. Rather, she prays for motionlessness, for "absorbing life without seeking it, and existing without individual sensation." She is, however, aware of her humanness and of the universe as horrible and full of "inscrutable inhumanities." She is also capable of spontaneous, "free" expression. "I never affect my thoughts, and I never adulterate any thoughts; but when I speak, think forth from the tongue, speech being sometimes before the thought; so, often, my own tongue teaches me new things."

Isabel does not present herself at this stage as a Poussin shepherdess. She is nonetheless capable of thought, of what, further, might be considered free or original thought and a conception of how to live in a hostile environment. With her surmise as to her relation to Pierre, made possible first by reading and then by writing, she loses all these capabilities. Before she acted upon her surmises of paternity and relation—and in each case I think Melville wants us to recognize how arbitrary and makeshift her conclusions are—she had the capability of being a "positive" Bartleby. Her surmises, then, are fictions, fictions unaware of themselves as fiction, fictions engendered by a desire to identify the father, a desire kindled by learning to read and made actionable by learning to write. For Isabel they do not bring about the prayed-for *Gelassenheit* existence, a harmonious living with things, much less with family, but rather despair and death.

Isabel is a demonstration of how the fictions created by reading and writing, when unaware of themselves as fictions, in contrast to the saving-space a knowing Ishmael creates for himself, facilitate if not coerce involvement with lines of fatal entanglement, the same sort of lines that Ishmael as Ahab's replacement bowsman avoids without difficulty (and his double, Steelkilt). Pierre is another, complementary example. Reading her letter—which claims him for her brother, but which gives no evidence for the claim—Pierre parallels Isabel's faulty reasoning. In true

Young Werther fashion, he declares: "Now I feel that nothing but Truth can move me so. This letter is not a forgery. Oh! Isabel, thou art my sister; and I will love thee, and protect thee, ay, and own thee through all."

The agency of this truth-certifying emotion is writing, the reading of her letter, which Isabel not inaccurately refers to as "the fatal line." If, as readers of the novel, we do not sense the fatality of the contact, the narrator assures us that Pierre has been given a wound that can never be healed, a wound that does away with the moral beauty of the universe *and* the assumed saintliness of his father. "Now, now for the first time, Pierre, Truth rolls a black billow through thy soul!"

The problem, as Pierre and his narrator will later find, is that this destructive experience is still less than the whole truth. For the moment, though, an inventory of what he loses may be useful. It includes no more pleasure in the exterior natural scene, no more trust in a benevolent deity responsible for that scene, disinheritance of the ancestral Saddle Meadows estate, estrangement from his mother, no marriage to the beautiful girl next door, Lucy, in favor of Isabel's mysterious company. And, per the narrator's comment, his attitude toward his father undergoes a radical shift from near-idolatrous reverence to suspicious skepticism.

As with Isabel, reading and writing lead to disclosure of paternity. Yet, when the text has been deciphered, the father literally isn't to be found. Language, through reading and writing, seems to promise a father and in the end only makes its users more keenly aware of his nonappearance. This awareness—if not gone through in the sense of beyond, not to locate some more distant rainbow, but to devise a means of dealing with the enforced aloneness—can conclude only in despair.

In Pierre's case, his reading of Isabel's writing conditions his reading of another text, his father's chair-portrait. Previously, he had been only vaguely intrigued by the ambiguous smile on his father's face as painted by one cousin Ralph. He had been intrigued by it, but it was an ambiguity he hadn't known how to read. The emphasis upon whiteness, a symbolism carried over from *Moby-Dick* and developed extensively in *Pierre*, in the account of his pre-Isabel reading of the portrait alerts us to the difficulties of perception, of right reading of "all those ineffable hints and ambiguities," in the context of a white world: "banked round by the thick-fallen December snows, or banked round by the immovable white August moonlight."

Having read Isabel's letter ("all mysteries ripped open as if with a keen sword"), Pierre recollects a number of hitherto unrelated clues for decipherment, particularly his mother's adverse reaction to the chair-portrait as opposed to the one she has hung in the Saddle Meadows mansion. He rereads the portrait and rejects it. When he does this, at the Black Swan Inn where he has gone with Isabel and her companion after departing the ancestral home, it is on the basis of a resemblance between his father and Isabel, a resemblance which is never quite fully seen but which serves as a further basis for the manifestation of "the tyranny of Time and Fate."

In reaction, Pierre burns the portrait. Watching "the painted scroll" burn, he is suddenly moved to save it, but to no avail. "Pierre darted his hand among the flames, to rescue the imploring face; but as swiftly drew back his scorched and bootless grasp. His hand was burnt and black-ened." Reading conditions reading. Isabel's letter, which offered no ac-tual evidence, motivates Pierre to *find* a resemblance, one which leads to the destruction of the father's ambiguous image. As he declares to himself after the burning, "henceforth, castout Pierre hath no paternity." At this point the loss of paternity, along with all the other related losses of the inventory, appears a necessary price to pay for his own personal freedom. It is a price he is willing to pay.

Pierre enacts his freedom in further writing. His attempt to write a book, stimulated by his conviction that he has now seen through the veils of appearance to absolute truth, is compromised from the start by his lack of reading skill. This is measured by his response to, besides Isabel's letter, the "texts" of Dante and Shakespeare. We're told that, while "the horrible allegorical meanings of the Inferno" are luckily imperceptible to the dilettante, these same meanings act upon the earnest and youthful "piercer" into truth and reality as a poison. For such a piercer is un-provided with the "uncapitulatable security" of the more mature sen-sibility (reader). Pierre examines the character of Hamlet, senses the moral of the play as prompting action over endless meditation, but does *not* perceive that Hamlet is, finally, a fictive creation "evoked by the wanton magic of a creative hand." The result is that Pierre's enaction of freedom as a writer is founded on half-knowledge. As the narrator com-ments, insight may reveal the depths and the heights, but "when only midway down the gulf, its crags wholly conceal the upper vaults, and the wanderer thinks it all one gulf of downward dark."

Caught midway down by his own immature comprehension, Pierre is doomed not to triumph over life's entanglements nor to achieve anything like freedom for himself through the creation of a fictional space. Presumably better educated than Isabel, still, like her in the end, he will not be able to weave such a space in his writing because his reading has not taken place at an adequate depth (and height) of understanding. Merely recognizing the existence of darkness in the world is not enough. The created fictive world, to recall Spenser, provides us with clues for the penetration of its surface: first itself, then perhaps our lives. Pierre leaps to the second without adequately grounding himself in the first. Inadequate readers do not make adequate writers.

Toward the end of the novel, when Pierre has set up a three-cornered household with Lucy and Isabel, we find other contributing reasons for his failure. The money needed for food and rent forces him to submit pages to the printer before the manuscript can be completed as a whole. Consequently, the printed pages dictate what must occur in the remainder. And, à la Heisenberg, he finds that the closer he approaches the truth in his writing, the more evasive it becomes. "For the more and the more that he wrote, and the deeper and the deeper that he dived, Pierre saw the everlasting elusiveness of Truth; the universal lurking insincerity of even the greatest and purest written thoughts." Too, he becomes physically exhausted because of the effort writing costs him, and his eyes, abused by the effort, even refuse to look on the, again, significantly white paper. "He turned them on paper, and they blinked and shut." The developing symbolism of whiteness could hardly be more apt. Exposed as he constantly is to it, the young writer must be even more careful than Lapland travellers to be equipped with protective glasses—that is, with symbolic language used in full consciousness.

Pierre, the immature writer seeking to write the mature book, is not so equipped, and his attempts at composition only result in self-immobilization—when his eyes fail him, he is described as remaining "suspended, motionless, blank"—and, not long after, his death by poison. He is very much a "negative" Bartleby. It is the same poison which Isabel takes. Lucy, who had accompanied Isabel to visit Pierre (in jail for shooting Glendinning Stanly), dies of shock. Thus all three die at the novel's close in a literal heap of entanglement. The poison is given as a "real" drug, but it should remind us of that other poison, the product of the uncomprehended allegorical meanings in writing, the one the "cause" of the other. It should also remind us of what all three characters lack: the uncapitulatable security of knowing the symbolic possibilities of language and of knowing how to read them and put them to use.

Pierre should not be taken as a later equivalent for Ishmael. While the narrative voice in *Moby-Dick* is not always in character (or is not always made evident as character), the narrator is always distinct from the character of the young would-be writer in *Pierre*. The narrator is always superior to the young writer. This is measured by the narrator's implicit skill in reading writing, in understanding the utilization of language's symbolic possibilities as "technique" for the purposes of a "creative hand,"—namely, play and survival. Isabel learns to read and write in order to identify her father. Pierre, an immature reader of her writing because much of his education as a reader has involved falsifying popular novels (falsifying because they neatly resolve all ambiguities in the end), reads for a similar reason and writes to reveal what he considers to be the previously veiled truth.

But the truth, in a universe that is consistently portrayed in *Pierre* as a shifting or stratified surface upon surface, a terrestrial sphere of ambiguities that is every bit as white and treacherous as the sea, cannot finally be stated. There is no ultimate unmoving ground. With every additional term used to try to pin the shifting down, the further one is removed from it.

The mature writer, necessarily a mature reader, does not attempt to still what cannot be stilled, does not attempt to build a house on such shifting surfaces. The available language, the coffin-buoy, is put to deliberate symbolic use to allow the writer to float on the margin of a world that is otherwise unreliable at best. The writer's uncapitulatable security resides in the ability to read symbolically—to use darkness to perceive the appalling whiteness, its bottomlessness—*and* to write symbolically to stay clear of those lines that would connect language users with the deceiving and destructive elements of the white world. Thus the narrator of *Pierre* is deliberately careless, tied neither to mimetic representation nor to the conventions of narrative sequence. Rather: "I write precisely as I please."

One would never suspect, judging from Olson's comments on the novel, that the reversible equation of reading and writing plays any part whatsoever in *Pierre*. In *Call Me Ishmael*, its subject is declared to be disillusion itself, "man undone by goodness." Later, Christ is given as "the subject and matter" of the novel. Still later, *Pierre* "is a Christ syllogism: 'I hate the world.'" In "David Young, David Old" it's acknowledged that the novel is endurable, that there are perceptions in it not to be found in *Moby-Dick,* but what these perceptions are remains unstated. In "The Materials and Weights of Herman Melville," the discoveries made by Freudian critics of *Pierre* are alluded to and left unspecified with the later summation that, after *Moby-Dick,* the "rest of his work is the defeat which is still our own." In "Equal, That Is, to the Real Itself," it's claimed, surprisingly enough, that the writer of the Hawthorne review was "essentially incapable of either allegory or symbol." And last, in "Reading at Berkeley," the self as foundation stone is given as the source of *Pierre,* which, according to Olson, is "one of the things that got me over."

Granted, my own account of the novel is far from complete (e.g., the Memnon Stone as a development of the white whale and as a text to be read). It is difficult to avoid the conclusion, however, that Olson has seriously misread *Pierre,* if not Melville generally. Pierre is not undone by goodness. He becomes the fool of truth, virtue, and fate because of his shortcomings as a reader and writer. Christ does appear frequently in the book. To cite three instances: he is mentioned in association with the Enthusiast To Duty, a half-formed personage who will not recognize a mortal parent or mortal bounds. He is mentioned in association with the condition of silence, "the most harmless and the most awful thing in all nature." He is mentioned in association with the Sermon on the Mount, which prompts in the soul of the enthusiastic youth an irreconcilable conflict between the biblical account of the world as depraved and the sermon's "soul-melting stream of tenderness and loving-kindness." Christ is surely important for these associations. He is intimately connected with whiteness—the very veil of the Christian's deity, son of the source of chaos—that engulfs the shifting universe and which would engulf all its citizens unless they as language animals devise linguistic strategems which will allow them to float on and over it.

There is, however, no indication that Christ, frequent term that he is in Melville's vision, is the central term for the novel. Olson's own constant reference to Christ as the element that spoils the work after *Moby-Dick* is a critical red herring. Further, the world as white-shrouded physical universe is not so much hated as dreaded. (The haters—Ahab and, in a different way, Pierre himself—go irretrievably to their doom.) No alternative spiritual realms are described or pined after in Melville. The question is always one of survival in this world. The self may be hard and obdurate, but the novel's major character, whose name means stone, fails not from insufficient will but from insufficient skill as reader and writer. It is one of the ambiguities of the novel, perhaps the penultimate one for our reading, that its major character's failure precisely indicates the success of its author's conception of fictional space, an intentional "inventional mystery."

There can be a number of reasons why Olson should so flagrantly misread Melville in public. They can be divided into two categories, two variations of the same thing: unconscious and conscious negative capability, something—as "Equal, That Is, to the Real Itself" shows—familiar enough to Olson. The first, something of a contradiction, is a lack, an inability. Under it I would put Olson's inattention to the use of fictional/symbolic devices in the Hawthorne essay, an inattention which has serious repercussions for his reading of the later work. That is, if the applications of language's symbolic capabilities aren't picked up on, then there can be little awareness of the purpose behind those applications.

This shows up clearly in Olson's early reading of Ahab as represented by "In Adullam's Lair," an uncompleted study of Melville written by Olson in 1939–40. This passage is typical:

> Torpor lies upon the prose of *Pierre* as death upon the people. A poet's line, like eyes, uncovers the health of his being and is this most true of such naked and spontaneous makers as Melville. Robed and bundled are his words in *Pierre,* smothered in sense, the breath of image put out. But "Enceladus" spoken, and the swathe is cut away. When the image is of the Past, "before man's brain went into doting bondage, and bleached and beaten in Baconian fulling-mills, his four limbs lost their barbaric tan and beauty," only then in *Pierre* does the line raise itself. Pierre is Enceladus.

Whether we agree or not with Olson's sense of the line in *Pierre,* the identification with Enceladus, Keats' titan who was defeated in direct confrontation with Zeus and buried beneath Mount Etna, is hardly positive.

The identification is symbolic of Pierre's inability as midway reader and writer. From the novel: "that moment the phantom faced him; and Pierre saw Enceladus no more; but on the Titan's armless trunk, his own duplicate face and features magnifiedly gleamed upon him with prophetic discomfiture and woe." Pierre has imagination, has the vision, but will not get beyond its prophecy because of his inabilities, which are so many amputations preventing not simply heroic struggle but also the creation of a saving fictional space. We should not forget the origin of his vision, the natural world, specifically "The Delectable Mountain" on the Glendinning property surrounded by pastures of the white amaranthine flower and grim scarred rocks which are given hostile motion by Melville: "on every side bristlingly radiating with a hideous repellingness." This *is* the white world. Pierre is the citizen and victim, the victim of his inability to read or to use allegory.

Olson, fixed on Ahab as a primitive Lear in this study, victimizes himself in turn by not understanding Pierre's failure as its author's successful allegory for the need of Ishmael's fictional, figurative space in a world where the amaranth will not die. "The immortal amaranth, it will not die, but last year's flowers survive to this! The terraced pastures grow glittering white, and in warm June still show like banks of snow." Olson's misreading of the visionary identification leads him to commit another. "This Pierre, the uncreated, the Ahab who kinged and captained no world because his creator had forsworn his Imagination for Christ, this man had a backward and a downward in him like a pyramid: 'The old mummy lies buried in cloth on cloth; it takes time to unwrap this Egyptian king.' Melville denied him." Not following the nature of, or the motive for, Melville's critique of his earlier work, Olson must cast Pierre as a failed Ahab. This Ahab shadow is supplied with the oldest of critical surmises to account for his failure to achieve the stature of his supposed forebear. Olson makes up an autobiographical fiction for the author's motivation he didn't understand in the first place. Like the pineal gland, Christ is the ever-ready, if unsubstantiable, *raison.* Caught in his fixation, Olson does not see that he has become the duplicate of duplicate Pierre.

By his own account, Olson's reading of Melville begins with "Benito Cereno," a fiction expressly about the difficulties of reading in a greyly ambiguous situation and one in which much symbolism and outright allegory (e.g., the "shield-like" stern piece of the *San Dominick*) is encountered. Whatever Olson's attraction, a reader who finds the author of "Benito Cereno" incapable of allegory or symbol is revealed, like Delano, to have inexperienced eyes.

Judging from the horatory "biblical" style of "In Adullam's Lair," it's possible to detect the hand of Edward Dahlberg, who was the early study's first critical reader and to whom part IV "Loss: Christ" of *Call Me Ishmael* is dedicated, on Olson's shoulder. It may be that the Christ perorations in Olson derive from the example of Dahlberg. I wish, however, to consider this other variation of negative capability, deliberate and conscious misreading, and to seek elsewhere for its animus. There can be little doubt about Olson's familiarity with the entire Melville canon. Per his own recommendation in his *Bibliography* for Ed Dorn, Melville was Olson's "one saturation job," the one writer he read exhaustively. I think—and his correspondence with Sealts would seem to support this—he did this essentially only once. But it is unlikely that such reading, both extensive and intensive, stopped there; rather, it seems to have been the locus of remembering and pondering for a lifetime. Melville is Olson's center and source that, once saturated, once "in himself," gave him the key to "everything else very fast." And Melville is the key to everything else, everything else he reads and writes, in Olson.

Part of the animus for Olson's deliberate misreading or misreporting of reading, I would suggest, is a proprietary desire to keep his central source to himself. Elias Canetti, on the "dynamics" of cannibalism in *The Conscience of Words,* is relevant. To gain power, you must defeat an opponent stronger than yourself, you must partake of that power (eat from the body, *magnum corpus*), and you must keep something of the once-stronger opponent as a souvenir of the power you now possess yourself. This has to remind us of Ishmael who, as his author's book's etymology and extracts prologue make clear, is a cannibal of texts. This sort of cannibalism allows what "experience" never could, the creation of fictional space. It is the fictional narrator cannibal, not Queequeg, who survives. It is a cannibalism which Olson is well enough aware of: "Melville's books batten on other men's books." (Cf. the misdirection rhetoric of "In Adullam's Lair": "Such a man as the Melville of *Moby-Dick* is only self-begot: he cannot begin in another, and the last loin for him is Christ.")

The imperative first sentence he took for his title has a doubly reflexive reference to the earlier cannibal and to himself, Olson, the later one. Understandably, Olson is rather coy in his discussion of the old State-secret. The secret is cannibalization of the source or father. Once he had identified his source, appropriated and made it "in himself" through reading, the problem became how, through writing, to keep it there.

Olson solves the problem by misdirection and by abstraction. The first has to do with his insistence on Melville's value as an author of physical detail and factuality; the second with turning this value into theory that, because of its growing autonomous complexity, can soon enough be discussed in its own terms, "projective" indeed and not referential at all. Again and again Olson cites "The Tail" chapter as evidence of Melville's concern with visible truth. Yet when we read the chapter, we find that Ishmael's conclusion is one of lack of mastery, even indifference to the physical object: "Dissect him how I may, then, I but go skin deep; I know him not, and never will." As has been seen in both novels, to put your trust in the external physical scene—in either of its particular manifestations, whale or terror stone—is to will your own perdition. The "facts" in *Call Me Ishmael* are manifestly Olson's facts. Olson, as previously noted, turns Melville's fictional space into a physical entity.

He does not, however, stop there. It is combined with another abstraction, America, and the two are pushed until, having collected other italic and all caps terms, there can be no thought of the source of it all. Item: "Space has a stubborn way of sticking to Americans, penetrating all the way in, accompanying them. It is the exterior fact. The basic exterior act is a BRIDGE. Take them in order as they came: caravel, prairie schooner, national road, railway, plane. Now in the Pacific THE CARRIER. Trajectory. We must go over space, or we wither."

A similar constellation is proprioception, which begins with the cavity of the body and ends with "the unconscious is the universe flowing in, inside." It would be hard to imagine anything more antithetical to Melville's vision, but by this time it doesn't matter. The abstraction has lifted free of its source which, of itself, would be difficult to guess even by laboriously reversing the abstraction motion or gesture.

Yet that antithesis is the point. The source will be left alone; the corpus, Melville, will be safe from the threat of despoilation. Not only is the source made safe, the new cannibal has emerged at the same time in his own right with the power of his own name and voice. Peculiarly, it is the need to misreport, to veil the source, that has prompted his eloquence. His writing is read as his own, self-begotten. In his *Bibliography* Melville is mentioned only once, on the basis of the accuracy of his description of how to cook a whale. Or, from *Causal Mythology:* "I won't quote, as one never does, one's own secrets, that's why you steal from others." The others constitute the titles of the bibliography, all having to do with external and abstract America, a list of misreading, *not* the lightly touched-upon source. If we read this list diligently enough, we will no doubt forget the last lines of *Call Me Ishmael's* headnote—"Loke, fahter / your sone!"—or its conclusion, a description of Proteus, "son of the father of Ocean," who changed his shape to evade philistine Aristaeus. Olson the son, Melville the father, but the cannibal son is protean in evasion.

Another recourse is vilification. Misreporting, misdirection, will have to do for *Moby-Dick,* already a "classic," which means it will be dutifully taught in the schools and dutifully "unread." That is, the book will be taught from obligation, read likewise, if at all, and not for active use by another reading writer. But who would be tempted to consider even glancing at something continually scorned, its author's (formerly valid) vision reduced to mere statement, its prose fatty, its characters absurd (Isabel) or abstract (Pierre), something judged, overall, a disaster? No one would, but someone did—the protean evader himself, the producer of these judgements, the self-consciously unself-begotten.

At some point in the remembering and pondering over his reading, it must have dawned on Olson that he had duplicated Isabel's (and Pierre's) learning to read and write. What guides his reading, what gives him any distinction over and against the "mischievous" academic critics he reviles in "Letter for Melville 1951," written to be "AWAY FROM" the Melville Society's 100th birthday party for *Moby-Dick*—readers who would presume to know the source's work but who have not come to it as usufruct beyond the furthering of their careers, that is, who have not come as true cannibal sons (and does not every son have to question the credentials of every other son?)—is the *Moby-Dick* "Manuscript" notes and marginal comments written by Melville in his set of Shakespeare. Olson's discovery of the set, his finding the handwritten notes and comments, duplicates Isabel's discovery of the handkerchief and the talismanic word written inside its booklike folds.

Thereafter—my guess would be that this speculative "at some point" falls between the first Melville study (1939–40) and "Projective Verse" (1950), one indication of which is the editing down of rhetorical vehemence and reference generally to *Pierre* in *Call Me Ishmael* as compared with the clotted chapters of the earlier study—Olson's every move is predicated on unmaking or, at the least, disguising the duplication. For the duplication is also an identification: it means Olson the reader become the writer through his reading is not so much the strengthened and "articulated" cannibal as victim of his source's "fatal line." Olson is the Loose-Fish whose reading made him Melville's Fast-Fish. Each successive critical theory, each new reader presumes a degree of superiority over the text. Nothing throws such presumption into question as Ishmael's inquiry: "and what are you, reader, but a Loose-Fish and a Fast-Fish, too?" Thereafter, Olson's project becomes the creation of a Loose-Fish identity for himself, an identity, moreover, to be established through writing. The question thus becomes how far can a conscious Fast-Fish remake himself, through the very medium of his "fatality," into an at least apparent Loose-Fish.

The critic Joseph Riddel, in his essay "Decentering the Image," has made a careful reconstruction of Olson's poetics. Despite several differences between us (e.g., I would argue that Olson does extend his "inquiry" to *Pierre,* that the privileged-text status apparently given to *Moby-Dick* is only one more pretextual maneuver of conscious negative capability), the essay is useful even for those more concerned with the writing of poems than with criticism. Let me pick out merely one element from Riddel's long essay. This has to do with displacement: "for Olson's poet, the first act is to displace the fiction of origins." Following Olson's *Special View of History,* Riddel notes that chance and accident precede and displace the fiction of original unity, generating history as a space of play.

He goes on to consider selection in the act of writing.

> Selection begins in seeing the local difference, in "factual observation," or looking. Looking is not perception, however, not the constitutive act of a subject. Nor is it empirical ordering. Looking is situated at the place where selection begins, in the first accidental marking of difference and relation, a grammar governed by neither subject nor arche, an an-archy, a multicentered field.

And:

> Language, however, is already informed with hierarchies. The language of poetry appeals to the unity of the Word, and thus to the commanding presence of the "Old Man (Juice himself)" who possesses all the "lightning." To recuperate the cultural origin in "selection" is to seize a beginning already begun, to recover the play of writing. Selection is not *aletheia,* but a productive interpretation, an act of appropriation.

Accurate enough as it is, the generality of this critical language would have to make Olson smile. Selection, indeed, can involve interpretation and appropriation, but in Olson's case it is more specifically cannibalism, eating and protecting the source of one's power. Related to Riddel's discussion, but not emphasized in it, is speed. I call attention to speed because Olson does and because it serves as an indicator of how central his duplication of Isabel and Pierre became for everything else he did.

To demonstrate this, I will gloss two Olson texts, "Projective Verse" (now almost the unexamined cliché he found Homer to be) for poetics, and "In Cold Hell, In Thicket," his finest "lyric," for the poetry. Each of the essays' first three theses—kinetics, principle, process—suggests speed (as do the terms of the essay's subtitle: projectile, percussive, prospective). The primary definition of the poem, in the first, could not be more direct. A poem is energy, a transfer of energy, a high-energy construct and discharge. The product or effect of energy is speed. The second, the principle, is not so immediately obvious. This is expressed in Creeley's "FORM IS NEVER MORE THAN AN EXTENSION OF CONTENT." The content of "In Cold Hell, In Thicket" is the difficulty of living in such conditions, translated conditions of the treacherous white world, and the corresponding need for a saving space. Thus the question: "how trace and arch again / the necessary goddess?" Not Greek, but the Egyptian Nut, the sky goddess, the goddess of space "arched, as she is, the sister, / awkward stars drawn for teats to pleasure him, the brother." The question is repeated through parts 1 and 2 and culminates in 3: "Who / am I?"

The questions are related. Unless the goddess can be arched again (and she is a fictive creation of language to begin with), then there's no chance for identity because there's little chance for articulate existence in the cold hell of the white world. The content is extended, in part II, to a question of self-revelation.

> And who
> can turn this total thing, invert
> and let the ragged sleeves be seen
> by any bitch or common character?

I take this total thing to be the source that has been eaten, that which has given power, allowed Olson to understand the need for a saving space created by language's symbolic functions and provided him "what / he has to say," that which has been the means of his standing up with a voice, Melville.

The direct answer points us at once to speed. It will be done by taking fixes (the plural is important), multiple readings. The act of such taking, and writing as its reporting, is difficult to maintain: "this / is the almost impossible." "This" is staying at speed, in motion, never letting yourself be trapped—as Olson the duplicate has been trapped—by a too-prolonged single reading, a fix become fixation. Going from this content to the poem's formal elements, we find aspects of speed everywhere. Some of these are: lack of conventional end punctuation; open-ended parentheses; rapid-fire multiplication of questions, so that no single "answer" can hope to satisfy them; reiteration of clauses whose subject is often remote, suspended, or left unstated in apposition. The content is the question of survival, the form is motion, and the product of that motion is energy and the feeling of speed.

If we have any doubts about the product, they are quickly removed by the term's appearance in thesis 3, process: "a matter of, at *all* points . . . get on with it, keep moving, keep in, speed, the nerves, their speed, the perceptions, theirs, the acts, the split second acts, the whole business, keep it moving as fast as you can, citizen." This only superficially has to do with Pound's don'ts of imagist composition. Rather: if you don't do this, you will become entangled as Isabel was, and you will entangle others, as Pierre and Lucy were. And if you are Charles Olson, *you* will be entangled, a Fast-Fish, stuck with a source whose identity will be disclosed (as yours will be concealed) by the stench of a writing that is *only* a duplication or reproduction of the first.

Gradually becoming a more aware reader and writer than either Isabel or Pierre, Olson becomes in turn a speed reader and writer. This is the point, per Riddel, of looking. Olson's poetics and poetry present the "almost impossible" attempt, through reading and writing, through the conscious use of language, to regain Isabel's condition before she could read or write, when she spoke and thought "from the tongue." It is an attempt to make surmises that have some precision in themselves and that leave the mysteries, their surfaces, intact and the reader/writer as unentangled as they can be. And when, as his poetry and poetics consistently demonstrate, he did speak, as the "Poetry and Truth" lectures at Beloit demonstrate in particular, it is with all possible speed, a "swirl." It is this very speed which permits Olson, having once duplicated Isabel's discovery and Pierre's midway inabilities, to recover himself as reader and writer, as his own Ishmael.

The answer to the first question, why Olson should so misread, is the answer to the second. His misreading—of which speed reading and writing, taken as a single relation or equation, is the final positive conversion or conscious negative capability, in effect another way to fail—is what keeps Olson in the play of language. As long as he can stay at speed, he is alive as "himself" in that play, making a space for himself as he goes. His central source is Melville, and he in turn is ours, the cannibals who come after. "That it is simple": a man is "for use, for / others."

A Picture
of Mystery
and Power

In time poets and their poetry become critical cartoons. The great value of Susan Howe's *My Emily Dickinson* is that it neither reproduces nor produces such criticism. What it does produce is a picture of mystery and power. The poet is a hunter consciously and aggressively active in the hunting process of composition. The poetry is what's hunted down and transformed by that process in a wilderness of language. Power has been exerted to be transformed and exerted again upon us as readers of the poetry. Because Susan Howe's reading is attentive both to the poet's historical contexts and to her texts—passionately attentive and open-ended in interpretation—the final mystery of the poet's motivation is respected, and the exertion of the poetry's power is given free play. It is a picture, but a picture that releases to mystery and power. It is a picture of Emily Dickinson, and it is a picture of the poet in the act of composition that applies to the practice of contemporary poets. Given the intricacies of its subject and their implications for contemporary practice, this is a compact, even short book. It is also a great and important one.

At least part of this importance, though not the major part, is as a corrective to the current preponderance of attention and thus authority granted to academic critical theory written by those who are not themselves poets. Students should be forgiven the impression that the function of poetry is to provide an occasion for critical theory. Perhaps, in the manner of Pierre Menard, Derrida has not only explained Ponge—not to forget Nietzsche—but has also improved upon the work. In Harold Bloom's terms, the critic has become the author of the poet *and* the climate generally.

To welcome such a corrective is not to deplore criticism in itself, nor is it to deprecate philosophy. It is to regret the obscuring of poetry by an ever-increasing overlay of prose commentary and critical theory. It is to be justifiably angry with the conduct (and reception) of philosophy as an autonomous activity, the products of which stand as self-sufficient Kafkaesque castles having no reference to poetry. Criticism turns poetry into prose that misremembers its source. While criticism aspires to this perceived condition of philosophy, a predictable enough by-product of modernism, philosophy itself may well be guilty of forgetting its origins in poetry. Heidegger is undeniably one of our century's preeminent philosophers, and his philosophy has served as a direct stimulus for the development of literary hermeneutics. It is doubtful, though, whether his thought could have come to definition, much less influence, without the poetry of Hölderlin, Trakl, and Rilke.

(Susan Howe's judicious utilization of some terminology from Heidegger is exemplary. The author of *My Emily Dickinson* is not an intellectual Luddite. If her readers find her utilization occasionally too breathless— e.g., "For the journey of a soul across the distance to being's first breath, true existence is in the Abyss"—they should recall her devastating questioning of Heidegger following her citation of Mary Rowlandson's narrative of her child's brutal murder by her Indian captors. "Where is the warm hearth Heidegger finds through Hölderlin's perception of what lies waiting at the summit of the central Self?")

The argument is not for the abolition of criticism or philosophy but for an alteration of attitude which recognizes the existence of poetry as distinct from its commentary and theory, if not as the originating site of the most fundamental element of all language, namely, metaphor. It is for an alteration in the balance of the agonistic debate between those, the poets, who have a vision to state in metaphor, and those, the commentators and theorists, who wish to be free of any such vision's hold and to disperse, if not altogether deny, the power of such vision's images. The debate is as old as Homer and Plato. *My Emily Dickinson* functions as a corrective to the current imbalance of this debate by its very style. For it is nothing like anything found in current commentary and critical theory. In fact, while there are whole sections of "normative" sentences and paragraphs, there is much that isn't prose at all.

What follows is taken from a paragraph responding to poem 1382 ("In many and reportless places") by Dickinson and which anticipates her poem 378 ("I saw no way").

On this heath wrecked from Genesis, nerve endings quicken. Naked sensibility at the extremest periphery. Narrative expanding contracting dissolving. Nearer to know less before afterward schism in sum. No hierarchy, no notion of polarity. Perception of an object means loosing and losing it. Quests and in failure, no victory and sham questor. One answer undoes another and fiction is real. Trust absence, allegory, mystery—the setting not the rising sun is Beauty.

Some of this might have been written by a critic with an unusually acute and insistent ear. Most of it, however, could have been written only by a poet accustomed to think in figures. What assertion there is spreads out in the complex horizontal branching of association and metaphor, oblivious to prose conventions of punctuation and syntax.

This is more crucial than a surface discrepancy of stylistics. Toward the end of Susan Howe's recent collection of poems *Defenestration Of Prague,* there appears a list following and answering two italicized questions: *what are eyes for? What are ears for?*

Tension
Torsion
Traction
Unction
Vection
Version
Vision

Lists in a variety of spatial displays figure prominently in this poet's poetry and "prose." When we come upon the beginning of her brilliant reading of "My Life had stood—a Loaded Gun—," what we find is a list of equations of identity for "My Life."

My Life: A Soul finding God.
My Life: A Soul finding herself.
My Life: A poet's admiring heart born into voice by idealizing a precursor poet's song.
My Life: Dickinson herself, waiting in corners of neglect for Higginson to recognize her ability and help her to join the ranks of other pubished American poets.
My Life: The American continent and its westward moving frontier. Two centuries of pioneer literature and myth had insistently compared

the land to a virgin woman (bride and queen). Exploration and settlement were pictured in terms of masculine erotic discovery and domination of alluring/threatening feminine territory.

My Life: The savage source of American myth.

My Life: The United States in the grip of violence that threatened to break apart its original Union.

My Life: A white woman taken captive by Indians.

My Life: A slave.

Unlike almost all criticism, there is no move to close off the play of these possibilities. Instead, it's allowed to flourish. Much later in the book another list appears, one which gives the possible relations generated by the same poem, both in itself and in combination with historical and literary associations it attracts to itself.

Gun in My Life
 My Life in Gun
  My in The Owner
   The Owner in My
    Catherine in Heathcliff
     Heathcliff in Catherine
      Edgar in Tom
       Tom in Edgar
        Panther in Boone
         Boone in Panther
          Doe in Rebecca
           Rebecca in Doe
            Killdeer in Deerslayer
             Hawk-eye in Kill-deer
              Serpent in Chingachgook
               Chingachgook in Serpent
                He in I
                 I in He
                  Childe Roland blowing Edgar's mad song.

Again, this contradicts the operative premise not only of academic literary criticism but also the criticism of many poets, including William Carlos Williams with whom the author expresses a sense of kinship in her introduction.

That is, it does not attempt to close off possibility in the interests of a single "right" reading. It lets the power of Dickinson's vision continue to play upon us even as she herself is included in that "us" of readers. By itself, then, Susan Howe's style demonstrates, in Eliot's phraseology, that the criticism of artists writing about their own art is of greater intensity and carries more authority than that of nonartists. The authority which this book carries cannot be that of any single right reading. Rather, it is the poem's own authority, the authority of the vision of Emily Dickinson's poetry, the result of passionate attention to words in tension, torsion, traction.

This connects with Susan Howe's refusal to go along with received feminist critical theory concerning Emily Dickinson. If a poet is to continue to think as a poet outside the poem, the poem's process of composition, if a poet is to remain true to the authority of her vision and what her eyes and ears perceive to be the vision of another poet—a vision moreover that is not static, but dynamic—then she will have to remain at odds with feminist criticism as much as any other.

The discussions of Helene Cixous and of Sandra M. Gilbert and Susan Gubar are to the point. Cixous is found wanting in her disregard for Gertrude Stein while elaborating a horatory program for the writing of women in the future. The authors of *The Madwoman in the Attic* are chided for their depiction of Dickinson as a sewing spider-artist. "This is poetry not life, and certainly not sewing." Prior to this statement there *is* agreement that gender difference does affect our use of language, and there is a distinction that matters. "That doesn't mean I can relegate women to what we 'should' or 'must' be doing. Orders suggest hierarchy and category. Categories and hierarchies suggest property. My voice formed from my life belongs to no one else. What I put into words is no longer my possession. Possibility has opened." If the poet is to be true to vision and possibility, to the continuing exertion of vision's power, then *all* the hierarchies and closures of criticism have to be resisted.

It is daring to do this. For there are several instances of agreement between the author of *My Emily Dickinson* and the feminist critics she parts company with. Yet remaining true to the authority of her vision and to that of her subject, she can only turn away from a society she might otherwise enjoy, a society which presumably would be only too happy to confer its authority upon her. To remain true in this way is to keep possibility open, even if it means, as it does, the enforcement of solitariness and isolation. Her readers, we are the beneficiaries of her courage to recognize that "a poet is never just a woman or a man. Every poet is salted with fire."

This courageous and *human* recognition sets *My Emily Dickinson* apart from the current varieties of academic literary criticism and, if only as a matter of degree, from much of the criticism written by poets. Pound, Williams, Olson, and the Possum want to be right. Therefore, the play of possibility is abridged, and the drive toward a single authoritative reading, however spectacular and unacademic in appearance, ensues. Despite a number of differences, the book's truest progenitor and peer is *The Necessary Angel*.

We should hear Stevens as we read Susan Howe's final paragraph. "Poetry is the great stimulation of life. Poetry leads past possession of self to transfiguration beyond gender. Poetry is redemption from pessimism. Poetry is affirmation in negation, ammunition in the yellow eye of a gun that an allegorical pilgrim will shoot straight into the quiet of Night's frame." She has written "stimulation" where Stevens would have written "sanction." Their different word choice comes down to "the same difference." Just as I'm persuaded that Dickinson will be acknowledged as the primary nineteenth-century American poet, so am I that Stevens will be likewise acknowledged for our own century. What persuades me is their awareness and confrontation of the ultimate problematics. What makes *My Emily Dickinson* so valuable is its open address to all who would read and its courageous confrontation of issues that go far beyond the current debate over aesthetic authority. The book is valuable because it confronts, like Dickinson and Stevens, those ultimate problematics of how to be alone and how to stay alive.

Timely and needed as the book's critical corrective is, that is not the major part of its importance. For that we must turn to its picture of the poet in the act of composition. It is true that an unusually useful—by which I mean attentive to textual questions and imaginative in dealing with them—work of academic criticism (e.g., Lyndall Gordon's "critical" biography of Eliot) may occasionally offer a glimpse of such a picture. Such works are not to be discounted. More typical examples of criticism, however, offer nothing of the sort for the same reason that sex doesn't occur in Henry James: they have no knowledge of the experience. A poet who has written some of the most mysterious and powerful poetry of our time, Susan Howe is certainly knowledgeable about the act of composition. What is authorized by her style and her own working knowledge is a picture of composition. The major importance of this book lies in the originality and depth of that picture and its potential for application by other poets.

To repeat, the poet is a hunter consciously and aggressively active in the hunting process of composition. The poetry is what's hunted down and transformed by that process in a wilderness of language. This restatement of the picture is a composite and condensation of several images that recur in the book. Not long after the list of possible equations for "My Life," there is this: "Power is pitiless once you have put it on. The poet is an intermediary hunting form beyond form, truth beyond theme through woods of words tangled and tremendous. Who owns the woods? Freedom to roam poetically means freedom to hunt." And somewhat later: "freedom to explore is a violation of Sovereignty and Avarice, and may be linked forever to loneliness, exile, and murder." This in turn should remind us of an earlier characterization of Emily Dickinson and Robert Browning wandering "a wilderness of language formed from old legends, precursor poems, archaic words, industrial and literary detritus." And to an even earlier sentence: "pursuit and possession. Through a forest of mystic meaning, Religion hunts for Poetry's freedom, while Poetry roams Divinity's sovereign source." Finally, moving past all of these citations to a sentence toward the end of the book: "all power . . . is utterly unstable."

There are other images contributing to the picture, but these are what I take to be the crucial ones. Their distribution throughout the book is not a matter of chance. That is, its disorganization, in terms of prose conventions and standard critical methods, is governed by the complex horizontal dynamics of association and metaphor. Through these dynamics the book grows, branching out into a mirror-maze of metamorphosis. Let us briefly consider these images.

The poet becomes a hunter by putting on power. Primarily, this means a power over language whether, as with Dickinson, over that of another contemporary poet's poem or over the inherited legends and literary detritus making up the wilderness that is language. The act of composition, assumption of power, takes place in the woods of words. In part, this should remind us of Olson's composition by field and its finest realization, "In Cold Hell, In Thicket." To make this assumption is to move consciously and aggressively, to move as a hunter. The poet does this in order to bring about a more powerful composition, literally to bring about composition.

How is the power of a poem measured? Susan Howe provides an insightful answer in her discussion of Jonathan Edwards and Dickinson: "subject and object were fused at that moment, into the immediate *feeling* of understanding. This re-ordering of the forward process of reading is what makes her poetry and the prose of her letters among the most original writing of her century." What can be a greater or more final manifestation of power than the reordering of the reading process? Prose is read forward toward conclusions. In an age characterized by advertising and in which the primary field of undergraduate study is business marketing, readers read toward those conclusions *at speed.* Such reading uses language up, particularly figurative language, which is discarded like so much fast-food packaging along the way. In this age as in any other, poetry resists any such rapid linear (or digital) consumption. While the silent reading of poetry involves the same physiological processes as reading prose, it is so composed, if it is to exert power, as to resist both speed and summary conclusions.

The poetry of power in any age resists such reading to the point of stoppage. (The speed urged by Olson is a compacting of perception, of metaphor process, rather than a rate of reading; if anything, compacting has to be a slowing agent.) It does this as part of the exertion of power in language. Whether it is done with any positive regard for readers is a good question. Pound's "to see again" presumes the reader will benefit as well as the poet. Notwithstanding the neatness of her manuscripts, we can't quite be sure that Dickinson herself was concerned with whatever well-being her poems might provide for others. We have to remain uneasy with such poets. When Susan Howe writes "together We will hunt and kill for pleasure," there can be no assurance the reader is included in the collective. The play of the poetry of power is never less than frightening (and not only to ethical culture moralists).

Emphatically, the poetry of power is never "a good read." In *My Emily Dickinson* there is a reference to the pioneer practice of fire-hunting, whereby hunters would "shine the eyes" of deer and thus secure "a fatal shot." The poetry of power threatens to transfix its readers by its vision, holding them utterly. It may be that this is what underlies the antagonism described by Eric Havelock between the Homeric poets and the Platonic philosophers. It is an antagonism that continues, though we may call it a debate and though the balance seems presently to be all on the side of criticism (aspiring as it does to the free-standing condition of philosophy). Understanding poetry as that which almost successfully resists the intelligence should not tempt us to forget that, in its complexity, there may be whole regions of language, composed parts of the woods, which *are* successful, impenetrable, in their resistance.

Two related terms entwine themselves around the spreading growth of the book. They are "concealment" and "revelation." "Poems and poets of the first rank remain mysterious. Emily Dickinson's life was language and a lexicon her landscape. The vital distinction between concealment and revelation is the essence of her work." The distinction is vital because the poem is not now one and then the other but *both* at once. "Dickinson went further than Browning, coding and erasing—deciphering the idea of herself, dissimulation in revelation." The poem's images may provide revelation, vision, *and* at the same time serve as concealments of what is most vital for the composing self. (Despite the earlier suspicions of musicologists, we have come to know the "secret program" of Berg's "Lyric Suite" only by chance.)

For there to be composition there must be hunting and killing. The power of the hunter poet is made all the more absolute when the evidence for the enacting of power has been concealed in a simulated revelation. Plausible metaphors for hidden metaphors. Aware of such power, we can only smile a Gioconda smile at the questions of critical decorum recently raised by Jonathan Culler: "does one deem empirical authors responsible for what is discovered in their texts? Does one allow oneself the possibility of treating authors as blind to the forces operating in and through their language?" We can only smile at the "new" argument of Michael Riffaterre's influential *Semiotics of Poetry* that poems are riddles saying one thing and meaning another.

Critical theory, by its rhetoric of authoritativeness, seeks to divert attention from its secondariness. The critic is a prose hunter in a forest which has been designed and already hunted over by the poet. The critic solves only those riddles which are left to be solved. There is always another part of the wood in a powerful poet's work. The true "super-reader" can be only the poet. As Dickinson's correspondence with Higginson demonstrates, *all* the poet's texts are artful and aware.

The implications of Susan Howe's images and their related terms of concealment and revelation are not, in the end, smiling matters. The freedom to hunt is purchased at a price. Freedom is always freedom *from* something. To hunt, the poet must tear away from all the somethings that would prevent entry into the wilderness. (Suddenly, Emily Dickinson's chosen seclusion appears in a new light.) What must be torn away from is all that which is represented by settlement, historically limited and approximate as that term may be, by all the settled usages of grammar and law, at and beyond the frontiers. "Really alone at a real frontier, dwelling in Possibility was what she had brilliantly learned to do." The several sections of *My Emily Dickinson* which remind us of the historical American wilderness and of the dangers of living there—for a Jonathan Edwards, for a Mary Rowlandson—continue to be apt.

Only now we must understand that the imperatives for staying alive in the America of real frontiers remain in effect for our encounter with and in language. Once we have torn away from the settled usages—and this is never done once and for all, but must be repeated with no cessation of pain or doubt—we must remain in motion. Whether it's *away from* or *toward,* motion must be maintained. If not, the poet risks composing nothing not already composed, an inert sort of hunting, or of becoming the hunted. For to hunt at all must certainly contain the possibility of becoming the hunted. There is only one possible protection, if there is to be any hunting and if power is to be put on, and that is to stay in motion. "Unconcealed consciousness out in pure Open must be acutely alert if *he* is feminine." We can affirm this and also affirm that *all* hunting consciousness in composition, male or female, must be acutely and continuously alert.

We have read that all power is utterly unstable. It is unstable because of the unceasing away from and toward motion of hunting. There can only be power in the motion, in the act (which may include the guarding and concealment of what has been hunted down). To take on, to maintain power, the poet must always be going into exile, must always act alone, and must know that the title of hunter could be exchanged, with equal accuracy, for murderer. If a further twist is needed, the "prey" that is hunted down in the wilderness of language will be identified by what the poet has been attracted to out of love and admiration. *Power is pitiless.*

The earliest of the cited images of the book's picture involves not only the forest of language once more but also religion and poetry in a relation of conflict. Religion hunts for poetry's freedom because it is dependent on the images of vision for its own existence and organization. Take away those images, and all the churches fall down. The church does not produce vision but enshrines and builds basilicas around it. Through these actions vision is turned into static dogma, suitably "stable" material for erecting an organization. Once an image is selected, all others are suspect and must be denied. To promote itself, religion becomes a demonstration of authority in the name of the chosen image. By definition, the hunter poet cannot be satisfied with the restricted movement permitted by the leash of dogma. There is no other recourse than rebellion. "Dickinson takes sovereignty away from God and bestows it on the Woods." And the woods are made of words.

Yes, this is a female triumph over organized male authority. It is also more than that. The poet's rebellion can hardly come to an end once the biblical He's have been dutifully translated to She's. And the righteous instigators of that translation will be no less energetic than their predecessors in the imposition of their authority.

The poet who would hunt and take on power goes to no church, however reformed. The obligation to stay in motion, to find ways to conceal and guard what has been hunted down, remains binding. It is noteworthy that Susan Howe has included this image in her book. It is not merely historical. Vision is the big picture, which includes apprehension of violent spirit powers. Its inclusion reminds us of those men and women who assumed the responsibilities of rebellion even as they mistrusted it and who went into exile and perhaps ignominious martyrdom as a result. We need to be reminded of the human seriousness of poetry in an age of advertising and marketing which would recognize its activity, insofar as it recognizes it at all, as a minor craftsmanship.

Finally, some readers of *My Emily Dickinson* may feel we've not read the same book. For them its attraction will be an unabashed feminine perspective from which an instance of the feminine overthrow of male authority is celebrated. This is a possible, though surely reductive, reading. If I read it differently, it is to call attention to the wider application of Susan Howe's picture of the poet for all those who would read or write. It is a great and important book.

An Ongoing Conversation

One way of reading Theodore Enslin's poetry is as an ongoing conversation or dialectic. In the past, for example, he has often cited the names of those, quick or dead, who have made contributions to this conversation in the margins adjacent to the poems. In *The Weather Within* there is a single citation for the entire poem in the form of its subtitle: *In Memory In Homage: George Oppen, 1908–1984.* This is a conversation, then, with one primary partner, with the voice—as remembered, made part of Enslin's own voice, though not always merely assented to— of George Oppen.

It may be useful to identify the reference of the poem's title. This is given in part no. 20, which I quote in full:

> There is rightness
> a standing up
> rectitude
> the integer vitae
> we will not claim
> all of it
> that is settled
> outside us
> yet a conduct
> a weather within.

The weather is inside, internal, something to be maintained—"a standing up"—against our own vicissitudes and those of the forces, physical and spiritual, outside us. Concern with "rectitude"—and an awareness going well beyond past or present received notions of correct deportment—sets both George Oppen and Theodore Enslin apart from many of their contemporaries. Like some of their diction, these two poets can appear old-fashioned, perhaps deliberately so, in this concern. In an age typified by hi-tech nominalism and an all-pervasive irony, an irony which, while once functional, threatens to become a disease, both these poets stick out in their standing up.

In such an age both are relatively out of place, though precedents—in Pound, in Zukofsky—can be found. What could be more incongruous than presuming some modes of behavior, beyond self-interest and "enlightened" pragmatism, are to be preferred over others, than presuming the presentation of one's work has something to do with one's life, than presuming one will be held accountable for how one conducts both activities. At a conference on the work of George Oppen (University of California at San Diego, 1986), a not unintelligent critic asked how students could be helped past the barrier of Oppen's constant "wisdom seeking." One can understand the question, and one can understand that it begs the question.

There are forty-eight parts in *The Weather Within,* two to a page. The parts are numbered (e.g., 3–4) at the upper outside corner of each page. (The parts appear in the same order, though in a somewhat reduced format and without numbers, in the offset edition put out by the Membrane Press.) Some mention should be made in passing of the Landlocked Press first edition as a handsome job of bookmaking. The typeface is large and readable, the paper is Ingres-Fabriano (cover and text), and there are front and back drawings by Kim Wilson.

Of the poem's forty-eight parts, I single out three sets of two each from the beginning, middle, and end, each of the three dealing with age. The parts on each page do and do not connect with one another. At the same time it should be noted that they aren't given, antiphonally, as separate statements from Enslin and Oppen. Both are from Enslin, both have "intertextual" allusion, directly quoted in some and only hinted at in others, to Oppen's work. Reading the parts, one overhears and is made aware of Oppen's voice through that of Enslin. In a variety of ways it shows through. Beyond "conversation" generally, perhaps the more specifically accurate analogue for the dynamics of the poem is a two-part motet, the "given" part coming from Oppen, the added and somewhat more "frontal" part from Enslin. We hear the whole of the motet at once, the one part showing ("bleeding") through the other.

In the first part we're told that consciousness, in relation to the life around and outside itself, is "out of scale." There is more of it, more going on in it than in the rest of "life." The problem, given this out-of-scaleness, is how to deal with it. As the work of both poets has demonstrated over the years, there is no "deal," but only the trying to deal. Or as Enslin drily comments in the final part of the poem, "I suppose / it is the human condition." It could also be called tragedy. Even out-of-scale conscious- ness "flickers"; it is both the "make and brake" of our lives. Oppen appears in this first part through the use of space breaks within lines, a practice that became more and more pronounced toward the end of his work, and through the reference to the consciousness as "the engine," which will be recalled from the serial poem "Image of the Engine" from *The Materials.* While consciousness can be a machine making for "clearing," understanding, it is at best "seasonal." It is at once not in proper sync with the world around it and yet subservient to the alteration of that world. It is this root contradiction which is tragic.

In slightly shorter lines, part no. 2 then takes up what can be done, granted such a condition, from the perspective of age. The given, either of consciousness or of the phenomenal world, is no longer a major concern. There is no gesture of dismissal with regard to what can't be dismissed, but simply: "Age is more adventurous." This is a marvelously free line, not flamboyant, but free and intrepid. The question then occurs as to what, having relegated the given to a less-than-privileged position, is to be done. Part no. 2 doesn't provide an immediate response. What follows, instead, defines and qualifies age. We read that this quality of adventuresomeness beyond the given is its gift to us. This is so much the case, "We might almost wish / that it were not so." For, as others have before us, we crave the known, the stable, the familiar. It is even more comforting to be confronted with the constant alteration of the given, which is at least constant in its alteration. For all its brevity, this part is full of careful qualification. Age is not simply presented as superior to all that came before it, an invalidation of those "prepatory" years, as it were.

Having declared that age is more adventurous, it's noted that that is its gift to and from us. Without being overly grim, the poem denies any external benefits as part of the "human condition." Rather, we're re- minded that all we can have, what we must have, is time, but that time is a gift *from* ourselves; what may be realized from or in age comes at the price of our own mortality. Thus it is "we might almost wish / that it were not so." We find ourselves in such a position because the gift must produce, sought after or not, an increment of consciousness which, as it grows, can only result in the further realization of being "out of scale." (Cf. Oppen's "The man is old and— / Out of scale" from "Seated Man," in *This In Which.*) Thus age is "poised," but it rarely takes "that last flight / above the peaks" that youth had vainly attempted to scale. The nature of the flight isn't further defined. My guess is that it amounts to vision, that awareness of "the big picture" which comes about when one is somehow released from, "above" the pull of the immediately given. In its relative independence from the given, age can come to vision, a bringing of the world and consciousness into scale, into a kind of harmony. This is a possibility. It is, however, only a possibility, one rarely taken, and if taken, the last.

This bittersweet, sfumato sense of age is something we are familiar with in Oppen, but in its accentuation, it is relatively new in Enslin. There had been darkness in the work, but it had been counterbalanced by light, hope however qualified, in the ongoing conversation or dialectic of his previous poetry. Now there has been a shift.

> The words themselves   older
> it does not seem so   possible
> that words which we   rearrange
> with no difficulty   should be that old
> without an ability to deflect
> our uses   yet in the largest sense
> they do resist   and elude us.
> They make it difficult just at the moment
> when they seem defenseless.
> In measure attempted
> they will assume nobility
> growing from the rubbish
> of our thoughtless assault.
> Oh   the words.
> Words live lives of their own.
>
> (no. 38)

There may be attempted measure, there may be nobility, but the nobility belongs to the words living lives independent of us, their unthinking users. The poem may be read as a motet's counterpoint to the heartlessness of words in Oppen's "Route" *(Of Being Numerous).* It is hard, even given the age's clichés of relativity, to imagine anything more devastating.

We encounter restatements of the same "themes" in the parts of the middle set, nos. 23 and 24. We are back to consciousness, this time to an awareness "that all has aged around us / we alone remain young." We're told this is the only way of looking out, that what is within does not age. At first glance, then, flecks of light against the darkness. Yet the reservations all but extinguish them. For if that is the only way of looking out, what we find is "only on the surface." If what's within resists aging, we still know only "our own part" of it. Our "youth" remains caught up with the superficial. Our consciousness continues to be out of scale and inharmonious.

The musical expression of this paradox of increasingly aware and increasingly delimited consciousness is developed in no. 24.

> What may be sung   well sung
> may well be sung   it is
> that pitiless singing   changes
> as the bells insist their tones
> again   the ringing in stages
> many stages   one after another
> ways in or out down corridors
> long stopped with dust   the
> velvet of neglect   done
> well done   may well be done.

The part begins with the closing lines of Oppen's "Song, The Winds of Downhill" *(Seascape: Needle's Eye)*. That poem is one of affirmation. Out of a deliberate impoverishment of the tradition, great or otherwise, one makes one's way, by "handholds" and "footholds," beyond the residential suburban plots of the anthologies, toward the poem "which may be sung / may well be sung," the supposedly originary condition of the traditional lyric.

Yet Enslin turns the affirmation of Oppen's poem around: "it is / that pitiless singing." Oppen celebrated the possibility of making one's way, of a kind of progress toward composition which, it's implied, is enough, that is, that the struggle to arrive, make something from the barest means, can be undergone and that the result will be somehow satisfactory, even to the point of casting some doubt on the tradition's mostly honorific gestures toward an origin in song. It *will* sing. Enslin accepts the possibility of singing and produces in true contrary motion a song of darkness. It is as though Gesualdo had reworked Thomas Tallis' "Spem in alium."

What has been won through—and this should be understood neither as an argument with nor as an ironic dismissal of Oppen—is a further realization which happens to be "darker": the song of our struggled-for composition is, finally, not our own at all but that of the words with their own autonomous lives. It is indeed a change, an instance of changes, playing on the chords of the older poet. But the playing, like the change-ringing of bells (clangorous relative of the motet), only serves to produce an image of darker and darker darkness. The ringing in stages leads to corridors "long stopped with dust   the / velvet of neglect." From Oppen's image of bare-headed struggle with the outside world (cf. "Carpenter's Boat," in *This In Which*), we have come to an antithetical, curiously interior scene.

One thinks of the steps in Kafka's insurance office, of Bartleby's law office and prison walls. What has happened is that we forsook the givens of tradition, struggled out in "the elements," only to find ourselves back on those steps and within those walls. Indefinite postponement and ostensive acquittal, indeed. And the little play on the vowels—from Oppen's "sung" to Enslin's "done"—is chilling. Even further, the free-floating syntax of the final "may well be done" phrase means this interior scene may very well be *the* scene of our existence.

I want to connect the change-ringing of no. 24 with "that open song" of no. 43. In the latter, the song is described as a single line which, with an added voice, would strengthen to cadence. The purpose of change-ringing is, by adding to a given or inherited subject, to come to something else, not simply further elaboration, but that elaboration *and* something else. (This is how discovery is made in music and poetry.) Confronted with anyone's sense of limitation, whether or not the weight of tradition is felt as an actual mass, there has to be some expectation that the addition of another voice will help, both for the immediate job of getting along in composition and for the desired end result of something distinct and "new."

This expectation, however, is denied twice. Having posited the possibility of cadence, Enslin insists that it still remains a single line and that "we must allow it all to end / without conviction." The poem circles back to the opening of song and the conjoint cadential line. The line is not so much denied—after all, this poem is fair evidence that it can be made— as is its ultimate "discovery" found wanting. "This little trickling melody is all we have." A cadence is a progression of chords, usually two, which gives the effect of defining and closing a "sentence." Here the chord changes, the words, have been attended to and put together with skill only to close with a literal line (melody or sentence) of failure. What we have, what we've made, is not enough.

The final set, nos. 47 and 48, begins with a reference to "But So As By Fire," one of the poems from Oppen's series "Some San Francisco Poems" (Seascape). That poem concludes:

> We have gone
> As far as is possible
>
> Whose lives reflect light
> Like mirrors
>
> One had not thought
> To be afraid
>
> Not of shadow but of light
>
> Summon one's powers

Enslin's reference to Oppen's line, like his other references, is indirect, more a variation than a quotation per se. And, importantly, the poem begins where Oppen's ends. Enslin, then, is not saying the same thing as Oppen. In this poem there is an awareness that not all shadows are threatening or, if so, that their threat may be truly insubstantial. "Yet / power does appear." We can read "power" here, following the reference to "But So As By Fire," as one's capacity to bring about vision (or perhaps the cohering power of vision in itself). Working with words in composition, some vision can appear. There can be melody, there can be "sense." Yet again, though, there is qualification. That power of clarity and resolution, power of light, may well only "summon shadow / long after the fact has vanished." What would be achieved by the power of vision is, in effect, an incapacitation, a haunting which would prevent any further discovery, if not any motion beyond our old fears. Our very capacity proves to be nullifying. We remain old men, out of scale and seated, stuck.

The final part of the poem returns to the image of the mind "in age." In this condition, as suggested toward the end of no. 2, there is a power beyond what was possible in youth. Now there is flight beyond mere aspiration; there is actual ascent and hovering. Yet again, though, there is complication. Once detached from the pull of the given, the mind "cannot come down." It is the tragic, unlooked-for opposite of Icarus. (Cf. Oppen's "Daedalus: The Dirge," in *The Materials*.) There is further complication in developing the image. "The turns are silent wheeling   shadows / high above the landscape." The shadows that had been simply ominous, instances of generic danger, turn out to be not true "signs" for threatening facts, much less the Erinyes, but the illusory products of our own minds. (It is difficult not to think of predatory birds in reading these lines, the power of the mind preying upon itself.) The problem of scale, of integrating an ever-enlarging consciousness with what it's conscious of, has been resolved. "All that / bewildered us" has been resolved by the vision of age.

There remains yet another problem, one revealed (in this rather disheartening process of revelation) as of distance. Just as things come together, the mind and its objects in "mensural" scale, their unity is found to be too distant, "so far off it does no good." At this point Enslin's voice gently, but meaningfully, interrupts (cf. the close of no. 14) the less "vocal" flow of the poem. "I suppose / it is the human condition." The very flatness of the statement is affecting. Having come so far in the process of age and of composition, it is a finale made all the more final for its quiet flatness. This is the human condition: that there is vision, coherence, "only at that place / where the fit is powerless." I first misread the last line to be somehow benign, a last "testament of acceptance." That *is* a misreading. Undemonstrative as it may be, it would be difficult to be "darker." The unactionable vision, product of the art so long to learn, exists as a design that is "perfect in its just   repose."

Earlier in the poem both words and axes are identified as things that cut. The words of the poem's penultimate line, so quiet and flat, could not be more cutting. They are not used as agents of revenge or retribution against another person nor against another politics. Certainly, they are not against George Oppen. The words came, entered composition as the result of vision, the human need for a more than incidental or merely local "given" coherence. In no. 30, symbol, metaphor, and synonym are all rejected. More than these, however crucial as language functions, is need: "we are in need / deep need of scene." With need comes obligation, the poet's obligation to make a scene, an operative or "realizable" design. Once it has realization, however, the mind's own flight in age distances us from it. Whatever perfection there may be belongs to the design in itself. We come to recognize that perfection, that encompassing coherence, only when it is unreachably remote from us, made so by our own need and obligation. The repose is the design's, not ours. The space break between "just" and "repose" in that last line is an instance of the perfection and of the heartlessness of words, of poetry as the art of words.

I don't know that such dark vision of vision can't be found elsewhere in Enslin, in *Forms* or *Ranger,* to mention two ambitious earlier works. What strikes me as new is its concentration. It is this concentration which gives *The Weather Within* a largeness of its own. Whether one reads it as the inevitable trap that must come of poetry's own self-troping or as tragic vision, the poem is large, not monolithic but inclusive and humanly generous within its inclusion.

Introduction

The vision seeks the man.
—Zora Neale Hurston

I came to jazz just as I was.

In the beginning it is a matter of supplication to be made a member of the sanctified church. Later it becomes the discovery, an apparently enabling discovery, of an informing source for poetry. Still later it becomes a prolonged and perhaps-not-to-be-released-from encounter with the sirens, both their song and the aftermath—bones among a field of flowers—of their song. I use the sirens as a figure for my encounter with the voice and with one of its primary instruments, the horn. There are other instruments, but in this area of decision, in the sanctified church of jazz, the horn is primary. A matter of supplication becomes a question of survival. What is to be survived is the power, the face-eating power to the third power of the voice.

Not knowing the power of the voice, I asked for the wrong thing. To ask to be made a member of the church is to ask for the wrong thing. When, in time and in the circle of repetition, I came to some knowledge of the voice, there was nothing but the stench of terror. To ask to be made a member is to ask for the wrong thing. What is to be asked for is how to stay alive.

The first jazz that made itself available to me was "The Drum Thing" on John Coltrane's *Crescent* album. It was a story, a narrative. It had something to do with a journey across a wide expanse. And it was with a journey or simply a straggling procession of musicians in mind that I began the poem. It's tempting to say the music gave me the poem. The contribution of the music, however, was more an instigation, a prompting to begin, than a complete template.

It was the first poem which truly pleased me. It seemed to exist apart from me, to have an object existence of its own. And I knew that, without the music of John Coltrane and Elvin Jones, it would have had no existence at all.

Helped in the ongoing work of composition and protected from becoming a parasite of personality, the poet is pleased and happy. What more could be desired? This was my feeling in writing the later poems prompted by jazz. Ornette Coleman's "Lonely Woman" on his *Shape of Jazz to Come* album involved yet another journey across a wide expanse. And Lester Young's playing, whether with the smaller Kansas City groups or with the Basie big band, had a behind-the-beat poignancy that involved him in a pursuit by green meteors and other personages of the night.

I made a grid from the sheet music for "Lonely Woman." The idea was that my lines, shaped in compliance, might take on some of the rhythmic character of the music. Even as I did this, I suspected it would not be enough to transpose already-transposed music into poetry. There would have to be transformation. Not "jazz poems," they would have to start from and go away from jazz. They would have to end up somewhere else.

The music could be blues—what Ornette always plays and what tends to come through whatever the context Lester was playing in—and the poems themselves could be elegiac occasions. In "Coming Forth By Day," the poem that takes off from Ornette, ponderous women move among the deaths of fire, air, and lands. In the Lester Young poem, the death is Lester's own, but reconsidered as a night scene. The music could be blues, the poems could be elegiac, but I was pleased and happy. What I had yet to hear was the voice behind the music. What I had yet to understand was the relation of the music, the voice, and my own defacement.

Several years later, when "Giant Steps" was written, I still had not heard nor understood. What more could be desired? Jazz was my church, my informing source. While I had gone on to listen to much more of it both before and after Coltrane, his music continued to be the center of my source. I had developed an unresting cadence, a cadence which in the motion of its going seemed to have certain affinities with his "sheets of sounds." And, by way of etymological research into the terms of his titles, the potential vocabulary of the poems was enlarged. Through this cadence and vocabulary the potential of composition was enlarged and expanded.

I was a willing, eager supplicant in the church of jazz, and it continued through all its various promptings to lead me on.

I do not remember at what moment I began to hear and to understand. No doubt, it was a gradual, not prepared for much less sought after process. I thought I was writing poems that started from jazz and eventually got away from it. What I thought was wrong. By the time I came to write "Not Quite Parallel Lines," I knew what I had thought was wrong. Two musicians appear in the poem: Coltrane and Albert Ayler. They are cited as exceptional natures which I am heir to and which nevertheless must be opposed. There must be opposition because they are players— and thus are played through—of the horn of the voice.

Who would have dreamed these exceptional natures must be opposed? I hadn't and didn't want to. It seemed blasphemous to go against those I most admired, those who had prompted me to discover the potential of my own composition. What I gradually began to hear through them, however, was the animal power of the voice. What I gradually and reluctantly began to understand was that the power of the voice meant my own powerlessness.

Composition is attention. If jazz is its instigation, that means leaning and leaning in more intently in listening to be able to write. With more intent listening come admiration and love. At the same time the listener becomes increasingly vulnerable, exposed, to what plays through the players and their instruments. This is the voice which eats the face away. It is the voice which turns the face of the listener, member among the members, into its excrement.

Odysseus encounters the sirens once. The growing, undeniable intensity of admiration and love and the existence of recordings mean a constant encounter and reencounter. In this circle of repetition there is always a call, there is always a being spoken to. *The vision seeks the man.* In the area of decision of jazz the members cannot help but to hear the call and what is being spoken.

Once having come to jazz, like language, there is no leaving. There is only the trying to decide against being turned into the called and be-spoken. There is only the constant trying to decide to stay alive.

Come Shadow
Come and Pick
This Shadow Up

We return to texts because something cannot be forgotten or because something has, indeed, been forgotten. Both are involved in my return to Louis Zukofsky's "Songs Of Degrees." Certainly, having thought and written about this series as key to the entire circle of Zukofsky's work, I have not been able to forget it. Nevertheless, having read Lisa Faranda's *"Between Your House and Mine": The Letters of Lorine Niedecker to Cid Corman* (Duke University Press, 1986), I am reminded that Zukofsky read and commented upon the first two of the songs in the course of an NET film make in 1966. I had seen the film but had somehow forgotten about it. I wish, then, to return to the first two poems in the "Degrees" series and to a comment made by Zukofsky in the film that the effect of these poems is "something like a prayer."

It will be useful to consider the following terms as indicated by the title for the series: "song," "degrees," and "valentine." I will define these terms as they occur in book 12 of Zukofsky's long poem *"A"* and in his critical study *Bottom: On Shakespeare.* I concentrate on their occurrence in these works because of their central importance for Zukofsky and for their chronological placement. Book 12 is the hinge or pivot of *"A"* and is in many ways the single most important of the poem's twenty-four books. According to a chronology drawn up by the poet's wife, Celia Zukofsky, the first two poems of the series were begun and completed in 1953. Book 12 was completed in 1951; *Bottom,* while not completed until 1960, had been begun in 1947. Both these works are of an importance and of a placement to have a bearing on the first two songs of the series.

In "a final note" to the Origin Press edition of *"A" 1–12* (1959), William

Carlos Williams remarks on his own initial bafflement with Zukofsky's poetry, which would not read right according to his imagist expectations. One reason for this was Zukofsky's relation to music, in particular to the contrapuntal music of Bach. Williams: "it wasn't simple. . . . It was never a simple song as it was, for instance, in my case." Zukofsky's never simple song can be defined in relation to Bach, the letters of whose name spell out the "theme" of book 12, and in particular to the contrapuntal principle and process called fugue. It is no accident that, immediately following the statement of the named theme on the second page of book 12, there should appear a reference to Bach's *Art of the Fugue* and to the composer's characterization of this principle and process as the behavior of reasonable men in an orderly discussion. Earlier, in book 6, Zukofsky asks what will serve as the presiding question for the entire composition of this long poem "of a life / —and a time":

> Can
> The design
> Of the fugue
> Be transferred
> To poetry?

(Zukofsky's recently published correspondence with Pound makes it clear he was aware of fugue "in the matter of musical approximation" no later than 1931.) Taking this as the presiding question for *"A"* as a whole and reducing Bach's contrapuntal music to an art of fugue, we can place Zukofsky's understanding and practice of song in an equation with fugue.

A few pages after the statement of the B-A-C-H theme and the reference to fugue, and after asking whether Bach didn't sometimes think like the Chinese, it's claimed "the important thing" is what the composer of the *Guerre-Lieder* says. This is Schoenberg, whose statements with regard to fugue may be taken as definitions accurate with respect to musical composition and sympathetic with Zukofsky's understanding of his own practice as a poet. In *Fundamentals of Musical Composition,* Schoenberg states that a fugue is a composition with "maximum self-sufficiency of content." The more such sufficiency is manifest "in the form of unity of material, the more all the shapes stem from one basic idea . . . from a single theme." And, as he states in an essay on Bach in *Style and Idea,* "one should not expect that new themes occur in . . . fugues, but that there is a basic combination which is the source of all combinations." What these statements confirm is that, while individual fugues may attain individual forms, fugue itself is not a form. Rather, it is a process of continual expansion or growth, the many from the one, based on the principle of imitation. In *"A"-12* the one theme or basic combination is stated through the letters of Bach's name which unites such distinct, but persistently entwined subjects for Zukofsky as *B*aruch Spinoza, *A*ristotle, his wife *C*elia, and Paracelsus, the last that "strange Renaissance personality so amply endowed with genius" whose original surname was von *H*ohenheim.

The statements of the theme in both the beginning and close of book 12 are further and specifically focused upon the poet's wife, the object of his love:

(beginning)

Blest
Ardent   good
Celia,   speak simply, rarely   scarce, seldom—
Happy, immeasurable love
        heart or head's greater part unhurt and happy,
        things that bear harmony
        certain in concord with reason.

(close)

Blest
Ardent
Celia
        unhurt and
Happy.

The "same" theme is given even greater distribution and focus in *Bottom*. Expressed as Shakespeare's theme, which is found to the nth variation throughout the entirety of the plays and poems, it is nonetheless Zukofsky's, *his* "Shakespeare theme": *love sees.* If the presiding technical question is whether the design of the fugue can be transferred to poetry, the presiding critical question is whether anything will be seen through the attempted transference. Admittedly, the two questions are but different aspects of the same question.

The transference can come about only by analogy. Zukofsky's poetry will have to be an "imagined music." The syllables, to quote from a statement concerning *Pericles* in *Bottom,* "are brought together *like* notes." The analogous motion for the process of fugue, this bringing together, is conceived as a weaving in both *"A"* and *Bottom.* Thus in the poem the figure of the weaver is picked up from the *Phaedo:* "Weaving, instead of unweaving, / A fiddle—Or Penelope's web." Thus Zukofsky's very "persona" in writing his critical study on Shakespeare is none other than Nick Bottom of *A Midsummer Night's Dream,* a weaver and, according to Thisby, "eke most lovely Jew, / As true as truest horse." And thus it should come as no surprise to discover that, complementing Schoenberg's statements, one of the preeminent musicologists of the first half of our century and author of "a humane and readable analysis" of the *Art of the Fugue,* Donald Francis Tovey, should define fugue simply as "a texture." For when we look for the root of this new term, what we find is the Latin *textura,* "a weaving."

Modeled by way of analogy with Bach's fugue composition, Zukofsky's song proceeds as a weaving of words and their syllables on the single theme of *love sees.* To quote from *Bottom:* "Up, down, outwards—for even inversions and exact repetitions move on—are the melodic statement and hence the words' sense: or after syllables have been heard before in contiguity, they may also be augmented or diminished, or brought to crowd answer on subject in a great fugue." To quote from book 12:

> We begin early
> And go on with a theme
> Hanging and draping
> The same texture.

The technical and critical question, again, is whether the transference can be done and, if so, whether it can be done with sufficient skill so that the song/text woven on this single theme will not only provide a guiding principle and process for the working out of the poet's composition but will also result in something to be seen. Judging from his comment about prayer and, earlier in the NET film, about how the two songs show what could be done with twelve words (cf. Webern on Bach's *Art of the Fugue:* "what else could this work be but the answer to . . . 'what can I do with these few notes?'"), Zukofsky was well aware of the question.

It will be recalled from Schoenberg's statements that, as there is unity of material, the shapes stem from one basic idea or single theme. Shapes are the earliest indications of form. They appear as such in the opening lines of book 12 when, following the most primary of motivations— *"deep need"*—and made singular, shape, they are given as the first products of composition.

> So goes: first, *shape*
> The creation—
> A mist from the earth,
> The whole face of the ground. . . .

It is shape—in coordination with the other firsts of glyph, dance, and body cited in Zukofsky's demographic of composition—that orders the poem's rhythm and style. And while shape as a first apprehension of form may order the "intermediate" working out of rhythm and style, it may also be understood as a result of that working. This leads us to the consideration of what particular shape, if any, results from the composition of poems conceived as songs defined by the weaving principle and process of fugue.

We are helped in this by the painter Paul Klee, who was himself something of a musician and who is mentioned with regard to form toward the end of book 12. Klee's Bauhaus lectures contain valuable insights about the composition process. In one of them he takes up the peripheral movement of color or the "canon of color totality." A canon is a condensation or concentration of fugue. As a term it derives from *fuga per canonem,* or fugue according to the strict rule. Webern, a student of Schoenberg and a composer partial to canons, provides a further definition: "a piece of music in which several voices sing the same thing, only at different times; often what is sung occurs in a different order." One of the orders is called mirror canon, a type of fugue which occurs in Bach's *Art of the Fugue* and with which Zukofsky was familiar. As he wrote in a letter to Lorine Niedecker (January 28, 1937) with respect to *"A"-8,* "I've let the intensity with which I've felt the material determine its order & the *effect* or *suggestion* is something like a mirror fugue in this section."

To connect this with the characteristic motion of fugue—weaving—it could be said that in canon the texture results from the weaving of the same kind of threads or the same thread. The effect of a mirror fugue or canon may be achieved when the "points" of syllables weave words into lines that define a plane. The effect is felt when, within that plane, the syllables and words reflect one another. In terms of music history, the form or shape which prefigures canon is the round. The visual shape we associate with such music is precisely what we find demonstrated in Klee's lecture, that is, a *circle* of color.

These observations are of interest because they suggest how what is essentially vertical, the song/text/poem, may be composed by means of a weaving and result in the effect of a circle which may also be "reflective." As Wilfrid Mellers writes in *Bach and the Dance of God,* a study which would have pleased Zukofsky for its linkage of Bach and Spinoza, "yet at the same time this existent passion is *objectified* since the canon is in mirror inversion" (my italics).

Besides the constant oscillation of Zukofsky's theme and its combinatorial subjects throughout all of *"A"* and *Bottom,* there are several references to circles in book 12. I would cite two variations. The first fuses language from Spinoza's *Ethics* to make up the opening three lines, which are then joined by what I take to be three of a more personal invention.

> Since no one cares about anything he does not love
> And love is pleasure that dwells on its cause
> He who loves keeps what he loves:
> An image inwreathed with many things
> That may flourish, that draws cause
> To light up.

In the second the same variation of the circle, the condition of being inwreathed, is joined with language that had been used earlier in the book to describe Bach's renewal of the arabesque.

> For all inwreathed
> This imagined music
> Traces the particular line
> Of lines meeting
>   by chance or design

These variations remind us of the critical question attendant to the poet's theme. It is a question which has its own insistent variations. Will love see? How will it see? What will it see?

The answer is that love will see by dwelling on its cause (potentially anything, but particularly the four subjects, with a special emphasis upon Celia). It will see by virtue of the image which has been made not so much as an imagist picture poem but as that which is held, kept and reflected, in the inwreathing circle of the woven "line of lines" traced by the imaginary music of the poet's song.

What will be seen can only be what has caused the poet's attention to be attracted to what is outside the poem and to what is within its composition—that is, what the poet loves. According to Zukofsky's poetics, this is sincerity, the care for detail, attention to the particulars of the outside world and to those within composition. Williams' bafflement is hardly surprising. The image matters for Zukofsky, who has written perceptively of Pound and Williams in both his critical essays and in the later songs of the "Degrees" series, but it is an image grounded in a shape primarily determined by a musical principle and process. It is primarily an acoustic or cadential image. Zukofsky's song = fugue, the shape of whose weaving motion is a circle which, mirrorlike, would hold or keep what is loved.

Zukofsky's song, which is also text and poem, can be placed in an equation with fugue. This can be done because words in his composition are treated *like* notes. This can be done, too, because the shape that is produced as effect or suggestion is, analogically, the same shape produced by fugue. The writing of song so understood moves toward a visual end. While related to imagist poetics, this is still distinct from Pound and Williams. For it does not *begin* as a visual report. The motivation behind Zukofsky's circular end and beginning, the creation of a musical or acoustic/cadential image, is to light up what is loved, to illuminate and to reveal the beloved as substantially as an object held in the mirror of that image. We must hear in order to see. We must hear and see in order to love.

In considering the second of the title terms, "degrees," we can follow the alphabetic order of Zukofsky's theme. That means starting with Bach and with the term's use in music. Here degrees indicate the position of a note with reference to a scale and are sometimes called scale-steps. Degrees in music locate the position of a note or tone with reference to a predetermined range or space. Degrees locate notes with reference to the total space of a scale (from the Italian for ladder) and with reference to the internal spaces—the intervals—within its totality.

Applied to poetry, this usage refers to the tones of individual words or syllables and to the intervals of their exact or recognizably "near" recurrence. It is a reference Zukofsky seems to have had in mind when, writing in *Bottom,* he mentions "the tones of the syllables . . . the relations of their intervals" and the previously cited "up, down, outwards" description of how words may be composed like notes in a fugue. Or, expanding on Spinoza's conception of bodily motions in a later talk, "About The Gas Age" (1970), how they twine as stems around one another, "and the intervals at which they twine are of interest only mutually—considered 'perfect' or 'short of perfect' as the case may be." The degrees are the tonal points in themselves and in combination with others in the twining or weaving motion of the words' syllables and their intervals of recurrence.

Having mentioned Spinoza, whose *Ethics* is organized according to the geometric method, we should not forget that in geometry and trigonometry degrees are defined as parts of a whole, which is considered as the circumference of a circle.

There is another "B" usage of degrees, this one from part one of *Bottom:* "love, the seed of the writing . . . moves all the leaves of his book to sound different degrees of 'Love's mind' or its relative failures of judgment." This statement about the one thing said by all Shakespeare's works develops from Helena's speech at the end of act 1, scene 1, in *A Midsummer Night's Dream:*

> Things base and vile, holding no quantity,
> Love can transpose to form and dignity:
> Love looks not with the eyes, but with the mind,
> And therefore is wing'd Cupid painted blind;
> Nor hath Love's mind of any judgement taste:
> Wings, and no eyes, figure unheedy haste.

The order of Zukofsky's statement makes degrees equivalent with failures. Love's mind fails because it is not in proper alignment with the eyes, with what attention to particulars through them can inform those who would look with something more than "unheedy haste." These degrees are differences of relative failure based on the wrong relation of love, eyes, and mind. Like all differences, they distinguish themselves one from the other and at the same time point or "relate" toward a common reference, the right relation negatively defined in this case, that is, love : reason : :

eyes : mind. Or: "love needs no tongue of reason if love and the eyes
are 1—an identity." It is then that love sees.

Nothing, however, will be seen unless differences, degrees, are acknowledged. It is the differences which identify the reference or theme.
Commenting on "Julia's Wild," his set of variations done as a "dark
valentine" on the line "Come shadow, come, and take this shadow up"
from *The Two Gentlemen of Verona*, Zukofsky notes that they ring "a
difference." It is the acknowledgment of difference which offers evidence
that eyes have looked without haste, with sincerity, and it is by means of
("through") such an acknowledgment that an image of the beloved object
may be constructed.

Of the possible "A" uses of degrees, I wish to consider one from book
12 and another from Aristotle, one of the four subjects of the book's basic
combination. From book 12:

> What is the worth of their
> Expounding the Torah:
> All a man's actions
> Should make him a Torah—
> So to light up   5
> Whether he moves or is still.
> Given a share, the body
> Comports the soul.
> It sees its reflection
> Only when it bends to it.   10
> It is not the same
> Asking a friend,
> The world is its place.
> It joins mouth and heart,
> The place and its presence   15
> Where each creature sings its song,
> It is ruled and acts
> First note to fourth,
> Because of its holiness
> Its song seems not holy at all,   20
> As in the "Section of Praise"
> Uniting the degrees:
> As it is, created—
> And—ashes and ear—
> Do you hear yourself,   25
> You must stop.

The passage is quoted at length for its demonstration of Zukofsky's way of working. Nearly all the lines derive from Hasidic sayings. My speculation is that they derive specifically from those collected in Martin Buber's *Ten Rungs: Hasidic Sayings* (1947), and I will use Buber's titles in the following list.

It is a list of the lines from this passage identified by number and their Hasidic sources.

> "To Say Torah and Be Torah" (1–4, 6)
> "Body and Soul" (7–8)
> "In Water" (9–10)
> "He Is Your Psalm" (11–12, 22)
> "The Beginning of Teaching" (13)
> "The Mouth and the Heart" (14–15)
> "All the Melodies" (16, 21)
> "Hiding and Revelation" (17)
> "Great Holiness" (19–20)
> "Two Pockets" (23–24)
> "On the Day of Destruction" (23–24)
> "How to Say Torah" (25–26)

Nearly all the lines can be derived directly from the Hasidic sayings. It has not been unusual since at least *The Waste Land* footnotes for a poem to have many and diverse sources. The extent to which Zukofsky has borrowed from the sayings, however, is remarkable. Because single words and phrases have been lifted from several different sayings and recombined in a compact unit of lines, it is not obvious there has been anything borrowed at all.

A reader might assume that all these lines have something to do with Rabbi Leib, the name printed with a full colon immediately before them. But that is not the case. What Zukofsky has done is to separate the words and phrases out from their original contexts to provide himself with a vocabulary for composition. So separated, they can be rewoven into a new song. What we have in this passage is the fully composed stage. What we have in *"A" 22–23*, in comparison, is the separated-out material which has been deliberately left at an earlier stage as an offering of material—"a raft of stuff"—for others to compose, mix down, into their own songs. Zukofsky's originality is as a weaver, an unweaver and a reweaver.

"Degrees" does not appear as such in the Hasidic sayings. What we find in "He Is Your Psalm" instead is: "the prayer a man says, that prayer, of itself, is God. It is not as if you were asking something of a friend. Your friend is different from you and your words are different. It is not so in prayer, for prayer unites the principles." And from "The Unity of Qualities": "emanating from God are ten qualities . . . seen with the true inner eye, they all form one simple unity. It is the task of man to make them appear a unity to the true outer eye, as well."

Zukofsky has translated Buber's principles and qualities into degrees. He has further translated them out of their religious context into one having to do with music, "where each creature sings its song." What were sayings concerned with religious experience become a vocabulary, a collection of "notes" newly released for composition. What is retained is the recognition, however radically translated, of the need for bringing the degrees into unity. It is through the unity brought about by the poet's weaving that "my song with an old voice is whole."

"Degrees" in Aristotle is a relative term of classification for analysis and argument. In book I of the *Posterior Analytics* its underlying reference is given in relation to more or less. "See if the terms cannot be compared as more or less, as is the case with a clear sound and a clear argument." They occur more significantly in the *Nicomachean Ethics,* where Aristotle opposes the Platonic position that pleasure is indeterminate because it admits of degrees. In opposition, Aristotle reminds us that a thing admits of degrees in two ways, abstractly and concretely. When a thing has oneness and simplicity (i.e., unity), it doesn't admit of degrees in the abstract. To quote from Aquinas' commentary on this part of the *Ethics,* "but it can be predicated according to more and less of such a form, as is evident in the case of light which is an undivided and simple form." The conclusion drawn from this is double: (1) light itself is not predicated according to more and less; (2) a body, however, is classified as more or less luminous as it partakes of light more or less perfectly.

To this should be added a later development in Aristotle's argument that pleasures, which in themselves admit of degrees by reason of their admixture, can be both determinate and good. One of the cited pleasures is that which results from musical harmony and which Aristotle extends to health as a harmony in human nature. Harmony, the simultaneous sounding of notes, is a synonym for wholeness, but one which is known in hearing a whole (complex) sound through more or less related individual sounds. Aristotle's use of "degrees" as a relative term of classification takes us back once again to music. What should be remembered is that in harmony we hear the one through the many. We can be aware of the one through the many; we can be aware of the whole—be made whole, returned to health—by unification of the degrees.

I will combine the last two subjects of Zukofsky's theme, "C" and "H," Celia and Paracelsus. Celia is the seen object that initially causes song, and she is the final object, the face of which is contained, lit up, reflected, and revealed as the image in the mirror surface or plane suggested by the woven circle of the poet's composition. There are other subjects in the theme, and Zukofsky has written in response to many others, if only as "episodes," outside it. Even a cursory review of the canon of his work, however, must recognize the persistence of his attention over the years to this one subject, Celia, "our genius" and "our tutelary spirit." Something of the poet's own understanding of the causation involved is described in book 12:

> So the instrument of knowledge
> Plays only when the beloved's head
> Turns from Passing to Being
> So learns by degrees.

Granted the basis of these lines in the *Phaedo,* what's learned by the poet is that his instrument, the mind or imagination, has nothing to play without a seen object. What we learn is that there are two objects. The first is the thing seen, in this case Celia; the second is the image, also Celia but reseen, a by-product of composition, which is experienced as an object.

This second object is necessary because the act of attention—sincerity, consciousness itself—makes for an increasing awareness of degrees, relative differences of more and less. Composition follows upon this awareness of differences—as an internal partitioning of the object itself and between subject and object—to unify the degrees, which are encountered as parts or aspects of the object and as measures of distance between the object and the desire of the poet's mind, to unify the degrees and to restore the object to harmony and wholeness. This is, at the same time, repeated on the level of language whereby words are more and more apprehended in their difference and are then resolved as a whole, complete song. There is, of course, the expectation that the poet's relation with the object, his love for her, is also restored.

This is the process of objectification which, with sincerity, is the other major term of Zukofsky's poetics. Celia is the initial cause, the seen object, but it is the poet's song as a composition which creates the reconstitution of the object, unification of the degrees, after the emergence of those degrees in the analytic multiplicity of consciousness.

The shape of Zukofsky's song is a circle. It takes that shape because of the fuguelike weaving of words and because of the poet's desire to hold and to light up the loved object. This is an image, a face, which, while never possibly complete in any literal sense, nevertheless suggests wholeness or the substantial (i.e., an object), as a result of the poet's care in observing the details/facets of the initial object and in attending to the details of composition. The second object is effect, an effect of the circle.

Many of the circles in book 12 derive from Paracelsus.

> Sane, vain and mad enough
> To call himself Paracelsus:
> In each (of Three Worlds) an urge to exceed
> And none wants to act with measure,
> To the end that balance be
> And no crooked thing,
> That nothing exceed the circle.
> Rests before the mirror
> Where its image rests. The image
> Is not sole object of knowledge. Nor is man
> Whose knowledge comes from outside him—
> The mirrored image he is.

These lines conflate and recompose the following statements which are to be found in the Bollingen edition of *Paracelsus: Selected Writings* (1951): (1) "thus man is like the image of the four elements in a mirror; if the four elements fall apart, man is destroyed. If that which faces the mirror is at rest, then the image in the mirror is at rest"; (2) "everything that man accomplishes . . . must have its right proportion; it must follow its own line and remain within its circle to the end that a balance is preserved, that there be no crooked thing, that nothing exceed the circle."

If something exceeds the circle, then the song's composition has been faulty. If the composition is faulty, then the mirror—if it can be made at all—reflects improperly, and the image of the loved object is distorted. The degrees will have to remain without unity. If the image is distorted, if the degrees have not been made harmonious, then there can be no rest (a term Zukofsky uses as equivalent to objectification). If there is no rest, there is no love.

I have emphasized the poet's love for the seen object. What should not be lost sight of is that, through sincerity and objectification, the poet seeks to make himself worthy of love in return. To exceed the circle is a double calamity. The poet enters composition with more than a casual interest. More is at stake than the production of a competent cultural artifact. Given such interest, the drive for completion becomes a serious matter. This is so much so that Zukofsky is faced with another critical question, one which is a consequence of the presiding question regarding the transference of fugue design to poetry. This is implicit in a later circle passage from book 12: "Once the circle is closed / It becomes very small / And very great."

We arrive at the appropriate critical question as we pay attention to the work. That is, the work proposes its own most appropriate and most exigent critical questions. The presiding one for Zukofsky may concern transference, yet that question leads to another of equal importance. This is not so much how there can be both a closed and open circle, but rather how—once the circle is closed—there can continue to be growth within its closure.

Playing these uses of degrees through Zukofsky's theme results in a complex but not inharmonious definition. Words and their syllables are treated like notes to compose a song whose shape is a circle and whose function is to hold the constructed image of the loved object so that it is reflected without distortion and lit up in the resolution of difference. The song's function is also to do this so that the maker of that rest-giving objectlike image is himself made worthy of being loved. Or, to quote from another poem from *Some Time* (1956), the collection in which the "Degrees" series first appeared, "So that even / A lover exists."

Both the first two songs of the series are dated and carry the subtitle "with a valentine." This gives the impression that they are somehow accessories to actual, physical objects. Zukofsky's reference, in the NET film, to the second of the songs—"It's a valentine"—makes it clear, though, that he considered the poems to be valentines in themselves. We can follow his example in taking this term, after "song" and "degrees," under consideration. We know that a valentine is a person chosen by another as a lover or special friend. We know that it is also a folded paper or card or letter, usually heart shaped, with verses "of an amorous or sentimental nature" sent on St. Valentine's day. What may be less familiar is that, as a verb, "valentine" means to greet with song, to sing.

"Julia's Wild," from *Bottom,* has already been mentioned in the consideration of degrees. What lends further interest to this set of finely realized variations on Shakespeare's line is that it is described by Zukofsky as a valentine. Yet when we read it we find nothing of an "amorous or sentimental" nature.

> Come shadow, come, and take this shadow up,
> Come shadow shadow, come and take this up,
> Come, shadow, come, and take this shadow up,
> Come, come shadow, and take this shadow up,
> Come, come and shadow, take this shadow up,
> Come, up, come shadow and take this shadow,
> And up, come, take shadow, come this shadow,
> And up, come, come shadow, take this shadow
> And come shadow, come up, take this shadow,
> Come up, come shadow this, and take shadow,
> Up, shadow this, come and take shadow, come
> Shadow this, take and come up shadow, come
> Take and come, shadow, come up, shadow this,
> Up, come and take shadow, come this shadow,
> Come up, take shadow, and come this shadow,
> Come and take shadow, come up this shadow,
> Shadow, shadow come, come and take this up,
> Come, shadow, take, and come this shadow, up,
> Come shadow, come, and take this shadow up,
> Come shadow, come, and take this shadow up.

Although "Julia's Wild" is included in Mary Ellen Solt's *Concrete Poetry* anthology, it properly belongs to the class of song and not the more literal object-compositions of either a Baude Cordier or an Emmett Williams. To quote again from Zukofsky's 1937 letter to Lorine Niedecker: "fugues in words don't really exist, because all the words go in one order—give one melodic line & can only suggest others between the lines going on at the same time."

What makes this poem a valentine is the suggestion of its technique. Certainly, the sentiment of Shakespeare's line can be understood as "love," if a darker and unsentimental version, and that should not be forgotten. Yet if it is not forgotten, it is because of the conscious and conscientious technique of Zukofsky, his care in weaving, unweaving and reweaving, all the degrees of this line. As he writes in a note in *A Test Of Poetry* (1948), "A poem is an emotional object defined not by the beliefs it deals with, but by its *technique* and the *poetic conviction* or *mastery* with which these beliefs are expressed." Unless all the words of the line—which is like a scale—all their combinations and their intervals, unless all the possibilities of the line are weighed and measured, there is no loved object and there is no "love object," no valentine. Both exist, and the poet with them, because of technique.

Shortly after the opening of book 12 there appears a "more literal" valentine. Within its outlined heart we read:

And under the outlined heart we read:

> Valentine's day because
> there are no hearts. There
> will be a heart because
> we will send you a letter
> that was from me to
> divide it in half.

Valentine's Day exists not to commemorate but to create. As the beloved may be said not to be, not able to turn from passing to being, until transformed by the lover's sincerity and objectification, there are no hearts—and no love—until they are made, composed and created. What is created is unification, from hearts to heart. We, Paul and his father, send you, Celia, "a letter," the valentine, in order that all three are unified and unfolded as one. The division allows for sharing and for a coming together. The valentine, variation on the circle, is closed, and the love of the family is made whole. All of this has taken place within the composition of a long poem of "a letter." It is the composition, its technique, which is the valentine.

It may be objected that if this is the case, then the shape of Zukofsky's canon is not so much a circle as it is one all-inclusive valentine. Given the dimensions of the canon—which in addition to the poetry includes a novel, a play, and a translation of Catullus—this claim will have to seem preposterous. There is simply too much of it for any one shape to apply to all its instances. Two factors, though, rule in its favor. One is Zukofsky's well-known belief that a poet writes one poem, one "continuing song" all his or her life. The other is the constant presence of highly conscious and conscientious technique. To quote Zukofsky quoting Wallace Stevens: "to every faithful poet the faithful poem is an act of conscience." This act is manifest in technique. It is also manifest in our reading: "an instant certainty of the words of the poem bringing at least two persons and then maybe many persons, even peoples together." Technique begins in the faithful care for detail, degrees of difference, outside and within the poem. It ends with the harmonious unification of all the degrees. There is a further bringing together in our reading the instant certainty of the words.

The world of Zukofsky *is* round. It is given a particular treatment or variation of roundness, the valentine, because of its author's weaving technique, which transcends the genres so that he could describe *Bottom* as prose and a long poem at the same time, and because of his theme: *love sees*. His technique and his theme—consciousness and conscience—are one. We, as his readers, are brought together with him and perhaps with others in reading his continuing song. It is in this way that the valentine-circle, while closed, can grow and become great.

In turning to the first two of the "Degrees" poems, I wish to return to Zukofsky's comment that their effect is something like a prayer. It is tempting, in making this return, to try to locate specific sources, other texts used for the weaving of these texts. Zukofsky's way of working renders such a temptation difficult and even misleading. As has been seen in considering the terms of the title, most of this material can be expected to come from those subjects within the basic combination of his ever-present theme. I think most of Zukofsky's material does come from these sources, but more as a grid of resonating individual words and phrases—the way we remember Bach and Shakespeare—than as a group of discrete texts which will read the rewoven text for us. Locating sources has value only as it calls our attention to the skill of the poet's weaving, as it calls our attention to how objectification has been brought about.

That said, I would cite two sources in particular for these poems. One is somewhat outside the basic combination, Plato's *Alcibiades Major* dialogue, while the other is very much from within it, a "reduced score" of passages from Shakespeare's *Pericles* as put together by Zukofsky in *Bottom*. In the dialogue Socrates defines "taking proper care" as "improving" and, in passing, mentions the art of weaving. Later, considering the dictum "know thyself," he asks Alcibiades if this would not then mean the eye should look at that in which it would see itself. Alcibiades concurs and identifies the objects in which we see ourselves as "mirrors and the like." Socrates suggests there is something of a mirror in our own eyes and, Alcibiades concurring, goes on to ask if he has observed that "the face of the person looking into the eye of another is reflected as in a mirror." Later in their exchange they agree that "he who is ignorant" will fall into error and that it is the obligation of those who would not be ignorant—who would know themselves and their own good—to look in the "bright and divine" mirror. Finally, Alcibiades having agreed to follow Socrates as a disciple, Plato has his teacher respond: "O that is rare! My love breeds another love."

In the *Pericles* reduction, the first passage is taken from the opening prologue as delivered by the "auntient" poet Gower, whose task is "to sing a Song that old was sung / . . . What now ensues, to the iudgement of your eye, / I giue my cause, who best can iustifie." Nothing could be more "conscious" than a poet quoting another poet's historic poet-character whose role is to produce a capitalized Song. We cannot help but be reminded of Zukofsky's conception of the poem as song, itself equated with the weaving principle and process of fugue. It is, further, an old song which the poet's son identifies in this pocket score of the play that appears as part of their own dialogue in the "Definition" section of *Bottom* as Shakespeare's *definition of love*. Gower's old song is his author's definition of love, which happens also to be that of the son's father, *his valentine.* The next passage, the single line "To glad your eare, and please your eyes," recalls the poet's musical sense of the image in order that the object of his love be illuminated and revealed. What follows, from Pericles' description of the princess "blithe and full of face," is an extolling of her beauty as "the book of praises."

It is because "thine eye" presumed to reach that book, reading Shakespeare's "reach" as both to create and to possess utterly, that "the whole heape" must collapse. I understand the heap as the lovers, their world and, by extension, the song itself. The next passage is noteworthy for the "myrrour/errour" rhyme. It is followed by a longer passage which develops a figure for vice as the wandering wind which spreads itself by blowing dust in the eyes of others. And yet the end of its action is "bought thus deare": "The breath is gone, and the sore eyes see cleare: To stop the Ayre would hurt them." Vice or error is overreaching presumption that would obscure the sight of others. This cannot be maintained, and the eyes of those who have been hurt in the blowing eventually see clearly, if only as a consequence of what they have undergone.

What provides solace, as it provides clarity, is the Ayre or song itself. I skip two passages to come to a longer one in which the passions are defined as those pleasures to be shunned by the eyes and the end result of which is a "life by care." We may skip other passages to come to the final two: Pericles' blessing on the birth of Marina ("Now the Gods throw their best eyes vpon 't") and Gower's line from act 4 ("Your eares vnto your eyes lle reconcile"). Hence we end with a blessing, which may have a bearing on the poet's attitude toward his own son and only child within the family circle, and with a line which once again recalls Zukofsky's desire that the image of the beloved be musical and so "lit up."

I have glossed portions of the dialogue and commented in somewhat greater detail on the play reductions as reflections of their prominence in the poet's resonating grid. The dialogue is suggestive. From it, for example, we learn to identify the mirror as existing within the eyes of another. The reduced play is more than that. It feeds directly into the poet's thought, in particular the need for an interweave of hearing and seeing. At the risk of seeming to reiterate the grid all over again, squaring the circle, I will cite a note from Spinoza's *Ethics,* quoted in *Bottom,* as usefully qualifying crucial terms for our reading of the poems.

> Unhealthy states of mind and misfortunes owe their origin for the most part to excessive love for a thing that is liable to many variations, and of which

we may never seize the mastery. For no one is anxious or cares about anything that he does not love, nor do injuries, suspicions, enmities arise from anything else than love towards a thing of which no one is truly master.

The terms given qualification are "error" and "care." The error, generally ignorance in Plato and the specific crime of incest in Shakespeare, is excessive love, one of whose expressions is care as in overreaching, "blinding" care.

All the twelve words of the poems can be found, with one exception, in the dialogue and play. Laid out as a scale or tone row in the order of their appearance in the first poem, they look like this:

hear   her   clear   mirror   care   his   error   in   her   is   clear

"Care," significantly, is repeated to give a total of twelve words. The one word which cannot be found in either source, "hear," I take to be the poet's variation on Gower's reconciliation of ears unto eyes, a variation which is in keeping with his own constant concern for an image which illuminates through musically grounded composition.

What follows is the third stanza and center of the second poem.

> Hear her
> Clear Mirror
> Care his error
> In her care
> Is clear

This stanza is a chiasmus in itself and for the poem as a whole. At the intersecting center of this center is "Care his error." The function of this line may be understood, analogously, as an operation in geometry. The line functions in the stanza and in the larger poem as a mirror by means of which the reflection in a plane of symmetry may be held. This is an operation which can be performed only in the imagination or "by an optical trick such as the use of a mirror." The trick (technique) of Zukofsky is a composition of words which produces an effect like that of a mirror reflection. It is an effect which is further enhanced by our understanding of the Platonic sense of the mirror as existing within another's eyes.

The stanza and poem may be said to engender an effect like the reflection in a plane of symmetry, a mirror, by the use not of exact imitation (same words, same sequence, only reversed) but by lines and syllables. That is, while the central plane line of the center stanza stands alone, lines 2 and 4 reflect one another, as do lines 1 and 5. Whatever the poem "says," its form would have everything seen and heard through the centermost plane of his error of care or excessive love. His error is the immediate motivation for the poem's composition, which seeks to restore what has been obscured by his presumption—face and eyes of the beloved—to a bright clarity. And the poet himself is redeemed in this restoration. If, formally, we do not understand (hear) the function of the mirror in the poem, we can't expect to understand (see) its cause (content).

It is a critical nicety taught to students that the first-person pronoun in poems is to be identified only with circumspection. The lyrical "I" is a construction not to be mindlessly equated with the historical personality of the poet. The circular consistency of Zukofsky's canon, however, allows us to put this convention "under erasure." There is only one "peeress" of Zukofsky's song, and we know her to be his wife, Celia. She is the "her" of the poem, and the poet is the "his." His error is Zukofsky's error. We do not violate propriety if we imagine the motivating circumstance of the poem as involving an embrace. For it is only in such an intimate "space" that the eyes of one can serve as mirror for another. What has happened is that he has been too grasping in his care and so blinded Celia *and* himself. The poem is an attempt to restore clarity, "clear care," to them both.

There are two stanzas before and after the central stanza. In the first of those coming before, the poet addresses himself with what might be called a self-apostrophe that her care, which is none other than his error, be heard and acknowledged. It is she, Celia and her eyes, who is referred to by the parenthetical clear mirror. The clearing up of his error lies in her care and in her clear eyes. The second of these stanzas reweaves "the same idea" with two more lines and with different punctuation.

> Hear her
> (Clear mirror)
> Care.
> His error.
> In her care—
> Is clear.

> Hear, her
> Clear
> Mirror,
> Care
> His error.
> In her,
> Care
> Is clear

In this reweaving we are made acutely aware, on an almost microtonal level of differences, of the degrees of the poem as a composition of words with their intervals of recurrence and as a composition of the relationship between the lover and the beloved.

The two "after" stanzas further break down the combination of words, the same twelve words, and so heighten our awareness of the degrees. The first of these two, having no punctuation, forces us to speak each word, "hearing" its own individual melody before going on to the next. Wilfrid Mellers has written of Bach's music that the density of its texture is "inseparable from the fact that each line, while making sense as an independent melody, contains harmonic implications that suggest or even create polyphony and tonal movement existing in time." What Zukofsky has done in this stanza, and what is borne out by his own reading in the NET film, is in effect to "sing" the entire row in slow motion. It is as though a fabric is being held up to the light so that the precise nature of the material, its individual parts and their combination, can be better appreciated. It is as though the fabric has been unraveled to threads which are held under a microscope where they appear as enlarged cross sections of shining microfilaments.

One by one we must sound the degrees or tones of the row. It is a sounding that quickens our sense of their individual differences—differences emphasized by the closeness of their sounds—and that quickens, in turn, our sense of their resolution or unification. The harmonic implications should be apparent. His error is redeemed only in her care, in her eyes. Her care is clear only if he perceives his error in her eyes. The tonal movement is toward clarity, resolution, to a cadenced closure of "is clear."

The final stanza adds ornamentation (arabesque) to the poem's slow movement. It does this by the addition of punctuation.

Hear
Her
Clear
Mirror
Care
His
Error in
Her
Care
Is clear

Hear
Her
Clear,
Mirror,
Care
His
Error in
Her—
Care
Is
Clear

These stanzas enact what we have learned from the consideration of song and degrees. They are exceptional in their fineness of realization. They reflect extreme technical skill which inextricably involves an extreme trust that the degrees of language and of consciousness itself, *all* the degrees of difference, can be resolved to harmony not only for the two pairs of eyes directly involved but also for ourselves whose eyes and ears are called upon to judge and to validate this valentine.

Rarely has so much been attempted with so little. In our time it has its truest parallel not in literature but in the few notes and intense "rests" of Webern. It is their extreme concision which, as Schoenberg wrote of Webern's *Six Bagatelles,* is their eloquent advocate, but it is a concision which also stands in need of advocacy. As readers who may benefit from the example of Zukofsky's skill and from his definition of love, we may satisfy this need by reconsidering the second poem in terms of those critical questions which the work proposes.

Those questions were whether fugue design could be transferred to poetry and whether, if it can, anything will be truly seen as a result. There is the further question of whether, if a circle can be made and thus "closed," there can continue to be growth. These questions can be combined with what we have found in the dialogue and play. A fugue is a process of continual growth, the many from the one, based on the principle of imitation. The identifying motion of this process is a weaving of words. The words of the second poem *do* compose such a motion, if only because they are always the same words, though differently lined and punctuated, and because their individual sounds are all so close one to the other. They *closely* approximate a chromatic scale.

Listening as we read, particularly to the last two stanzas, what we have to hear is a continuous half-step weaving with a single thread. Recurring, reflecting again and again as sounds that are almost but never quite the same sounds, these same twelve words give the effect of a circle and a rather tight one at that. Within this circle, its centermost plane suggested by the syllable-points combined to make a line, the further effect of a mirror is suggested. What the chiastic organization of the poem holds is the plane of a mirror, her eyes, which hold "Care his error." What is held as well within that plane is the solution of her care. That is, her care resides in the clarity of her eyes, themselves a mirror for the poet who must permit them to exist as such, to see, in his embrace. His image has existence only in hers.

The sincerity of the second poem is severely internal. The world of the lover and the beloved is restricted to the intimate space of their embrace. The attention to detail is focused on the weave of the same twelve words, which always must be experienced as the same, but yet different. By restricting himself to such a row, the poet forces our own reading attention to focus closely on the degrees of difference between individual words and each word's same, but still always different, recurrence. Our eyes and ears can agree in judging the poet's sincerity to be of high order because his severe restriction must result in a like severity of exposure of his technique. T. S. Eliot: the great poets show us how *bare* poetry can be.

Objectification proceeds from sincerity as an effect. If the technique of composition has been sufficiently conscious and conscientious, then it will produce rest. The reader will feel no desire for further information, further words. As there always will be further information and words, this is where the *art* of poetry enters in. This finite number of words, the same twelve words, has been so composed that we desire no more and no more of their combinations. We feel as though we know the poem's emotion as substantially as an empirical object. As Zukofsky writes in *Bottom:* "a song when heard has that sense of the *substantial* rather like the seeing of the eye."

To repeat, there are two sorts of objects. One is the poem as a composition of words, the other is the image suggested by that composition. In the second song, the two are one. The composition, modeled on fugue principle and process, suggests a mirror—per Mellers with regard to Bach's objectification through a canon in mirror inversion—. There *is* a mirror directly referred to in the text, the clear mirror of her eyes in which his error is held and clarified (clear and "cleared up"). The poem's mirror composition, as a whole structure, promotes rest insofar as it does not exceed its circle, that is, doesn't use words not present in the original row. The poem's mirror image promotes rest insofar as, going back to Paracelsus, that which faces the mirror—both the poet and ourselves—is at rest.

While the image of the poem may be said to be complex, it is clear: his error is reflected in her eyes, whose clarity resolves him back to light and sight, his own rest, so that both exist in the loving interaction of a "seeing" embrace. Pulled in by its close weaving of degrees, pulled in and held, this is what we see in the image, mirror, of the poem. We are given rest, and the circle, while undeniably closed, has also grown greater. For what we see through the hearing of Zukofsky's song is none other than his *definition of love* which, mirrorlike, also has been made to hold within itself, to hold as a bringing together, ourselves, its closely engaged readers.

Prayer is not a subject in Zukofsky's basic combination, nor is it prevalent in those that are. For example, Spinoza, in a letter to William Van Blyenbergh not quoted by the poet, writes: "I do not deny that prayers are very useful to us" and "for those who are not prepossessed by prejudices and childish superstition, it is the sole means of attaining to the highest degree of blessedness." So far as I know, these are the only prayer statements to be found in Spinoza. Going over the canon, we find only scattered references. There are several incidental ones in the Henry Adams essay (1929), and in *80 Flowers* (1978) there appear the "prayer-plant eyes" of the zinnia. Also, there are occasional references in connection with his father's death in *"A"-12,* and Celia reported in a 1978 interview that the poet's parents had a rabbi or biblical student attempt to teach him to say his prayers in Hebrew and to read the Hebrew prayer book, "but that didn't last very long either." In one of his prose pieces, *Ferdinand* (1942), we read what could be a self-portrait: "This friend had nevertheless steeped himself in English and American scholarship to a degree emulating the devotion of his parents to their religion about which he never thought." In general, Zukofsky's attitude would seem to be that of a line from his novel *Little* (1968): "fortunately a brief prayer."

The exception to this is what we have found in the Hasidic subtexts of book 12. "He Is Your Psalm" and "The Unity Of The Qualities" identify prayer with unification of the principles or qualities (degrees) and state that "the task of man" is to make them appear as a unity to the true "outer" eye. This, I think, is Zukofsky's understanding of prayer as he uses it in the NET film. Factored into his poetics, prayer is the condition of unity or objectification. Its function is, through the object effect of the image, to bring rest. If a poem has something like the effect of prayer, then what it has, or suggests, is such unity. If a poem gives us a sense of this effect, if we are so affected through its technique of composition rather than its ostensive subject matter or its author's beliefs, then it is an effective valentine and an effective prayer. If the more typical usage of prayer as entreaty has any application, it would be the working assumption or trust that a composition of words can bring such an effect *into effect* for others and for the poet. Unless this can be done, we must live our lives in a state of unrelieved need, a "life by care" which can never be given rest, however momentary.

The correlation, too, of Zukofsky's explanation in his letter to Lorine Niedecker ("the *effect* or *suggestion* is something like a mirror fugue") with his NET film comment on the "Degrees" poems ("and the effect . . . it's something like a prayer"), a correlation spanning nearly thirty years, is striking in its exactness. Prayer, in effect, is fugue, whose characteristic shape is a circle (or, modified, a valentine), the embodiment of completeness or unity which affects us as an object and thus promotes rest. Zukofsky has not been "born again" outside his experience as a weaver in composition. He has, though, introduced another term into the circle of his terms. Not surprisingly, any consideration of one must end up as a reflection of all the others.

As something of a test for what I would claim to be Zukofsky's understanding of prayer, we can put it up against what has been claimed for another poet, Wallace Stevens. While Zukofsky's original masters were

Pound and Williams, it is Stevens with whom he came to feel he had the most in common. As he states in his 1971 talk on Stevens, a talk which entwines the career of the speaker around his subject, "reading him . . . I felt that my own writing . . . was closer to his than to that of any of my contemporaries in the last half century of life we shared together."

In her critical biography of Stevens, *The Early Years: 1879–1923* (William Morrow, 1986), Joan Richardson connects Stevens with his contemporary Mina Loy and their predecessor Emily Dickinson. The language of her rationale immediately, if not completely, reminds us of Zukofsky, a further connection Richardson herself would appear to be unaware of. That is, the poets of her connection "wrested continuing possibility from the threat of conclusion" by forcing attention on the particular, by expanding instants of being, and by investing "any and every object" with the quality of sacredness. All of this, she tells us, is involved with the sounds of their words. Further: "each of their poems . . . was and is a prayer, a celebration exquisitely attenuating the lived moments." A few pages later, she links seeing each poem as a prayer with seeing each one as a "sacrament of praise." This she takes to mean that, for Stevens, the poem functions to celebrate "each moment of conscious-ness it instances." It does no harm if Richardson's claims are conflated and recomposed into one proposition: what identifies a poem as a prayer is the attenuation of consciousness.

It is not difficult to read the "Degrees" poems according to the Richard-son proposition. In fact, "exquisitely attenuating" seems a peculiarly apposite phrase for these poems and for much else in Zukofsky. To attenuate is to make thin. But it *is* difficult to imagine how poems of such complexity could keep that complexity and be made thinner still. A quick glance attests to this. But reading Zukofsky is not a glancing matter. The fourth stanza of the second poem forced us to speak each of the same twelve words in order that each is heard in its own melody and in its larger collective harmonic implications for the entire row. The point of this slow-movement stanza is to accentuate, hold up to the light, and thus heighten our sense of the degrees. Without such a sense or conscious-ness, there is little if any corresponding sense of (or need for) unification of the degrees, of objectification and rest. The fourth stanza is not the final stanza, nor is it the central mirror or plane of the poem.

Difference is ultimately of more interest than sameness. Even as there is no difficulty in reading Zukofsky according to the Richardson proposition, the different motivations of these poets in conceiving the poem as a prayer, which in itself is something of an overstatement, should be paid attention to. If Richardson's depiction of Stevens' motivation is accepted, the poem, with its emphasis upon sound and particulars, is that which seeks to forestall closure. In the terminology of Stevens' poetics, reality and imagination have been released for yet another meditation (i.e., a poem), concerning their relation and possible coordination to make a green poetry qua poetry. So long as poetry remains possible—and un-realized, an always open horizon—individual poems may continue to be written.

Zukofsky, however, is motivated by a deep need to close the circle. And he reads Stevens according to that need. Thus the statement, in his talk, about how the instant certainty of the words of a poem may bring people together is preceded by a quotation from Stevens' "Lack of Re-pose": "A few sounds of meaning, a momentary end / To the complica-tion, is good, is a good." The difference between the two poets comes down to a distinction of Aristotelian more and less. For Stevens such a momentary end is *a* good; for Zukofsky it is *the* good.

It is also the source for critical questions and for whatever distinction the work may possess as the response to those questions. Zukofsky's consciousness is not merely a technician's self-consciousness about his work considered as a job. While both poets, in the company of Dickinson and others, may conceive the poem as a prayer or as having the effect of prayer, Zukofsky's own motivating desire is that the circle not be ex-ceeded *and* that there be growth within it. The latter can be accomplished in more than one way, but all of them involve the active engagement of the reader. In these ways, whether as the reflective mirror of the second poem or as the "Precomposed" raft of stuff of *"A"* 22–23, ears and eyes are reconciled so that *love sees.* In that seeing, the poet's cause—his need to correct his error and to manifest his love, bringing rest to the beloved and to his readers—may be justified. In the figure of an embrace, as many as recognize the need for unification, having recognized the de-grees of difference, may be brought together by the poet's composition of words, but in such a way that they can see and can be seen clearly.

Allow me to let Zukofsky speak for myself. In his preface to An *"Objectivists"* Anthology (1931) and in between a phalanx of quotations from Pound that rivals my own from him, he notes, "but a critic-poet-analyst is interested in growing degrees of intelligence." It should be evident why this is so. Beyond sources, definitions, and critical questions—all of which, as they are proposed by the work, are to be taken seriously—there must be a growing awareness of the degrees, the degrees of the poem's language and of our experience in the world outside the poem, if we are to be alive or conscious at all.

The poetry of Louis Zukofsky is an incitement to such growth. As there is a growing awareness in reading it, so also is there an awareness that, for all its circular perfection, the work's own possibility for growth within its circle depends, as the justification of its cause depends, upon our own ears and eyes. Recently, literary criticism has been preoccupied with the recognition that texts are not passive creations for passive consumption. In this recognition poets are viewed as products of intertextuality, their lives lived in a context of texts (or library of Babylon). There is, in response, no denying the uneasiness that anyone may feel—trapped, grasped utterly—in reading Zukofsky. First there is bafflement with his musical conception of the image and his extreme concision, then there is incredulity and a proportionate discomfort with the realization of just how absolute his reflective symmetry is. There is the feeling, finally, of being trapped in a circle, all of whose "sides" mirror all the others.

We will remain trapped in this poetry so long as we do not read it with an attention that approximates the care of its composition. Perhaps such reading is necessary for all art of power, no less for Zukofsky than for Bach and Shakespeare. This is how, in fact, Zukofsky has read his own sources and so achieved an originality of weaving (and liberation from a predicative intertextuality). Eliot came to feel, reversing himself, that poets were sufficiently freed from Milton's reputation to approach the study of his work without danger. Zukofsky still enjoys no certain reputation, and I feel no need to reverse myself. Poetry of power is never approached without danger. What I have grown to learn in my return is that, for there to be a way out, a liberation, the circle of Zukofsky's poetry must be entered as a dwelling. In Spinoza's definition, we must dwell upon it as love dwells upon its cause. Otherwise, our attention is glancing, unheedy haste, and we remain haunted by a shadow that has not been properly picked up.

To Go Down, to Go Into

In 1974 John Wilson asked me to review George Oppen's *Seascape: Needle's Eye* for his significantly named magazine, *Occurrence.* It was then that I was confronted (confronted as I was by the need to have something to say) by Oppen's gaps. And it was a confrontation. Writers reading other writers they admire are free to move in their reading, to move like Yeats' long-legged fly upon the waters. They are looking for what have become familiar ways of writing and thinking, the admired sources of their admiration, and they are looking for what they might beg, borrow, or steal.

What they are not looking for are problems, the unfamiliar, which in turn may cause problems for their own writing and thinking. We are all anxious to praise ever-advancing progress in the career of the work, but we seem to be more certain in our praise when such work belongs to the past. Yeats, for instance. It is radically different when the work is truly contemporary. Thus it was that I found myself confronted by the appearance of gaps of space in the *Seascape* poems. I could offer several analogies for what this experience felt like, but the essential root all such analogies would share and return back to is fear. The experience was, in Melville's phrase, "a fearful thing."

If I had gone back to the beginning of the work, to *Discrete Series,* and moved forward from there, my reaction might at least have been more qualified. Having recently gone back, I have found not volumes of the familiar and then, in the later work, an abrupt departure into the unfamiliar and thus fearful-making, but rather a steady and, indeed, logical development. What this leads us to—as readers and writers in the present—is, it seems to me, the vital question. It is a question, however, which for its vitality to emerge fully requires a going back to come forward in the work.

There are no gaps in *Discrete Series*. Taking "Party on Shipboard" as representative, what we find are solid dashes of various lengths along with considerable internal punctuation. The longer dashes are at the ends of lines, the shorter ones are in the interiors.

> Wave in the round of the port-hole
> Springs, passing,—arm waved,
> Shrieks, unbalanced by the motion——
> Like the sea incapable of contact
> Save in incidents (the sea is not
>   water)
> Homogeneously automatic—a green capped
>   white is momentarily a half mile
>   out——
> The shallow surface of the sea, this,
> Numerously—the first drinks——
> The sea is a constant weight
> In its bed. They pass, however, the sea
> Freely tumultuous.

The poem begins with a lovely and functional ambiguity, the wave, which can be that of the sea or of the "arm waved" from the party. The commas are used, like alliteration in Hopkins, to spring or to project the wave. The combination of commas and dashes in the first few lines creates considerable energy. The wave is first made to stand out, almost like Francis Bacon's painting, a deliberately arrested thing, then it is juxtaposed, almost violently, with the waved arm of the party. The punctuation goes along with the words' sense. A syntax is achieved, "sense," but it is at odds with usual sentence sense, and consequently there is an imbalance. It is a deliberate imbalance readers are made to feel having been held by the commas, then held longer by the dash, then held by further commas and a longer dash after the word "motion."

In fact, the poem goes on holding until "The sea is a constant weight / In its bed." Holding is not quite accurate. What is going on in the poem is constant juxtaposition and the torsion created by juxtaposition, a matter of words and phrases put side by side with few verbs and prepositions as connectors. Their juxtaposition is accentuated, made to feel more abrupt and unavoidable by punctuation and dashes, not to forget the parenthesis, which acts as another sort of hold and as an indication of a temporary, if slight, voice modulation. Down to the sea in its bed, which is given tremendous, even portentous force by coming at the end of the poem's own discrete series, we have had to feel an ever-tightening torsion and, as a consequence, an ever-closer fusion between the sea and the party, between the physical universe and ourselves.

Without the dashes, in particular, the composition of this sentence would lack force. The sea would not be felt to be a constant weight, and the linkage between the sea and ourselves would not be felt to hold. In addition, the final lines of the poem—"they pass, however, the sea / Freely tumultuous"—would not be given the almost giddy and fate-attracting quality which they surely have if it were not for the dashes. The dashes function as guy wires in tubular sculpture, the wires holding the poems' sentences together by virtue of the tension established between the jointed parts or sections. The dashes establish a spine, however imbalanced, of tension. It holds the poem together, and it gives the poem power, which is all the greater as it is never fully released. The final lines of "Party on Shipboard" are laconic, almost prosaic, and one feels the certainty of the approaching event of shipwreck.

The dashes are still there when we come, after that much-discussed gap in time, to *The Materials*. There are fewer of them, there tend to be no commas in combination with them, and they are all of a uniform length. I will take the second section of "Blood From The Stone" as an example, specifically the third stanza of this section.

> As thirty in a group—
> To Home Relief—the unemployed—
> Within the city's intricacies
> Are these lives. Belief?
> What do we believe
> To live with? Answer.
> Not invent—just answer—all
> That verse attempts.
> That we can somehow add each to each other?
>
> —Still our lives.

The dashes make us feel the isolation of the group, almost their alienation from any sort of group, even though they themselves are just that, a group brought arbitrarily together by chance and imposed necessity. It is the failure of other groups—family, neighborhood, even friends—which has led them to join or rather to be joined with this group, which is the group of the isolated, the unemployed, those who could not find a place within the city's intricacies. The three dashes of the first two lines so break up and truncate the syntax that we are forced to realize the apartness of these people who are a group only insofar as they are apart. Like the party on shipboard, they are "incapable of contact / Save in incidents." We come to realize that not only are they apart at a particular moment in history, the thirties, but also that their lives may always be so.

And we are led to wonder about our own lives, the chance of being employed, being part of something larger than ourselves, the city. If things had been only very slightly different, perhaps we too would be members of this nongroup. And there is a suspicion that, ultimately, perhaps we are. There is a suspicion that the only group or collective identity we may truly share is that "of being numerous"; that whatever larger or unisolate identity we may feel is the product of incidents, those of history and of the physical universe, both of which are seemingly outside our control and which are almost always calamitous as their energy, experienced in terms of mass, impinges upon us.

Given this, it is not surprising that what follows in the poem so insistently questions belief and social belief in particular. The poem, verse generally, is the attempt to answer those questions. Here, too, dashes enter in. They are first used, almost conventionally, in a pair to set off and give emphasis to "just answer," as opposed to inventing yet another theory of self and society, yet another sociology textbook. The restated question is whether, as a group, we can be anything more than merely numerous.

The last line of the section uses a dash with a difference, namely, at the beginning of the line. So far as I know, this is the first such usage of the dash in Oppen's poetry. It does not separate units off from a larger syntactic flow; it does not slow down the rate of that flow as does, for example, a dash at the end of a line. What it does do is act as an "anticipatory" rest in music. It gives greater gravity, literally weight, to what follows: "Still our lives." What is given weight by this pause of anticipation is the fact that, whether we believe we have any sort of answer to the question of the possibility of society or not, we still must live out our lives. Positive or negative, they are all we have.

"The Undertaking in New Jersey," another poem from *The Materials,* is of interest if only because it contains both a dash and an ellipsis, the single such combination in the book.

> The bird's voice in their streets
> May not mean much: a bird the age of a child chirping
> At curbs and curb gratings,
> At barber shops and townsmen
> Born of girls—
> Of girls! Girls gave birth . . . But the interiors
> Are the women's: curtained,
> Lit, the fabric
> To which the men return.

The dash gives emphasis to the speaker's wonder, a combination of sympathy and perhaps incredulity that girls, who may be taken no more seriously than the bird's voice in their streets, are nonetheless responsible for the existence of the supposedly graver, at least graver-sounding, "townsmen." The ellipsis functions similarly, but not identically. It is a pause, produces a pause, but it is a pause to indicate the process of birth itself, a process by which girls become the mothers of townsmen. It also provides time to consider that process, which results in the grave-sounding townsmen who now exercise what "town authority" there is. What follows, the interiors, suggests that the town exterior has been taken over by the men who, in their role as townsmen, may treat women, girls and mothers, as meaningless bird voices.

Dashes and ellipses occur in the middle and at the end of lines in the *This In Which* poems. In "Street," both occur at the end of lines. This raises the question of why two different marks should be used to do the same thing. But of course they only appear to do the same thing. Both marks are holds, enforced pauses or hesitations, which may also serve as connective devices between blocks of language, but their "quality" is different. The dash is one smooth, uniform gesture. The ellipsis is that same gesture given graduation. It is like the high-contrast photograph on slick paper and the same photograph reproduced on newsprint, all the dots of the reproduction process standing out. The ellipsis gives grain or texture to the blankness of the dash.

In "Street," for example, the dash at the end of the second line emphasizes further the comma pause of the first line and makes more finally emphatic the end-stopped "Bergen street" that follows. Coming immediately after is an ellipsis, which also follows a comma pause.

> Humiliation,
> Hardship . . .
> Nor are they very good to each other;
> It is not that.

The ellipsis invites us to consider other conditions that might accrue to the poor—homelessness, perhaps. This invitation and the physically different look of the ellipsis slow down our reading, giving weight, density, "materiality" to our pausing. This is especially so at the end of poems. Here we are not pausing between lines, but between poems. We pause and more than pause between "Street" and "Carpenter's Boat." We reflect at length on the prospective unhappiness of the righteous little girls among the poor who expect to be so good and who will find that goodness may be a luxury they can't afford, reflecting on the collision between ethics and conditions, on how conditions may render any notion of ethical choice nonexistent if not slightly ridiculous. Still reflecting, for this applies not simply to poor little girls of our own time, we turn to "Carpenter's Boat" and to "how wild the planet is."

The ellipsis, as used by Oppen, does not vary from the dash in terms of grammatical function. Both are marks for division and separation. Both are holds, deliberate hesitations. The ellipsis differs from the dash in its suggestion of graduation or process. It notates and gives material definition to those periods of duration between words and lines. It gives weight and density to silence. At the end of the poem, it encourages us to reflection, in the process of which we turn the page to be confronted with another moment of vision, one more picture in the continuing larger serial picture.

In *Of Being Numerous* there continue to be combinations of dashes and ellipses. Rather than elaborate a taxonomy of their functions, which remain largely unchanged from those in the earlier work, I will take a single example of each, examples which are new in their usage and implication. No. 29 of the title poem contains two ellipses, one coming immediately after the other.

> And in the sudden vacuum
> Of time . . .
>
> . . . is it not
> In fear the roots grip

The poem begins with a question of what the poet can say of living, as an apology or excuse, to his daughter. The term "happiness" comes up and is dismissed as unsatisfactory. There is an attempt at some sort of group—family or society generally—assurance that the poet tells himself "only what we all believe" to be true. What the poet says is what we all believe. It is not merely personal. This, of course, is rhetoric. *Someone* is presuming to speak the belief of the group, the numerous.

The presumption, which I am inclined to accept, is of a darker, starker version of Williams' "Spring and All." There, despite a constant cold wind, "they"—bushes, small trees, and persons—grip down and begin to awaken. They have a certain dignity of entrance. Williams is oddly distanced, essentially an observer on his way to the contagious hospital. He is at least more distanced than Oppen, who obviously includes himself in "The baffling hierarchies / Of father and child." Those hierarchies *are* baffling, and they are nevertheless not enough to protect us from either Williams' cold wind or this other, more frightening thing: time, "from open / Time."

The first ellipsis can be read as illustrating almost a kind of onomatopoeia, the sudden vacuum of time. The ellipsis, read in its most conventional sense, means something has been taken out, something was once there but is no more except for these ghost dots. What further takes the something out, increasing our awareness of its taking, is the second ellipsis. All the uses are active—division, separation, hold, hesitation, graduation, process, weight, density—and all are further activated by the meaning of the word "vacuum." This second ellipsis reminds us of the dash at the beginning of a line in "Blood From The Stone." Like that dash, the ellipsis is anticipatory, but it immediately follows another ellipsis so that all the uses, their effect, is doubled. A sudden vacuum is made to occur in the poem, and the openness of time is given actuality of definition.

These ellipses effectively give definition to the almost-undefinable, open time, and project, as a kind of tension, its threatening mass. This is paralleled by the ellipsis at the beginning and end of a single line in "Power, The Enchanted World" and by the dashes in the same positions for a line in "Ballad." While the front-and-back balancing is relatively new, the function remains the same. Both marks are there to divide and hold, to graduate and give weight, to define and project. Besides the immediate focus of any moment (e.g., vacuum), there is a larger purpose in Oppen's usage of these marks.

This goes back to imagism. As Williams points out in his *Autobiography,* imagism lacked measure. As Oppen points out in his interview with L. S. Dembo, he learned from Zukofsky the need—coming after the imagist position—for forming a poem properly. Previously, I have said the dashes in Oppen's poetry operate as so many guy wires holding it together by way of tension. What I would now say is that both dashes and ellipses act to establish form or structure—what Zukofsky would call objectification or rested totality—by way of tension. What is distinctive about Oppen's practice is that it is a structure which is so composed as to contain—almost preserve—all that which is most threatening, the openness of time, the abrading grain of silence. This practice distinguishes Oppen not only from Zukofsky but also from the fragmentations of Pound and Eliot. It is what keeps Oppen contemporary and not merely modern.

If, as I've suggested, there is a logical development in the work, it is one which escaped me when I was originally confronted by the gaps in *Seascape.* My reaction then was fear made more fearful by a presumption of familiarity with what came before that book. My reaction might have been less extreme had I presumed less and paid more attention to what was on the page.

Granted the relatively sudden and predominant appearance of gaps in the *Seascape* poems, they still also contain, as do those in the *Myth Of The Blaze* section of the *Collected Poems,* dashes and ellipses. These marks, however, are now used in even more special ways. For example, the conventional number of three dots has been done away with. Now, further emphasizing the grain and relative duration of silence, there may be two dots ("West") or four ("The Little Pin"). Similarly, there is a dash at the beginning of a line ("Anniversary Poem"), and there is an internal dash ("The Speech At Soli"). All of these examples are qualified by gaps. In "West," the line reads ". . . sea [gap] from which . ." In "The Speech At Soli," the line reads "blazing sun of the farms—[gap] return."

In both instances, it is as though the mark is leading to, is a kind of graduation to, what has to be felt as the more silent silence of the gaps. In Bergman's movie *The Silence*, a small fan runs throughout the scenes with the blond translator sister, literally underscoring the silence and isolation of her life when she's confined to bed in the chilly, silent hotel room. It would not be incorrect to say that we *feel* the silence in these scenes. With Oppen's poetry, it is as though these dashes and ellipses lead us to a condition of further, deeper silence in which the fan itself has been removed.

I think this silence is surprising, if not exactly fearful. In fact, reading from and back to *Seascape* intensifies the surprise. It is as though we had gone through a process whereby our hearing becomes more and more acute, only to reach a point at which there's nothing further to hear. Or perhaps there's nothing other to hear than that which we have heretofore been avoiding, not the "sound of silence," but the sound of a wild planet—physical or spiritual—that silence suddenly makes audible and even, we may feel, inescapable. What I want to consider is why it should be done and what, in the terms of what I've previously called the vital question, it leads us to as readers and writers in the present.

Allow me to rephrase my consideration by way of language from Paul Celan's essay "Conversation in the Mountains" (1959): "and the silence no silence at all. No word has come to an end and no phrase, it is nothing but a pause, an empty space between the words, a blank—you see all the syllables stand around waiting." The question is whether this steady development toward gaps, a development which culminates in the *Primitive* poems, where *only* gaps—no dashes, no ellipses—appear, is toward "actual" silence or a pause, an empty space for rhythmic and rhetorical purposes as we find, for instance, in the poetry of Marina Tsvetayeva. This is a question about how to read gaps or what has apparently been deliberately left out. To answer it, I turn from the poems to Oppen's *Daybook*, to use the title now given to those pages of jottings and notes in the collection of the Archive for New Poetry, University of California at San Diego.

Readily enough, we find references to gaps in these pages. In fact, the following appear among the very first entries in a sample selection recently published by Cynthia Anderson under the title *"Meaning Is To Be Here."*

> That man, the space of the mind, is a flaw, a
> gap   a besieged and doomed
> sanctuary which is able to hold *everything* at arm's length—
>
> I am far from believing that it does not exist. I believe
> that it exists, that it cannot be understood, that that
> fact is lethal, and that there can be no help for us
>
> the most violent who cannot be appeased, who smash that
> empty bubble of the mind against the absolute solidity
> of being.
>
> The flaw the gap which is aware of being, tho it is
> within it. The flaw on which being presses.
>
> If we are able to imagine ourselves outside, we see
> that it was our home.

A gap is a flaw, is the space of the mind, is somehow the essential thing about persons, the essential human thing. It is a besieged and doomed sanctuary on which being presses, and it is our home.

A gap is a flaw as it disturbs, disrupts the syntax of a line or the overall pattern of anything. We are nearly desperate in our drive to perceive the world in terms of wholes, coherent patterns. Oppen goes against that drive or rather qualifies its basis. The motivating agent for our rage for order can only be the mind which itself, as consciousness, is the break in the chain and other patterns of being. The mind may be distressed by this, try to reduce or abridge it, and yet it is doomed by the opposing weight, the absolute solidity of being (felt as the sea in its bed or open time) which bears down upon it as upon a bubble.

We might suppose that this would lead Oppen to compose poems which are as airtight as possible, as *flawless* as Williams' yachts. As we know, however, this is not the case. The development in the poetry is toward a greater and even exclusive use of gaps. In one of the *Daybook* entries, Oppen faults William Bronk for not permitting any gaps to exist within the statement of his poetry, gaps which he further identifies in this entry as "gifts." Oppen's understanding of gaps is not simple. For while gaps are linked with the mind, with the space-making faculty of consciousness and thus with that which we believe to be most essentially human, they are also flaws in the larger poem as perhaps we ourselves are in the larger scheme of things. Not devolution, but "deruption." As those in small or large boats must learn to live with the sea if they are to stay out on it and stay alive, we must so live in the world, in the world of being, which eventually overtakes us whether by "acts of God" or by the remorselessness of open time itself. It is curious, then, that Oppen should refer to gaps as gifts and that he should turn to them more and more often in the development of his poetry.

Oppen's understanding, his use and conception behind that use of gaps, is not simple. It is perhaps even less so than what we find in Celan, who refers to a pause, an empty space, an unreal or merely temporary silence and who—one year later in his "Meridian" speech—makes a passing reference to a pause for breath in which hope and thought take place. Both "references" are present in Oppen. While we have begun with the dark sense of gaps as indicators of a besieged and doomed sanctuary, there are other senses. These come in with space. I take gaps to be Oppen's signs for the space of the mind, the space made by the mind, the space made by the mind for itself.

Such a space allows for consciousness, the construction of a protection—however doomed—from the constant assault of being, the motion of which is characterized by the constant weight of the sea. Now the supreme product of consciousness is language. Yet the purpose of the gaps cannot be to generate an ever-accelerating proliferation of language. They go all the other way. That is, the space of the gaps is necessarily associated with silence.

In the *Daybook* entries assembled by Bradley Westbrook under the title "Series Two: Notes, Jottings, Etc.," there are a number of references to silence. We read, for instance, that Oppen's intention—"as nearly as possible"—was the creation of silence in *Discrete Series*; that the first book was done as an effort to have art efface itself so as to permit things to shine forth on their own. This, however, changes. He comes to resign himself to coming on stage, to talking. The basis of his resignation is the conviction that silence is nothing and is, in itself, literally nothing. Yet it is in the condition of silence that the poem begins. What this condition gives us is wonder, the inexpressible. The notes and jottings make it clear that Oppen thought of the creation of space, gaps, in the poem as a means of establishing silence. "When space is not silence, the matrix of silence, it is chatter, noise." The desired condition is obviously not chatter. It is not desired because it gets in the way of vision. To quote from the *Daybook* entries collected by Cynthia Anderson with regard to the *Primitive* poems, "the world stops in silence but is illuminated" and "temporary pauses, stops—moments of vision." Without gaps there is no space, without space there is no silence, without silence there is no vision. Or, to borrow one of Thelonious Monk's titles, there are no brilliant corners.

When silence enters the poem, there may be vision, moments of vision, brilliant corners. These moments are illuminated as the opacity of words—what Celan refers to as veils—is removed. There is no more opacity, there is no more chatter. What we see with illuminated clarity is our world, which for Oppen is dominated by the elements ("weather-swept") and for whom the single predominating factor is the sea. The sea has several moods in Oppen, but the moments of vision tend to reveal it as primarily a huge force or form of energy which—like its abstract correlative, open time—is never less than threatening. Their revelations are not unlike what Pip encounters in *Moby-Dick,* the unwarped primal world, the heartless, ever-juvenile eternities. Or as Ishmael himself puts it: "To grope down into the bottom of the sea . . . to have one's hands among the unspeakable foundations, ribs, and very pelvis of this world; this is a fearful thing."

This *is* a fearful thing, and yet this is what Oppen has deliberately, with an astonishing deliberation, set out to do. As he writes in one of the *Daybook* entries, "the undertaking of the poems (and of all I have done . . .) / To go *down,* to go *into.*" The conventional associations of those words are religious. Such associations are not relevant for this poet. When one goes down and into with Oppen, as with Melville, what one encounters is not the radiant rose of certain faith but darkness and turbulence, where the only certainty is uncertainty. It is in reaction to what we encounter in the "light" of the gaps that the poet urges us to summon our powers. Indeed, "One had not thought / To be afraid / Not of shadow but of light."

If George Oppen is a religious poet, he is surely an unconventional, an uncertain or errant one. He himself understood this in terms of motion. The poems are kept in motion by the gaps and lack of end punctuation. They are not allowed to come to rest, the typical aspiration of religious or devotional poetry. Reading them, we are subjected to a constant going down and going into. The process, a constant encounter with uncertainty, is never over, never allowed to come to rest.

Certain facets of Oppen's thought are reminiscent of Simone Weil, whose *Waiting For God* is quoted in *Seascape.* What these facets remind me of, however, are two sections from her notebooks published under the title *Gravity and Grace*—"Decreation" and "Self-Effacement." Creation, in Weil's understanding, is a perpetual act of love. Our existence is God's love for us, but God can only love himself. This love is manifested (for himself) through us. "Thus, he who gives us our being loves in us the acceptance of not being." For Weil the desirable attitude becomes one of self-effacement, whereby the decreating person can give God's being back to him. Her wish, which is close to Oppen, is to disappear "in order that those things that I see may become perfect in their beauty from the very fact that they are no longer things that I see." Or: "to see a landscape as it is when I am not there."

Weil's desire is to be taken up, assumed into the Godhead. This is where she and Oppen part company. Weil does not hesitate to pronounce the condition of our existence an affliction. She takes that condition as indication of God's love. Her decreation and effacement of self, though, are based on the possibility—however grim it may strike us (like certain passages in Messiaen)—of grace.

Oppen is anxious to leave the world as it is. This is one of the consistent preoccupations running throughout his work. And it is out of this preoccupation that he comes to silence: first with dashes, then ellipses, and finally gaps of white space. These are all devices, signs for silence in which the world is stopped and illuminated, in which there can be moments of vision. They are provided, almost as inducements, to go down, to go into. When we do so, however, we do not come upon radiant petals of a radiant rose. It is, instead, a wild planet, characterized by the constant weight of the sea and the openness of time. To use two of Oppen's favorite figures, it is the tyger and it is the leviathan we come upon in the silence of these gaps. As both Blake and Melville were aware, the sublime contains and elicits both wonder and terror. Or from "To Make Much,"

> . . . and it seemed so beautiful so beautiful
> the sun-lit air it was no dream all's wild
> out there. . . .

The moments of silence and vision elicit wonder and terror. We stop the chatter to hear what is always there to be heard, the "ground" under everything else. In one of the series 2 *Daybook* entries, Oppen notes that words flow continuously through the mind. What they provide in their flow is not hope but opacity. They shield us, veil us from the world. There are those who would recognize all of this and argue for the nonstop use of words. One thinks of Stevens and Ashbery, of Antin and Silliman. It may be that they have heard and seen, and that, as a result, they are determined to keep moving—sticking and sliding—with language as the vehicle of their incessant surface motion.

In contrast, Oppen chooses with a development of steady deliberation to stop language, to take away its shielding and veiling in order to keep going down and into. This *is* a fearful thing. Not only is it fearful to go down into the unspeakable foundations of being, there is also the danger of the mind creating its own, exclusive solipsistic space. Left to itself, in its own exclusive space, "mind / will burn the world down." By the use of gaps Oppen provides a sanctuary space for the mind against the constant weight of being. They make some room, as he writes in the *Daybook,* for us among all the subatomic particles. Room is made for us, the mind freed momentarily from distraction, only for there to be a keener realization of just where it is we find ourselves: a world where "all's wild." I have said Oppen's use and conception of gaps is not simple. The opposition of sanctuary and of clarified terror, one not more primary than the other, is responsible for this. With reference to his criticism of William Bronk's noticeably Ahabian poetry, Oppen's gaps are, indeed, peculiar "gifts."

I think, however, we do well to recognize them as gifts. They do provide us with temporary pauses, which make a counterpoint of silence against the opacity of words, the poem's words, a counterpoint against the pull of the poem's syntax. The gaps are gifts of silence in which we may go down, may go into the unspeakable foundations. The generosity of Oppen's gaps, a generosity that increases in time, is remarkable. Alive as they are to several often-antagonistic possibilities and anxious to bring some sort of order to their composition, most poets attempt to seal off possible contradictions, to focus intensely within a fairly narrow range and only within that range.

George Oppen is at least as aware as others of the possibilities in composition and at least as anxious to bring whatever coherence he can to his poems. The emphasis on construction, on materials and their proper use, is unremitting in the work. And that emphasis throws the importance of the gaps into relief. The gaps are not casual gestures of artistic freedom. Oppen has no use for such gestures. The gaps represent what he came to feel, going against all his interest in construction, was absolutely necessary. The gaps are there as so many effacements of self and of construction. They are there to remind us of the silent ground out of and within which words exist. They are there so that the mind does not trick itself into believing, Ahab-like, that it can take on the world in direct confrontation.

The gaps encourage us to find our own minds, to do our own going down and into. There are two dangers in this: direct encounter with the wildness of the world and a kind of "rapture of the depths." Not only can we be terrified, like Melville's Pip, to the point of madness by such encounters, we can also become enraptured so that, oblivious to everything else, mind does in effect burn the world down.

These are the dangers of depth, of depth-seeking. Perhaps because we are only too aware of those dangers, dangers which seem to go hand in hand with an earnestness that is considered extreme and suspicious in its extremity, we have increasingly opted for an art of surface. I am thinking of a painter such as Frank Stella, of such painters as Barnett Newman and Mark Rothko. As much as I may prefer the latter to the former, I can only concur with an observation made early on in Stella's Norton lectures, which have been published under the title *Working Space:* "the aim of art is to create space—space that is not compromised by decoration or illustration." And: "great painting creates space and spreads the light."

George Oppen does, I think, deliberately create space in his poetry and with a minimum of decoration or illustration, what he would call chatter and commentary. Yet the light in the space of his poetry is not to be glibly taken as an automatically "positive" medium. At a later point in his lectures Stella remarks that the most obvious and difficult truth the artist reveals is that the viewer is after the fact. "The viewer is shut out for an instant in order to receive the surprise of participation without consequence." We can acknowledge the application of Stella's truth and, at the same time, acknowledge just how limited, in the case of George Oppen's poetry, that application must be. All readers, whether they are also writers or artists, come after the fact of composition. *Reading is secondary.* Reading the work of another, we are never better than second. Where the application ceases or must be highly qualified is indicated by the gaps, these zones of white space on the page, these zones of silence. They are the gifts which may be missing in William Bronk, but which are more and more prevalent in the development of Oppen's work.

The gaps encourage our participation in the work and in its vision. A by-product is an experience of depth. If we did not sense this in reading Oppen, then the gaps would be nothing more than Celan's blanks. They are more than blanks, and we do go down and into. As we do this, we experience a sense of depth. Not only does our experience suggest an enlarging space, it also suggests an enlargement of meaning. We are familiar with Oppen's insistence on the valuation of the little words, on the commonalities of nature and their nouns. What may be less familiar is how that insistence is coupled with an equally insistent drive to get to the ground of being for those things.

The gaps exist in the poems as opportunities to explore that ground. I don't mean to sound overly optimistic. The poet's generosity is not in question. He has an exact—and thus not mawkish or sentimental—regard for the disregarded, for common and often-overlooked details of the natural and social landscape. I don't mean to sound overly optimistic because it would be out of keeping with George Oppen's vision. We go down in the gaps of the poems, and we encounter moments of vision which in their illumination reveal a world where all's wild. If we do go down, if we do consciously participate in the gaps, that motion of participation has to alter how we view the world and ourselves. The poems are not changed, but we are. These gaps or gifts are consequential. They could hardly be more consequential.

To be earnest, to try, to seek depth earnestly is not now in fashion and, in fact, may always be under suspicion, suspected of heresy by those enlisted to dogma, suspected of pretentiousness by those who would classify poetry and the arts generally as entertainment, suspected not least by those who feel, however vaguely, that they have reason to fear what such an effort might entail. Not all these suspicions are without merit. But, unassuming and even hesitant as his poems appear to be, Oppen is intransigent. He is in earnest, he will try to go down and go into.

I know of no finer love poem than "Anniversary Poem." Part of its fineness is its resoluteness: "To find now depth, not time, since we cannot, but depth." A painter such as Rothko would have concurred with such an ambition and would not have scrupled to identify it as religious. Despite the existence of moments of vision encountered by way of the gaps, despite the existence of a whole vision in the poetry almost from the very beginning in *Discrete Series,* Oppen's poetry is not religious. It does not come to rest. The poetry and the poet are intransigent. This is a fearful thing. What happens to Pip—in the depths and bobbing on the surface of a ringed horizon—*is* a possibility. We have to remind ourselves, in a time of surface agitation—a time which, I fear, may be only an agitation of surface by so many long-legged flies—just how different this is from either Ishmael or his author who, in the retirement of his last years, would caution, like Captain Vere, about the advisability of going along with the measured, conventional forms of life.

It is this refusal to settle down, to come to an accommodation with what he saw in his poetry's moments of vision, which gives us a clue as to what our own role might be. I have spoken about how the use of gaps promotes participation. As readers, we are more and more frequently being asked not only to bridge the gaps—to get from one boundary of syntax to another—but also to enter, to go down and into the ever-deepening and enlarging space of the gaps.

In "Till Other Voices Wake Us," the final poem in *Primitive,* the need for our participation is made explicit. The poet remembers when, as an adolescent, he and his father had stared at monuments "as tho we treaded / water stony / waters of the monuments." They had turned from the monuments before they might grow tired "and so drown." This memory is then connected with another, that of writing *Discrete Series.* The later memory is concerned with the idea of series. The importance of this is that, according to one of the series 2 *Daybook* entries, it is the serial poem which permits the use of space and of silence. Thus we experience the poem "as opening, an opening, which is to say it is music." In "Till Other Voices Wake Us," space and silence having been created, the lights as an all-powerful music—the lights emanating from events set free by the poet's deliberate effacement—enter us.

This is the condition of rapture. It is a condition produced by the poet's own mode of composition. We should recognize that *all* of Oppen's poetry is serial in nature. All of it is concerned with the creation of space and silence. All of it is concerned with going down into that space and silence to find depth. Concentrated with such concern over the years, the poet can no longer flee and, frankly, is in danger of drowning in the light or music of his own vision.

This is where our active participation enters in and where, contrary to Frank Stella and also to Eliot—who, in the last line of "Prufrock," has us abruptly drowning because we've been wakened from a mermaid fantasy by human voices—it has consequence, actual as not simple nor simply optimistic consequence. We are the other voices. Participating, going down into the gaps of space and silence in George Oppen's poetry, we are given gifts of momentary vision which, however wild the world that is revealed, are experienced as a kind of light and as an enlargement of depth. Despite the poet's desire that we experience what he has experienced, there is an unavoidable divergence. We miss the point, we notice different aspects, we ask questions which are perhaps not the right questions, we are "other."

We will not benefit from the poet's gifts nor will we be of use to the poet unless we are those other voices. And neither our voices nor our otherness will matter unless we get beneath the surface, not a lingering in mermaid fantasy, but an active—different, questioning, "other"—"groping / down a going down." Nothing will matter unless we cease lingering, unless we cease moving like long-legged flies upon the waters. This is a fearful thing. Yet it has consequence: it prevents the poet, the poet's work from drowning in itself. It helps keep the work and ourselves from drowning either in a sea of being or of enraptured self-consciousness. It provides the only sort of group, the only sort of society in which we are likely to have more than incidental contact.

Works Cited

Some versions of the cited titles have been superseded by later or more inclusive editions. When only one such "reversion" has taken place, both titles will be given in one entry. When more than one has taken place, for example, a "collected works," the most current/inclusive edition will be given first, followed by individual entries for earlier titles. Only those earlier titles are cited that were used in the writing of the essays.

Ahearn, Barry, ed. *Pound/Zukofsky: Selected Letters of Ezra Pound and Louis Zukofsky.* New York: New Directions, 1987.

Andrews, Bruce. *Film Noir.* Providence: Burning Deck, 1978. Reprinted as part of *Getting Ready to Have Been Frightened.* New York: Roof Books, 1988.

Aquinas, Thomas. *Commentary on the Nicomachian Ethics.* 2 vols. Trans. C. I. Litzinger. Chicago: Henry Regnery, 1961.

Aristotle. *The Basic Works of Aristotle.* Ed. Richard McKeon. New York: Random House, 1941.

Ashbery, John, and Elliott Carter. *Syringa.* CRI SD 469q, 1982.

Booth, Marcella. "The Zukofsky Papers: The Cadence of a Life." In *Louis Zukofsky: Man and Poet,* ed. Carroll F. Terrell. Orono, Maine: National Poetry Foundation, 1979.

Bronk, William. *The Empty Hands.* New Rochelle, N.Y.: Elizabeth Press, 1969.

———. *Finding Losses.* New Rochelle, N.Y.: Elizabeth Press, 1976.

———. *Life Supports: New and Collected Poems.* San Francisco: North Point Press, 1982.

———. *Light and Dark.* Ashland, Mass.: Origin Press, 1956. An unrevised second edition of this volume was published by the Elizabeth Press in 1975.

———. *The Meantime.* New Rochelle, N.Y.: Elizabeth Press, 1976.

―――. *My Father Photographed with Friends and Other Pictures.* New Rochelle, N.Y.: Elizabeth Press, 1976.

―――. *Silence and Metaphor.* New Rochelle, N.Y.: Elizabeth Press, 1975.

―――. *That Tantalus.* New Rochelle, N.Y.: Elizabeth Press, 1971.

―――. *To Praise the Music.* New Rochelle, N.Y.: Elizabeth Press, 1972.

―――. *The World, The Worldless.* New York: New Directions, 1964.

Buber, Martin. *Ten Rungs: Hasidic Sayings.* New York: Shocken Books, 1978.

Canetti, Elias. *The Conscience of Words.* Trans. Joachim Neugroschel. New York: Seabury Press, 1979.

Celan, Paul. "Conversation in the Mountains." In *Collected Prose.* Trans. Rosmarie Waldrop. Manchester, Eng.: Carcanet, 1986.

―――. "The Meridian." Trans. Jerry Glen. *Chicago Review* 29, no. 3 (1978).

Coleman, Ornette. *The Shape of Jazz to Come.* Atlantic 1317, n.d.

Coltrane, John. *Crescent.* Impulse Stereo A-66, 1964.

Copland, Aaron. *Twelve Poems of Emily Dickinson.* Adele Addison, soprano, with piano accompaniment by the composer. CBS Masterworks 32 11 0018, 1967.

Cox, Kenneth. "The Poetry of Louis Zukofsky: '*A.'*" *Agenda,* double issue: vol. 9, no. 4, and vol. 10, no. 1 (1971–72).

Dembo, L. S. "The 'Objectivist' Poet: Four Interviews." *Contemporary Literature* 10, no. 2 (Spring 1969).

Duncan, Robert. *Derivations: Selected Poems, 1950–1956.* London: Fulcrum Press, 1968.

―――. *The Truth & Life of Myth: An Essay in Essential Autobiography.* Fremont, Mich.: Sumac Press, 1968. Reprinted in *Fictive Certainties: Essays by Robert Duncan.* New York: New Directions, 1985.

Enslin, Theodore. *Forms.* 5 vols. New Rochelle, N.Y.: Elizabeth Press, 1970.

―――. *Ranger.* 2 vols. Berkeley: North Atlantic Books, 1978.

―――. *The Weather Within.* Orono, Maine: Land-locked Press, 1985. Reprint. Milwaukee: Membrane Press, 1986.

Faranda, Lisa Pater. *"Between Your House and Mine": The Letters of Lorine Niedecker to Cid Corman, 1960 to 1970.* Durham: Duke University Press, 1986.

Fiedler, Leslie. *No! In Thunder.* Boston: Beacon Press, 1960.

Forster, K., and P. Boyde. *Dante's Lyric Poetry.* Oxford: Clarendon Press, 1967.

Frye, Northrop. "The Realistic Oriole: A Study of Wallace Stevens." In *Wallace Stevens: A Collection of Critical Essays,* ed. Marie Borroff. Englewood Cliffs, N.J.: Prentice-Hall, 1963.

Gilbert, Sandra M., and Susan Gubar. *The Madwoman in the Attic: The Woman Writer and the Nineteenth Century Literary Imagination.* New Haven: Yale University Press, 1979.

Gordon, Lyndall. *Eliot's Early Years.* New York: Oxford University Press, 1977.

Heidegger, Martin. "Language." In *Poetry, Language, Thought.* Trans. Alfred Hofstadter. New York: Harper and Row, 1975.

Howe, Susan. *Defenestration of Prague.* New York: Kulchur Foundation, 1983. Reprinted as part of *Europe of Trusts.* Los Angeles: Sun & Moon Press, 1990.

———. *My Emily Dickinson.* Berkeley, Calif.: North Atlantic Books, 1985.

———. *Pythagorean Silence.* New York: Montemora Foundation, 1982. Reprinted as part of *Europe of Trusts.* Los Angeles: Sun & Moon Press, 1990.

Klee, Paul. *The Thinking Eye.* Ed. Jürg Spiller. New York: Wittenborn, 1961.

Lévi-Strauss, Claude. *The Raw and the Cooked: Introduction to a Science of Mythology.* Trans. John Weightman and Doreen Weightman. New York: Harper and Row, 1969.

MacCaffrey, Isabel G. *Spenser's Allegory: The Anatomy of Imagination.* Princeton: Princeton University Press, 1976.

Mellers, Wilfrid. *Bach and the Dance of God.* New York: Oxford University Press, 1981.

Melville, Herman. "Hawthorne and His Mosses." In *Hawthorne: The Critical Heritage,* ed. J. Donald Crowley. New York: Barnes and Noble, 1970.

———. *Moby-Dick; or, The Whale.* Berkeley: University of California Press, 1981.

———. *Pierre; or, The Ambiguities.* Evanston, Ill.: Northwestern University Press and the Newberry Library, 1971.

Olson, Charles. "A Bibliography on America for Ed Dorn." In *Additional Prose,* ed. George F. Butterick. Bolinas, Calif.: Four Seasons Foundation, 1974.

———. *Call Me Ishmael: A Study of Melville.* San Francisco: City Lights Books, n.d.

———. *Causal Mythology.* Bolinas, Calif.: Four Seasons Foundation, 1969.

———. "David Young, David Old." In *Human Universe and Other Essays,* ed. Donald Allen. New York: Grove Press, 1967.

———. "Equal, That Is, to the Real Itself." In *Human Universe.* New York: Grove Press, 1967.

———. "In Adullam's Lair." *Archetypes,* no. 1 (1975).

———. "In Cold Hell, In Thicket." In *The Distances.* New York: Grove Press, 1960. Reprinted as part of *The Collected Poetry of Charles Olson,* ed. George Butterick. Berkeley: University of California Press, 1987.

———. "The Materials and Weights of Herman Melville." In *Human Universe.* New York: Grove Press, 1967.

———. "Projective Verse." In *Selected Writings,* ed. Robert Creeley. New York: New Directions, 1966.

———. *Poetry and Truth: The Beloit Lectures and Poems.* Ed. George F. Butterick. San Francisco: Four Seasons Foundation, 1971.

———. "Reading at Berkeley." In *Muthologos: The Collected Lectures and Interviews,* vol. 1, ed. George F. Butterick. Bolinas, Calif.: Four Seasons Foundation, 1978.

Oppen, George. *The Collected Poems of George Oppen.* New York: New Directions, 1975.

———. *Discrete Series.* Cleveland: Asphodel Bookshop, 1966. This is a reprint of the 1934 Objectivist Press edition.

———. *The Materials.* New York: New Directions, 1962.

———. " '*Meaning Is to Be Here*': A Selection from the Daybook." Ed. Cynthia Anderson. *Conjunctions: Bi-Annual Volumes of New Writing,* no. 10 (1987).

———. *Of Being Numerous.* New York: New Directions, 1968.

———. *Primitive.* Santa Barbara, Calif.: Black Sparrow Press, 1978.

———. *Seascape: Needle's Eye.* Fremont, Mich.: Sumac Press, 1972.

———. *This in Which.* New York: New Directions, 1965.

Paracelsus. *Selected Writings.* Ed. Jolande Jacobi. Trans. Norbert Guterman. Bolligen Series no. 28. New York: Pantheon Books, 1951.

Plato. *Dialogues.* Trans. B. Jowett. 2 vols. New York: Random House, 1937.

Pound, Ezra. *The Cantos 1–95.* New York: New Directions, 1956.

———. *Drafts & Fragments of Cantos CX–CXVII.* New York: New Directions, 1968.

———. "Ta Hsio: The Great Digest." *Confucius.* New York: New Directions, 1951.

Raine, Kathleen. *The Land Unknown.* New York: Braziller, 1975.

Reich, Steve. *Drumming, Six Pianos, Music for Mallet Instruments, Voices, and Organ.* Performed by Steve Reich and Musicians. Deutsche Grammophone, DG 2740-106, 1974.

———. *Writings about Music.* New York: Universal Edition, 1974.

Richardson, Joan. *Wallace Stevens, A Biography: The Early Years, 1879–1923.* New York: William Morrow, 1986.

Riddell, Joseph, "Decentering the Image: The 'Project' of 'American' Poetics?" In *Textual Strategies: Perspectives in Post-Structuralist Criticism,* ed. Josue X. Harari. Ithaca: Cornell University Press, 1979.

Riffaterre, Michael. *Semiotics of Poetry.* Bloomington: Indiana University Press, 1978.

Rosenmeyer, Thomas G. *The Art of Aeschylus.* Berkeley: University of California Press, 1982.

Samperi, Frank. *Lumen Gloriae.* New York: Grossman Publishers, 1973.

———. *The Prefiguration.* New York: Grossman Publishers, 1971.

———. *Quadrifariam.* New York: Grossman Publishers, 1973.

Schoenberg, Arnold. *Fundamentals of Musical Composition.* Ed. Gerald Strang and Leonard Stein. London: Faber and Faber, 1967.

———. *Style and Idea: Selected Writings of Arnold Schoenberg.* Ed. Leonard Stein. New York: St. Martins Press, 1975.

Sealts, Merton, Jr. *Pursuing Melville.* Madison: University of Wisconsin Press, 1982.

Shapiro, Karl, and Robert Beum. *Prosody Handbook.* New York: Harper and Row, 1965.

Solt, Mary Ellen. *Concrete Poetry: A World View.* Bloomington: Indiana University Press, 1970.

Spinoza. *Selections.* Ed. John Wild. New York: Scribners, 1930.

Stella, Frank. *Working Space.* Cambridge: Harvard University Press, 1986.

Stevens, Wallace. *The Collected Poems of Wallace Stevens.* New York: Knopf, 1951.

———. *The Necessary Angel: Essays on Reality and the Imagination.* New York: Knopf, 1951.

———. "Notes toward a Supreme Fiction." In *The Collected Poems of Wallace Stevens.* New York: Knopf, 1964.

Stravinsky, Igor. *Poetics of Music in the Form of Six Lessons.* New York: Vintage Books, 1947.

Taggart, John. *Dodeka.* Milwaukee: Membrane Press, 1979.

———. *Peace on Earth.* Berkeley, Calif.: Turtle Island Foundation, 1981.

———. *Prompted.* Kent, Ohio: Kent State University Libraries, 1991.

Tovey, Donald Francis. *The Forms of Music.* Cleveland: Meridian Books, 1956.

Waldman, Diane. *Mark Rothko, 1903–1970: A Retrospective.* New York: Abrams, 1978.

Webern, Anton. *The Path to the New Music.* Ed. Willi Reich. Trans. Leo Black. London: Universal Edition, 1963.

Weil, Simone. *Gravity and Grace.* London: Routledge and Kegan Paul, 1987.

———. *Waiting for God.* Trans. Emma Craufurd. New York: G. P. Putnam's Sons, 1951.

White, Robin. "Interview with Steve Reich." *View* 1, no. 4 (1978).

Williams, William Carlos. *The Autobiography of William Carlos Williams.* New York: New Directions, 1951.

———. "A Final Note." In *"A" 1–12,* by Louis Zukofsky. Kyoto, Japan: Origin Press, 1959.

———. "A New Line Is a New Measure." *New Quarterly of Poetry,* Winter 1947–48.

———. *Selected Poems.* New York: New Directions, 1963.

Zukofsky, Celia, et al. "A Commemorative Evening for Louis Zukofsky." *American Poetry Review,* special supp. (January/February 1980).

Zukofsky, Louis. *"A" 1–24.* Berkeley: University of California Press, 1978. *"A"* is a long poem and has a proportionately long publication history. The following are the earlier editions used by the author: *"A" 1–12* and *13–21* (2 vols.). London: Jonathan Cape, 1966 and 1969. *"A" 22–23.* New York: Grossman Publishers, 1975. *"A" 24.* New York: Grossman Publishers, 1972.

——. *All: The Collected Short Poems.* New York: Norton, 1971. The poems appeared earlier in two volumes published by Norton: *All: The Complete Short Poems, 1923–1958* (1965) and *1956–1964* (1966).

——. *Arise, arise.* New York: Grossman Publishers, 1973.

——. *Bottom: On Shakespeare, with Music to "Pericles" by Celia Zukofsky.* 2 vols. Austin, Tex.: Ark Press, 1963. Reprinted (as a single volume, not including Celia Zukofsky's setting) by University of California Press, 1987.

——. *Complete Short Poetry.* Baltimore: Johns Hopkins University Press, 1991.

——. *80 Flowers.* Lunenberg, Vt.: Stinehour Press, 1978. Reprinted in *Complete Short Poetry.*

——. *Ferdinand, including IT WAS.* London: Jonathan Cape, 1968. Reprinted as part of *Collected Fiction.* Elmwood Park, Ill.: Dalkey Archive Press, 1989.

——. "For Wallace Stevens." In *Prepositions: The Collected Critical Essays of Louis Zukofsky.* Berkeley: University of California Press, 1981. This is an expanded version of the edition of Zukofsky's essays published in London by Rapp & Carroll, 1967. The following essays by Zukofsky are also from *Prepositions* (both editions): "An Objective," "A Statement for Poetry," "Ezra Pound," "Work/Sundown."

——. Interview and reading. National Education Television, WNDT (August 19, 1966).

——. *A Test of Poetry.* Highlands, N.C.: Jargon/Corinth, 1964. Reprint. New York: C. Z. Publications, 1980.

——, ed. *An "Objectivists" Anthology.* Le Beausset, Var, France: To Publishers, 1932.

Acknowledgments

The author wishes to acknowledge and to thank the editors of journals in which many of these essays first appeared:

John Wilson, editor of *Occurrence,* no. 3 (1975)—"Deep Jewels"; no. 7 (1977)—"The Spiritual Definition of Poetry";

Michael Cuddihy, editor of *Ironwood,* no. 11 (1978)—"Reading William Bronk"; no. 22 (1983)—"Of the Power of the Word"; no. 26 (1985)—"George Oppen and the Anthologies"; nos. 31/32 (1988)—"To Go Down, to Go Into";

Carroll Terrell, editor of *Paideuma,* Winter 1978—"Zukofsky's 'Mantis'";

Douglas Messerli, editor of *Sun and Moon: A Journal of Literature and Art,* no. 8 (Fall 1979)—"How to Do Things with Words";

John Witte, editor of *Northwest Review* 19, no. 3 (1981)—"The Poem as a Woven Scarf";

Robert Bertholf, editor of *Credences: Journal of Twentieth Century Poetry and Poetics* 1, nos. 2/3 (1982)—"Louis Zukofsky: Songs of Degrees";

Dennis Barone, editor of *Tamarisk,* Fall 1982—"On Working with Dancers"; Summer/Fall 1983—"Play and the Poetry of Susan Howe";

Bradford Morrow, editor of *Conjunctions: Bi-Annual Volumes of New Writing,* no. 11 (1987)—"A Picture of Mystery and Power"; no. 12 (1988)—"An On-Going Conversation";

Don Wellman, editor of *O.ARS,* no. 6 (1988)—"Introduction";

Lee Bartlett and Peter White, editors of *American Poetry* 5 (Winter 1988)—"Come Shadow Come and Pick This Shadow Up";

William Spanos, editor of *Boundary 2: Journal of Postmodern Literature* 16, no. 1, ser. 2 (1989)—"Call Me Isabel, Call Me Pierre."

Permissions

"Zukofsky's 'Mantis'" has been reprinted in *Louis Zukofsky: Man and Poet,* ed. Carroll Terrell (Orono, Maine: National Poetry Foundation, 1979).

"Of the Power of the Word" has been reprinted in *Conversant Essays: Contemporary Poets on Poetry,* ed. James McCorkle (Detroit: Wayne State University Press, 1990).

"To Go Down, to Go Into" was given as the 1987 Oppen Memorial Lecture under the sponsorship of the Poetry Center, San Francisco State University.

"Introduction" has been reprinted as "Afterword" in *Prompted: Poems by John Taggart/Drawings by Bradford Graves* (Kent, Ohio: Kent State University Libraries, 1991).

Bruce Andrews. *Getting Ready to Have Been Frightened.* Copyright © 1988 by Bruce Andrews. Used by permission of Roof Books.

William Bronk. *Life Supports: New and Collected Poems.* Copyright © 1949, 1955, 1964, 1969, 1971, 1972, 1973, 1975, 1976, 1977, 1978, 1979, 1981 by William Bronk. Used by permission of the author.

Theodore Enslin. *The Weather Within.* Copyright © 1986 by Theodore Enslin. Used by permission of Membrane Press.

Reprinted from *Pythagorean Silence* and *The Defenestration of Prague* as collected in *Europe of Trusts* (Los Angeles: Sun & Moon Press, 1990). Copyright © Susan Howe, 1982, 1983, 1990. Reprinted by permission of the editor.

Charles Olson. *Collected Poetry of Charles Olson.* Edited/translated by George Butterick. Copyright © 1987 Estate of Charles Olson [previously published poetry], © 1987 University of Connecticut [previously unpublished poetry]. Used by permission of the University of California Press.

George Oppen. *Collected Poems.* Copyright © 1960, 1961, 1962, 1963, 1964, 1965, 1967, 1968, 1972, 1974 by George Oppen. Reprinted by permission of New Directions Publishing Corporation.

Material from *Primitive,* copyright © 1978 by George Oppen. Reprinted with permission of Black Sparrow Press.

Index

About The Author

John Taggart is Professor of English and Director of the Interdisciplinary Arts Program at Shippensburg University, Pennsylvania. A major postmodern poet, he has published nine volumes of poetry. The most recent of these are *Loop* (Sun & Moon Press, 1991) and *Standing Wave* (Lost Roads Publishers, 1993). He has also published a volume of translations, *Aeschylus/Fragments* (Parallel Editions, 1992), and a series of prose meditations on the painter Edward Hopper entitled *Remaining In Light* (SUNY Press, 1993). He was educated at Earlham College, the University of Chicago, and Syracuse University.